THE PLAYWRIGHT'S MANIFESTO

T0353546

THE PLAYWRIGHT'S MANIFESTO

How You Can Be The Future
of Playwriting

Paul Sirett

methuen | drama

LONDON • NEW YORK • OXFORD • NEW DELHI • SYDNEY

METHUEN DRAMA
Bloomsbury Publishing Plc
50 Bedford Square, London, WC1B 3DP, UK
1385 Broadway, New York, NY 10018, USA
29 Earlsfort Terrace, Dublin 2, Ireland

BLOOMSBURY, METHUEN DRAMA and the Methuen Drama logo are
trademarks of Bloomsbury Publishing Plc

First published in Great Britain 2022

ISBN: HB: 978-1-3502-0429-4
      PB: 978-1-3502-0428-7
      ePDF: 978-1-3502-0430-0
      eBook: 978-1-3502-0431-7

Typeset by RefineCatch Limited, Bungay, Suffolk

To find out more about our authors and books visit www.bloomsbury.com
and sign up for our newsletters.

For Bert and Stella, Natalie, Joe and Elena.
And for all playwrights – past, present and future.

CONTENTS

ACKNOWLEDGEMENTS

I would like to thank all the playwrights, directors, actors and other theatre people I have worked with and who have inspired me over the years. A list far too long to include here. My life would have been a poor thing without you.

I would also like to thank the many students I have had the privilege of teaching; without them I might never have developed the ideas in this book. I would particularly like to thank Chloë Lawrence-Taylor, who read and fed back on drafts and diversions of this book with such acuity and encouragement. This book would not be this book without Chloë's feedback. Thanks are also due to Lucy Davidson, Skye Hallam, Ryan Leder, Matthew Pettle, Philippa Quinn, Rachel Tookey, Isla van Tricht, and Charlotte Cromie for conversations during the early development of this book, and to Anna Connolly-Quirós for her later comments.

I also want to thank my agents, Cathy King and Alex Bloch, and Dom O'Hanlon at Bloomsbury for commissioning this book and for having the patience to wait for me while I attempted to come to terms with a family bereavement. Also, my daughter, Elena Sirett, for her brilliant help with the research for the chapter *Write a Postdramatic Play*, along with Cecil Castellucci, Emma Muir-Smith and John Rwothomack for their contributions to this book.

Finally, I owe the biggest debt of gratitude and love to my wife, Natalie, and our children, Joe and Elena. Life with a playwright can be a complicated thing. Thank you for your love and forbearance.

PREFACE

Playwriting is hard. So hard. I myself have tried, as I foolishly thought that the years I have spent working with writers had seeped into my DNA. The various mantra of plot, structure, character intentions and emotional arc informed my own process but my ability to dare to take risks or to dig deep into the psyche of a character eluded me. To be a playwright you have to be brave and own an ocean of emotional intelligence, and to dare to pick off the scab, open the can of worms and lift the lid of the pressure cooker.

As a theatre director I have had the privilege of working with some extraordinary writers, of whom Paul Sirett is one.

I have a vivid memory of Paul and I being stuck on the logistics of draft three of *Reasons to be Cheerful*, our Ian Dury-inspired musical. I found myself acting out the various roles trying to phantom my own response to the issue. Paul watched, bemused, safe in the knowledge that being open and honest with where he was at, was a step in the right direction of problem solving. He knew what to do, of course he did, he was the writer.

He just needed space.

I love my conversations with writers and a Graeae conversation has the added value (challenge) of bringing the aesthetics of access into the mix. Asking a writer to contemplate audio description becoming part of a narrative sends alarm bells ringing: 'Jenny, you need to realise, writers do not write about what is happening on stage, they write the dialogue of the characters playing the action.' My reply is, 'Try it, see what happens.' And what has happened has been some glorious plays which have really embodied access in a proactive, creative, accessible way.

Writing is hugely individual and, as a cohort, playwrights cannot be pigeon-holed. New plays are the lifeblood of theatre, and a diversity of voices is an absolute MUST.

This book not only covers what we can learn from past playwrights and how they can inspire you, but it also asks you to embrace the poet within in you and to think theatrically about how you can tear down that fourth wall with the story you want to tell.

It is a reminder that, as a writer, you do not have to know everything! This is where directors and the cast come into play. They can unearth some of the undiscovered gems that lie within your text. Writing is notoriously lonely, but it does not have to be. Directors are always there as a soundboard, but it is worth remembering it is your play, not theirs – this is note to self! I need to be reminded of my role within the process and be mindful and sensitive to the nerves of all writers when they deliver a first draft.

You writers put your soul, wisdom and intellect into your craft and for that I am truly grateful.

Embrace this book and let the pearls of wisdom propel you forward to be the writer you want to be and to have the courage to make your voice heard.

Jenny Sealey, MBE

PROLOGUE

On 25 October 2012, I was on my way to teach a postgraduate class in dramaturgy at the Royal Academy of Dramatic Art in central London. As I crossed the road in Russell Square, I was hit by a taxi. I fractured three ribs, my collarbone split, my eye socket cracked, my neck broke in two places, and I had a massive bleed on the brain, otherwise known as a subarachnoid haemorrhage. Fortunately, I lived. Fortunately, I suffered no brain damage. Fortunately, I recovered and there have been no long-term problems. But an accident like that makes you think; it makes you think about who you are; it makes you think about what you have done with your life; it makes you think about what you are going to do with the rest of your life. The conclusion I came to after much deliberation and deep reading into philosophy, psychology and neuroscience was that I was glad I had given my life to playwriting, and that it was time to pull together all my thoughts and ideas about my chosen artform, to analyse and evaluate everything I had learned during my thirty-plus years as a professional playwright and dramaturg, and then give it all away. And that is why I have written *The Playwright's Manifesto.*

This book is in three sections. In the first section, I explain why it is important to write plays. I believe that the best way to understand ourselves, and others, and the world we live in, is through art. Specifically, for me, through writing plays. A play has the potential to help us learn and grow and thrill and reflect and challenge and potentially become better people. I believe that as a playwright you need to identify and prioritize what is most important to you. And then you need to write about it. Most importantly you need to write about it in the way that only you can write about it. You need to seek what you are best at, and then do it. Here, I am referring to that mystical thing called the writer's *voice,* which isn't anywhere near as mystical as some might think. I encourage you to stand on the shoulders of giants, to define your vision, to embrace your inspirations and your idiosyncrasies, and to strive to prioritize being different.

In the second part of this book, I look at the craft of writing for the stage. Here you will find everything I believe you need to know to write a well-crafted modern play. Then, I challenge you to do it differently. I argue for the importance of knowing your craft and then exploding it into a thousand theatrical pieces because it is vital that we progress. Stand still and we will ossify. Most books I have read on playwriting written in the last one hundred years basically do the same thing; they explain how to create a believable character, who speaks like a real person, in a story driven by cause and effect. That story, naturally, has a beginning, a middle and an end, at the conclusion of which, our 'believable character' either does or does not get what they want. They teach us how to write naturalistic, causal drama. And why not? It is a fantastic formula. It works beautifully. I will show you how to do that. But there is more, so much more, to playwriting than this one idea. There is something these books almost always seem to leave out. They seem to have forgotten about one vitally important thing: theatricality. This book is a cry for the theatrical in playwriting. It is also a challenge – a challenge to write plays that break rules; plays that delight in their use of form, image and language; plays that paint vivid abstract pictures; plays that are big in imagination; plays that put the poetic before the prosaic; plays that engage our imagination and intelligence as well as our emotions; plays that will be the future of playwriting. This book is a manifesto for the future of playwriting. And I want to challenge you to be part of that future.

In the third part of this book, I look at the process of writing, the nature of collaboration and the importance of coming to terms with the impact of writing plays on your practical, financial and mental well-being. Being a playwright is not an easy life. It can be wonderfully rewarding, but even the most successful playwright must learn to live with ridicule and self-doubt from time to time. In this section I try to paint an honest picture of life as a playwright and provide strategies for dealing with the highs and lows of our chosen profession.

Theatre is a living artform and I believe the time has come for us to fully comprehend the importance of the work we do. It is time to celebrate theatre's uniqueness, to think theatrically again and to truly embrace the primal, imaginative thrill that a live theatre experience can offer us.

So, I want you to take your playwriting seriously.

I want you to take the business of being a playwright seriously.

I want you to take your mental health seriously.

Importantly, I don't want to tell you how to write your plays – that's up to you. This book is not a didactic, pedagogical model, but a prompt for self-knowledge, for reflection, for learning and dreaming big. I want to suggest options you might not have thought about and encourage you to think differently, to become the future of playwriting in the most individual way possible.

Never forget: **the most exciting thing you have as a playwright is you.**

PART ONE

1.1 WRITE PLAYS

After my near-fatal encounter with a taxi, I concluded that writing plays was a profoundly important thing for me to do. The key words here are *for me* – I knew that writing plays was important *for me* because it was how I expressed myself. I would rather put an idea or an emotion or a provocation in a play than shout about it from a soapbox or paint it on a wall. Playwriting was what I turned to when I had something to say. I didn't have to analyse my compulsion because it came naturally to me. It was my statement of who I was, the things I knew, the things I had experienced, what I believed. I didn't feel the need to qualify my belief in the importance of playwriting to anyone else until a concerned playwriting student confessed to me that she was worried about making a commitment to writing plays when she could be doing something more useful, like becoming a doctor, or a lawyer, or giving her time and energy to working for a charity. Why become a playwright when all these more *worthwhile* occupations were available?

I did my best to reassure her that writing plays is just as important as any of the professions she mentioned, babbling on about the shared experience, primal forms of human communication, and our need to tell stories, but I was acutely aware of how inadequate my floundering answer was. So, I decided to give it more thought to see if I could better articulate my conviction.

I believe that if you want to be a playwright, it is as good a choice as any in terms of what you can do with your life. If you want to be a doctor, be a doctor; if you want to be a human rights lawyer, be a human rights lawyer; if you want to be a playwright, be a playwright. If it is what you genuinely want to do, you should do it; it is as good a way as any to live a good life and to make an impact on the world we live in.

It seems to me there are two strong arguments for becoming a playwright. The first is to do with the uniqueness of the job; the second is to do with the importance of the job. Or, to put it another way, the first is to do with being a little bit selfish; the second is to do with making a meaningful contribution to this thing we call life.

Let's start by addressing the concern that you should suppress your desire to write plays to become a lawyer or a doctor instead. Here's a thought: why even contemplate becoming a lawyer or a doctor, when, as a playwright, you can create your own lawyers and doctors who can save the world from all kinds of tyrants and diseases? And you don't need to limit yourself to doctors and lawyers, you can become a king, or a queen, or a peasant, or a toad, or a dog, or an anthropomorphic chest of drawers. You can be all the things you ever wanted to be and a whole lot more besides. You can be a superhero, an anti-hero, a devil, a serial killer, an angel. Who else gets the chance to slip in and out of skins like these on a daily basis?

And that's not all, as a playwright, you can live in any period of history you choose. Want to live during the reign of Henry VIII? Off you go then. Want to know what it was like in Greece at the time of Plato? Off you go. How about sampling life during the *prohibition era* in Chicago? Sure. And you can change history too. How cool is that? What other job allows you to change history! Don't like how that last election turned out? Change it! If you like, you can save the planet. Or you can save the entire universe. Or move between parallel universes. Come to that, you can create the universe. You can be God! Or, if you find that a bit too much, perhaps just a minor deity. Or perhaps I'm getting a bit carried away and you are just a mortal who likes to write plays – that's enough.

When you think about it, a career as a playwright is the opportunity to invent worlds and explore every career, every occupation, every love, hate, birth, life and death that has ever happened and that has never happened. What job could possibly be better than that?

As a playwright, no moment of your life is ever wasted. For instance, the much-abused receptionist you observe during your two-hour wait at the dentist might find their way into your next play – as might the storm that blew the roof off your house or the dream you had about seagulls attacking you.

You can be anyone, be anywhere, and every moment of your life has the potential for inspiration. Not a bad way to live your life.

However, writing plays is not just about creating the universe, living hundreds of lives, and never wasting a moment, it's also about doing the most important thing that any human being can do: *making art.*

Friedrich Nietzsche wrote that 'art is the supreme task and truly metaphysical activity of this life.'[1] I take his words to mean that the true meaning of life is to make art that helps us to see, feel, reflect, and perhaps, come to terms with our own finite existence. We live in an insane world. We like to think we are in control, but we are not. We like to think that we understand, but we do not. The only way we can even begin to contemplate the meaning of our peculiar little lives on this strange little planet is by making and experiencing art that engages with our emotions, that makes us think, that reflects our existence back to us. Art that enables us to experience *being* with all our senses. We did not create sublime nature, but we can make art, and we can all appreciate the sublime in great human art.

Art is the most honest and beautiful assessment of who and what we are that human beings have invented. In art, we recognize ourselves, our feelings, our virtues, our vices. We experience ideas articulated in ways that we might never have contemplated if a playwright or painter hadn't imagined and illuminated them for us. That moment of recognition when we are watching a great play, that spark of empathy, that shiver of fear, that pulse of love, that moment when thoughts and ideas and emotions we have struggled to articulate, are suddenly made coherent. To speak to the darkness and the light, to go deep into the recesses of the human experience and come back with something to say. That is our job. As playwrights, that is what we can do.

We can create art that reaches out, art that can heal, and, as Eric Bentley notes, art that 'serves as a lifebelt' and helps us rediscover our 'personal dignity.'[2] I sometimes think the reason why there is so much hate in our world is because of our ignorance of the lives of others. If we don't see and experience how others live, it can be hard to feel a connection with them. We fear difference. A play can tell us stories we might never hear about people we might never meet. And familiarity with the stories of others teaches tolerance and brings us all closer together. It helps us to understand that we are all human. As Elinor Fuchs wrote, 'art shows us how to live.'[3]

If you want to investigate life, if you want to ask BIG and small questions, if you want to create a living art that speaks to the immediate moment and will never exist in the same way ever again, there is nothing to equal theatre. Thornton Wilder said:

> I regard the theatre as the greatest of all art forms, the most immediate way in which a human being can share with another the sense of what it is to be a human being. This supremacy of the theatre derives from the fact that it is always 'now' on the stage.[4]

Theatre is *now*. It isn't a movie that was filmed last year, it isn't a portrait that was painted sixty-three years ago, it is *now*. This moment. The present. Theatre is the only artform that exists, with us, in the present because it is the present moment, the *now*, as art. And that's not all. Every production of a play is a new, living, breathing, changing thing, alive for a moment in time, to be reborn another day in an entirely new representation. Every production of a play is the play reborn. No other artwork can be regenerated this way. A play is a perpetual Lazarus. A play that you write today records the world you live in today, even if it is not about today. It is a document of your time. A measure of your time. Your message to the future. A message that can be revisited and reinterpreted for the time in which it is later produced. A play that you write today has the potential to speak to thousands of people in a multitude of ways over millennia, it is a work of art that can exist time and time again in innumerable manifestations with a multiplicity of collaborators over generations. No other artform is so versatile. No other artform offers living, breathing immortality.

Playwriting is a living art through which we glimpse the meaning and ephemera of existence. Before the players perform their play in the court at Elsinore, Hamlet tells them that 'the purpose of playing . . . was and is to hold, as 'twere, the mirror up to nature'.[5] Claudius and Gertrude literally see themselves reflected in the performance of the players, but the mirror doesn't always need to be literal. Sometimes just catching a tiny glimpse of a reflected half-image is enough. And if you don't like the idea of simply reflecting the world we live in, perhaps you can take inspiration from Bertolt Brecht, who allegedly said we should take a hammer to it to re-shape it instead.[6] Not only can you reflect the world, but you can also shape it into a better place. We have the power to write and respond now. Because theatre is *now*. Playwrights have the power to advocate for change. So, what's it to be, the mirror or the hammer? You can reflect what you see, or you can smash it all to pieces and reshape it. It's up to you.

And there's more, so much more. A play is the most primal form of living human expression. It speaks to who we are. It speaks to what we are.

It is our human story in living human form. Before there was language, there was performance – performance as communication, performance as warning, performance as prayer. Performance became a story. A story of people. A story about a fight. A story about the prey that got away. A story to make you cry. A story to make you laugh. When words began to be spoken, we told our stories, we acted out our stories. When words began to be written, we recorded our stories for others to tell, for others to act out. Our stories are performed, and in return our stories tell us who we are. This is what we do. This is what a playwright does.

Perhaps we would all do well to remember what our fellow playwright (and philosopher and statesman) Lucius Annaeus Seneca once wrote: 'Art is long, life is short.'[7] It bears repeating, *Art is long, life is short*. Sophocles wrote *Oedipus Rex* around 427 BCE. He lived to the ripe old age of ninety, not a bad lifespan, but his play has lived for two and a half thousand years. Proof that life is relatively short compared to the potential lifespan of a play.[8]

If you want to be a playwright and you are willing to work hard at getting better at it, you should do it. I think it is better to live by doing what you love to do, than it is by forcing yourself into a profession in which you will never be able to say and do all the things you want to say and do – the kind of things you can say and do in a play.

If you think you would make a better doctor or lawyer than a playwright, become a doctor or a lawyer. But if you think you might prefer to be a playwright, pursue it with everything you have got, and if you are still worried, write a wonderful play about a doctor or a lawyer to inspire someone to do the work that you didn't do (and perhaps might not have been very good at doing in the first place).

If you have taken the plunge into the depths of playwriting but, one day, find yourself in the middle an existential crisis and in need of a little reminder about why you decided to do what you are doing and why it's important to keep doing it, at the back of this book you will find over 100 further reasons why becoming a playwright and writing plays is a very good

idea. These are just thoughts I have noted down, and the list certainly isn't exhaustive, but it's a start, and if you ever need a bit of inspiration or encouragement or comfort, they are there wating for you. Feel free to amend the list and add more, or, better still, just have a quick glance and then go and do something really important . . . like write a play.

1.2 WRITE WHAT IS IMPORTANT TO YOU

I am fortunate in that I had twelve of my plays produced over a period of twenty-five years at the Theatre Royal Stratford East in London. I knew a lot about the theatre and its history long before I worked there. It had been the home of Joan Littlewood and her Theatre Workshop, an enormously important company in the history of British theatre – a company with working-class practitioners that made important, politically engaged, aesthetically innovative, intelligent work for working-class audiences without ever patronizing them. As a young, working-class man with dreams of being a playwright, I felt the pull of this theatre like no other. The first play I saw at Stratford East was a production of Shakespeare's *Pericles* directed by Ultz in 1983 soon after I graduated from university. Sitting in the auditorium for the first time I was acutely aware of the spirits of playwrights past who had worked in that theatre, writers like Brendan Behan and Shelagh Delaney. The first time I set foot on the stage was like stepping onto hallowed ground – a place that had seen the birth of plays like Behan's *The Hostage*,[1] Delaney's *A Taste of Honey*,[2] Theatre Workshop's *Oh What a Lovely War*.[3] One of the leading actor's during Joan's time at the theatre was Murray Melvin. In later years in-between acting jobs Murray worked as the theatre's archivist and in the early 2000s Murray hung two manifestos written by Joan Littlewood and her collaborators on the walls backstage. These manifestos – dating from 1936 and 1945 – champion the role of theatre in facing up to the problems of its time, being a popular theatre that reflects the dreams and struggles of ordinary people, and making theatre that is great art.

I had never seen these manifestos before, but reading them backstage for the first time I understood even more acutely why I had always wanted Stratford East to be my home: they were the same ideas that powered my own writing. Inspired by reading these manifestos, I decided to have a go at writing my own. It was a lot harder than I thought it was going to be. Working out what is at the core of why you write is hard. I borrowed some ideas from Theatre Workshop and eventually came up with a bloated statement of several thousand words. What follows is the heavily edited version:

Writing Manifesto

I will write plays that:

- are inspired by the stories of ordinary people. Reflect the dreams and struggles of ordinary people. Appeal and speak to ordinary people.
- have something to say about the world we live in, the events, frustrations, problems, inequalities, exploitation, upheavals and human suffering of today.
- confront people's fear of difference by placing what is different about others before them.
- stimulate the desire to build a better world.
- are humane.
- are engaging.
- are accessible.
- are entertaining.
- are aesthetically ambitious.
- are intrinsically theatrical.

Having done this, I now knew what was important to me and I decided that before I wrote a new play, I would check the importance of writing it against my list. If the play didn't match the reason why I wrote plays, I wouldn't write it. And that is what I have done ever since. It's not always good for the bank balance, but it's good for the soul.

Most playwrights don't sit down to work out their manifesto before they start to write plays. Many don't even realize there are specific things that are important to them in their work until an academic or a critic or their Wikipedia page points it out to them. I once found a much more succinct and perceptive summary of what I do on the Soho Theatre website. I am an Associate Artist at Soho and my profile read, '*Paul is a leader in new work that engages current political debate in a dynamically entertaining way.*' If only I could see myself with such clarity.

I think we can save ourselves a lot of time if we can work out what is important to us. If we know what we want to write, we can avoid the things we don't want to write. If we can work out where our priorities lie as playwrights, we can prioritize the work that is worthwhile.

So, what would your manifesto look like? Perhaps start by asking yourself what is important to you. And be honest. You don't have to want to change the world. This isn't about who you want to be, it's about what you want to write about. You might want to be the next Sarah Kane, but you are never going to be Sarah Kane so you might as well try to work out who you are instead.

What appeals to you intellectually? What appeals to you aesthetically? Make a list. Go on! Look at the plays you've written, or if you haven't written a play yet, write one, then look back at what you've written, I wouldn't mind betting that you can find clues. Have you ever written a play that you're not happy with? Is that because of the style or content or both? So, don't write any more plays like that. Look for threads to follow. And if you can't find any, think harder!

If you can't find the answer to these questions buried in your work, if you can't seem to excavate the things that are important to you, go for a walk, take a bath. Do whatever you need to do to find out. List the plays you love. Work out why you love them. There are clues everywhere.

Why do you want to write? Because you want to expose hypocrisy? Because you want to tell us life is shit, then we die? Because you want to tell us life is a beautiful thing and it's about time we realized it? Paula Vogel said that she writes all her plays with the purpose of 'trying to understand what disturbs me.'[4] Lucy Prebble said she is motivated to write when she feels 'an itchy sense that something is not being said.'[5] But what about you? What motivates you to write the plays you want to write?

Amongst Aristotle's six elements of tragedy is something he refers to as *thought*. *Plot* is the most important thing, followed by *character*, and third is what he refers to as *thought*. What is *thought*? There would appear to be an on-going academic debate about the meaning of this element, not helped by the fact that the text in Aristotle's *Poetics* is somewhat gnomic. He seems to be saying that *thought* is the writer's ability to express through his characters a course of action appropriate to that character, in other words, *thought* is what a character says and does. Or he might be saying that *thought* is the idea or theme behind the play as manifested in the things a character says and does.

Although it remains a bone of intellectual contention, the playwright in me is drawn to the idea that *thought* refers to the *idea* or *theme* of the play as made manifest through the characters the playwright has created; that a tragedy should have a message, or lesson, or be posing an important question of some kind. The notion being that the *thought* behind the play is the unifying content of the play. It is the playwright's originating idea as demonstrated through the characters and seen in the action of the play, in other words the intellectual thinking (*thought*) behind the play.

Think about one of your plays. What is the *thought* behind it?

Theatre critic and playwright, Eric Bentley, chooses to refer to the subject of *thought* as the intellect, the ideas, the theme of the drama. He champions the primacy of *thought* over plot and character and makes the claim that *thought* represents the writer's philosophy and that this might stand 'as the aim and object of playwriting.'[6]

If you agree with Bentley, and I do tend to agree with him quite a lot, understanding what is important to you, what your philosophy is, what you might write in your manifesto – these things represent what should be most important to you about playwriting. If you don't know what is important to you, why are you doing this?

However, Bentley is not entirely convinced by the word *thought* and suggests that 'Vision, is perhaps a better word . . . a play presents a *vision* of life', and it is the playwright's job 'to share this *vision*'.[7] Your *vision* is your driving force. Your job is to share your *vision*. It is the playwright's compelling question. It requires you, the playwright, to ask what you want from the work you intend to create, what you intend to say and how you intend to say it. It demands that you interrogate the idea behind your work and how you intend to pursue that idea.

Your *vision* will suggest the theme or idea for a play; you will use your intellect to develop that theme or idea – to construct plot, to create characters, to invent dialogue, to theatricalize, to utilize musicality and spectacle. Your *vision* is rooted in your philosophy. And it isn't pretentious to link playwriting to philosophy. There have been some great philosopher-playwrights – Seneca, Denis Diderot, Machiavelli, Albert Camus, Václav Havel. And there have been philosophies that have influenced playwriting trends – Auguste Comte's *Positivism* had a huge influence on naturalism in the second half of the nineteenth century; *Existentialism* and *Absurdism* were influential for writers like Beckett, Pinter, Genet, Arrabal, Ionesco. What is the philosophy that fires your playwriting?

Don't write plays to impress other people. You need to work out what is important to you. Don't waste your time writing plays about things that aren't important to you. You only get one life, write what you want to write about. Write the plays that you would want to go and see. I can't look inside your head. I can't tell you what is important to you. Work it out. Identify your *vision*. Write a manifesto. Write *your* playwright's manifesto. Then revise it. And revise it again every time you start to doubt yourself. Maybe it will change entirely as time progresses. It doesn't matter, what matters is making sure you are writing the plays it is important to you to write.

1.3 WRITE LIKE ONLY YOU CAN WRITE

In Caryl Churchill's play, *A Number*, the character of Michael points out that every human being has 99 per cent the same genes as every other human being.[1] This isn't a fiction. Believe it or not, genetically speaking, you are 99.81 per cent the same as every other human being on this planet. Every one of us has 3 billion genetic building blocks, or base pairs that makes us who we are, but of those 3 billion base pairs only 0.19 per cent is unique to you. *0.19 per cent.* That tiny fraction is what makes you, you. That's all you've got: 0.19 per cent.

Why am I telling you this? Because I like to relate this incredible statistic to the quest to find your voice as a playwright. We all grew up on planet earth, we have all experienced many of the same things, our brains are very similar, but it is the things about you that are different that will make you stand out as a writer. And I believe it is the things that make you stand out that you should prioritize in your search to find your authorial voice. We can all learn the craft of playwriting, but the magic ingredient is YOU – the tiny, original, weird, peculiar, obsessive, unique things that constitute your 0.19 per cent of difference.

The problem is that, in my experience, most new playwrights tend to overlook what is different about them when they start writing and try to write like the playwrights they most admire. This is usually most disastrous when the new writer is in thrall to playwrights like Caryl Churchill, Harold Pinter, Samuel Beckett or Sarah Kane. Trying to imitate these writers is a transparent admission that you haven't found your voice yet. By all means throw in a repeated scene, or a pause, or a bit of slapstick, or some idiosyncratic pagination in homage to these great writers, but please don't try to write an entire play like them.

And it isn't just new writers who fall into this trap. I fell into it myself not that long ago when I really should have known better. I thought to myself, who's getting loads of work and I alighted upon James Graham (author of *This House*)[2] and Peter Morgan (author of *The Audience*).[3] It seemed to me that both these writers were doing incredibly well, so I asked myself what I could learn from them. They were writing naturalistic, intelligent, witty, political plays. So, it seemed to me, the obvious thing to do was to write a naturalistic, intelligent, witty, political play. Right? Wrong. Firstly, it's really hard to write plays like this. Secondly, it just isn't how I write. I like to write politically engaged, entertaining theatrical adventures, usually with songs, not the fraught inner machinations of political intrigue. After months of intense playwriting pain, I finally gave up trying to be them and got back to being me.

I needed to remind myself who I was and how I wrote. I rarely write fourth wall naturalistic drama, and even when I do, I tend to put songs in the production to serve as a musical metaphor and remind the audience that we are in a theatre having a live experience. I like to play with the relationship between the audience and the actors. I like to gently – and not so gently – position my socio-political point of view. I like to have a bit of fun. I like to say serious things with a wicked grin on my face. Because this is who I am. Music and theatricality are at my core. I left school to play in a punk band. I went back to school so that I could get the exams I needed to go to university to study drama. I left university to play in a band. I got kicked out of the band and decided to get a proper job – writing plays. This is who I am. I love writing the kind of plays I never got to see when I was growing up because no one was writing them – or if they were, I didn't know about them.

I'm an odd mixture of things, and it is these oddities that constitute my 0.19 per cent. My challenge to you, is to tap into your 0.19 per cent. How do you go about doing that? Easy. Just be you. It sounds easy, but it isn't. Because finding that 0.19 per cent is about taking risks. It is about stepping out of your 99.81 per cent comfort zone and exposing your 0.19 per cent of difference. Your 0.19 per cent comprises the voices in your head, your emotions, your opinions, the strange things you think and dream that you don't usually tell anyone about. Your 0.19 per cent is the way your mind works. Because only your mind works in the way it works. Only you have lived the life you have lived. Only you have experienced the things that you have experienced in the way that you have experienced them. Only you sequence words and ideas in the way that you do. Are you ready to step beyond craft and expose that?

You are an amalgam of preferences, wants, needs, sentiments, aspirations, likes, dislikes, loves, hates, feelings, attitudes, tastes, values and beliefs. These are the kinds of attributes that set you apart from others. These are the things you need to use to help you find your unique voice as a dramatist. And the only way you can do this is by being brave, by being honest, by being brutal, by being prepared to risk total humiliation, by being prepared to write the things that it scares the hell out of you to write. This doesn't have to mean autobiography, it doesn't have to mean focussing on the bad things that have happened to you, but it might mean understanding some of these things in the context of who you are. In essence, it is the way you approach things, how you think your way towards things, being honest about these things and not trying to obscure them in verbiage. You need to dig into your core and write what you find there. Truthfully. Authentically. You need to think about the way you think. And then write like you think. And to hell with anyone who doesn't like it. It is what you bring to your writing that is distinctive about you that is the most important thing for you to strive for. YOU. In all your glorious, mad, strange, happy, sad, peculiar, messed-upness. The 0.19 per cent of you that says: I am different. The 0.19 per cent of you that is impossible to imitate. It is here that you will find your voice, along with other great playwrights like Bryony Lavery, debbie tucker green, Moira Buffini, Zinnie Harris, and Annie Baker who have dared to take a risk and show what is different about them in their work.

The tricks and talent of many playwrights can be taught; it is, more often than not, possible to break down what a playwright has done, and then, explain how they did it. Yet, for some, for the best (like those mentioned above), this is impossible. They have such original voices it is almost impossible to explain how they do what they do. It is impossible to teach their technique. Their writing is exclusive to who they are. They have learned to trust their instincts, their way of thinking, their 0.19 per cent. This is something to celebrate. In a world bursting with the desire to explain and categorize everything, what these writers do is a total conundrum. And we need to thank them for that. They have manifested their 0.19 per cent.

It takes strength to write as you really are, but without it, you will be just another, ordinary playwright. Don't be ordinary.

There is an irony to what Michael says in Caryl Churchill's play, *A Number*, when he reflects on the news that he has been cloned, by being comforted by the knowledge that he is 99 per cent genetically the same as everybody else, that irony being that Caryl Churchill is one of the most original playwrights of the last fifty years. She is anything but a clone, she is a constant innovator and inspiration. Unlike her character, Michael, Caryl Churchill found her 0.19 per cent of unique genetic code a long time ago, and she has been drilling deep down into that code for many years. My advice for any writer seeking to find their voice is simple: Don't be a clone, be a Churchill (Caryl, that is, not Winston).

1.4 STAND ON THE SHOULDERS OF GIANTS

Confession: my 1993 play *Worlds Apart* – my second play at Stratford East – begins with a character telling a long, politically infused joke directly to the audience. This moment was inspired by the opening of Arthur Miller's play *A View from the Bridge* which begins with the lawyer Alfieri telling a story about something amusing that has just happened directly to the audience.[1]

Another confession: the opening of my musical *The Big Life*, first produced at Stratford East in 2004 before transferring to the West End a year later, was inspired by the magnificent street scene set on Broadway that opens of *Guys and Dolls*.[2]

I am not alone in being inspired by the work of others.

Talking about the playwrights she admires, the inspirational Paula Vogel confessed that, 'I write almost every play with a valentine to Thornton Wilder.'[3] Paula doesn't hide the fact that Thornton Wilder has been a huge influence on her work, she celebrates it. You can find evidence in the introduction to her published play *The Long Christmas Ride Home* where she writes that she'd 'appreciate it if directors would read the one-act plays of Thornton Wilder for guidance.'[4] You can also find evidence in her play *Indecent*[5] which, like Thornton Wilder's play *Our Town*[6] begins with the character of the Stage Manager introducing the play and setting the scene, which Paula is happy to confirm 'is absolutely a valentine to the stage manager of *Our Town*.'[7]

Sending valentines is about acknowledging our influences. It is about standing on the shoulders of those that came before us. It isn't about plagiarism; it is about channelling the spirit of the writers we admire. It is about letting them teach us. I firmly believe that we send valentines all the time in our work, sometimes we know we are doing it, sometimes we don't. But we all do it. Me. Paula Vogel. And you. Admit it.

In a letter to his friend, the scientist, Robert Hooke in 1675, Sir Isaac Newton wrote: 'If I have seen further, it is by standing on the sholders (sic) of giants.'[8] Newton acknowledges that he owes a debt to the achievements of scientists that came before him. Similarly, I believe, we should not be afraid to admit that we are inspired by the work of other playwrights. Isn't this what got us writing plays in the first place? Didn't we all see and read plays that made us think, I'd like to do that! Don't we continue to see and read plays that inspire us? The question for us is what do we do with these inspirations? Many of us begin by trying to write like the writers we admire, we want to be them, so we try to write like them. But we soon learn that pastiche-Pinter isn't going to get us anywhere. We need to take our influences and marry them with who we are as writers. The point is to be inspired and take this inspiration somewhere new. But how do we do this? Do we borrow? Do we steal?

You may have heard the variously paraphrased maxim, *good writers borrow, great writers steal.* But what does this mean? Where does it come from? If you google this quote, you are likely to see it attached to the name of the poet and playwright, T. S. Eliot. So, is Eliot advocating that we plagiarize another writer's work? Not at all. Eliot's original quote is far more interesting than any of the paraphrased versions. Discussing the indebtedness of the dramatic poet to their predecessors, Eliot wrote:

> Immature poets imitate; mature poets steal; bad poets deface what they take, and good poets make it into something better, or at least something different. The good poet welds his theft into a whole of feeling which is unique, utterly different from that from which it was torn; the bad poet throws it into something which has no cohesion. A good poet will usually borrow from authors remote in time, or alien in language, or diverse in interest. Chapman borrowed from Seneca; Shakespeare and Webster from Montaigne.[9]

Good dramatic poets like Chapman and Shakespeare took what inspired them and made it into something better. Most importantly, they made it 'unique ... utterly different from that from which it was torn.' If we want to become better playwrights, one of the best places to start is with the work of the playwrights we admire. And, if we are to take the advice of

Eliot, we don't need to go too far back, Montaigne died in 1592, the same year that Shakespeare's career as a produced playwright began. And the wonderful world of playwriting was a dog-eat-dog business back then, plagiarism didn't exist, every playwright had to use whatever they could to stand out. And borrowing from Montaigne or Seneca or Horace was an important part of establishing an identity.

JUST TO BE CLEAR: I am NOT advocating plagiarism. When it comes to being inspired, I suggest we allow the best work of the writers we admire to inform our own thinking, endeavour to make those inspirations our own, and, where necessary, make sure we acknowledge those influences. In other words, don't steal their words, don't steal their ideas, celebrate their influence, their qualities, their artistry, and make it known. Tell the world you are standing on the shoulders of giants. Don't stamp on their heads. And I am most definitely NOT advocating appropriation. My musical, *The Big Life*, was inspired by Shakespeare's *Love's Labour's Lost*, my experience of playing in ska bands, and the story of post-war Caribbean immigration to the UK. I wrote this musical with the composer, Paul Joseph, in the early 2000s supported by an incredible team, the vast majority of whom had West Indian heritage. Today, I would not write this musical. As a white Englishman I do not feel it is appropriate. However, I cannot undo having written it, so if it is ever produced again, it will be re-written with a writer with an authentic West Indian background and voice. This isn't revisionism, it is simply a desire to be part of an industry that is prepared to learn, to change, and to respect ALL its practitioners and audiences. Sometimes we need to step down from the giant's shoulders to make room for others.

I didn't hesitate to stand on the shoulders of Shakespeare when I wrote *The Big Life*. I tend to agree with Harold Bloom who said, 'There is no God but God, and his name is William Shakespeare.'[10] But, as T. S. Eliot suggests, even Shakespeare wasn't born a genius. He learned his craft. He acted, he worked out how plays worked for an audience, and then added his unique voice. Shakespeare didn't appear from nowhere. His plays were the result of two thousand years theatrical gestation coupled with his virtuosity. Shakespeare didn't invent his stories, he borrowed them from other sources; he didn't invent the idea of writing in blank verse, he built on the writing of Christopher Marlowe and Thomas Kyd, who built on the writing of predecessors like Sackville and Norton, who built on the English Renaissance rediscovery of Horace and Seneca, who built on the iambic patterns of the great Greek playwrights and ideas of Aristotle.

Shakespeare wasn't the first to telescope history into a chronicle play; he wasn't the first to use a five act structure; he wasn't the first to mix the serious and the comic; he wasn't the first to show bloody deeds on stage; he wasn't the first to focus on a protagonist; he wasn't the first to use devices like a ghost, or a chorus, or a soliloquy, or a confidante; he wasn't the first to write a pastoral comedy; he wasn't the first to use a sub-plot. He studied. He learned his craft. He borrowed. Then, and only then, did he do what makes him stand out – he dug deeper into character and developed a use of poetic dramatic language that has the power to transcend all. He added what was unique about him – his imagination, his use of language. He stood on the shoulders of giants.

We need the ambition to stand on Shakespeare's shoulders. Then, we need to have the courage to add our own unique ingredient, whatever that may be. We inherit. We reinvent. And then we innovate.

What are some of the things that Shakespeare could teach us? Firstly, to know what we are doing. Then, to take risks. Shakespeare's plays are deliciously theatrical. They are packed with intrinsically theatrical techniques that sit waiting for contemporary playwrights to exploit. A quick glance at some of the things Shakespeare does can be inspiring. Perhaps challenge yourself to mix prose and poetry, the colloquial and the lyrical, the bloodthirsty and the beautiful. Try to write a play that is both serious and funny, a mixture of comedy and tragedy, high art and entertainment. Talk directly to your audience. Get your characters to articulate their innermost thoughts. Write a play rich in imagery, and metaphor, and simile, and hyperbole. Invent a few new words. Enjoy some unlikely coincidences. If you haven't got the answer to a research question, make it up! Embrace anachronisms. Change the facts about an historical character to make them more interesting. See what happens when you let yourself off your twenty-first-century creative leash.

I will unpack these and other Shakespearian inspirations in more detail later in this book. In the meantime, why not explore some of your favourite playwrights – ancient, classical, contemporary – analyse precisely what they do and how they do it. You might spot the influences of other playwrights in their work, you might even spot some of their techniques already at work in your own writing.

AND just in case you're still worried about this, I would like to say again that EVERYONE DOES IT. Even if they sometimes don't do it consciously. EVERYONE DOES IT.

And it's not just other playwrights you should look to for inspiration. Phoebe Éclair-Powell's Bruntwood award-winning play *Shed: Exploded View* was inspired by an art installation by Cornelia Parker that presented the contents of a shed blown apart by the British army and frozen as if in mid-explosion. Éclair-Powell's play borrows the sub-heading of Parker's, *Cold Dark Matter: An Exploded View*, and uses this fractured artwork to invent a fragmented story and structure about the splintered relationships within and between three couples. A perfect example of ethical theft.[11]

Look around you, be inspired by art, music, books, anything and everything that resonates with you. Study what you love. Steal from it. And if 'steal' is still too harsh a word for you, perhaps remember Paula Vogel's advice and think of it as sending a valentine.

If a playwright was an animal, they would probably be a magpie. We love to hoard the shiny, sparkly things we find in other stories or scripts or productions. We are all influenced by something or someone. Don't be afraid to love your inspirations. If you want to write a musical, create a combustible mixture of the music you love and the stories that resonate. The mega-hit musical, *Hamilton*, is strewn with shout-outs to the musical traditions that helped to birth it, 'both hip-hop (*DMX, Grandmaster Flash, and the Furious Five*) and musical theatre (*South Pacific, The Last Five Years*).'[12]

The old master and apprentice system worked most effectively when the apprentice took the work of the master to a higher level. Don't shy away from your inspirations. Ask yourself how you can go one step further. When asked about the playwrights she admires, Lynn Nottage namechecked, Lorraine Hansberry, Tennessee Williams, August Wilson and Arthur Miller.[13] And, to varying degrees, you can see these influences in her writing, but Lynn Nottage is Lynn Nottage, she has a distinctive voice, and like many of the best, she isn't frightened to admit to where her understanding and love of the craft of playwriting came from.

We borrow. We grow. We stand on the shoulders of giants. Thornton Wilder himself admitted to being indebted to James Joyce's *Finnegan's Wake* for his play *The Skin of Our Teeth*. He also stated that he 'should be very happy if, in the future, some author should feel similarly indebted to any work of mine.' I can't help thinking he must be very happy with the valentines Paula Vogel has sent him. Not only that, Wilder also stated that for him great writing should be a 'torch race rather than a furious dispute among heirs.'[14] Paula Vogel picked up the torch and ran with it. And Paula, in her turn, has been hugely influential on a whole generation of American playwrights. The theatrical genius of plays like *Baltimore Waltz* and *How I Learned to Drive* and *Indecent* will inspire playwrights for decades to come.[15]

Are you ready to take the torch? You should be. Because great playwriting doesn't spring into being from nowhere. You are highly unlikely to write a great play without ever having seen or read one. It isn't a bolt of lightning from the heavens.

Be inspired. And don't be afraid to admit it. I am indebted to writers from Sophocles to Shakespeare to Genet to Wilder to Vogel in my work. What about you? Beckett? Kane? Birch? Gupta? Might be time for some of these playwrights to buy some shoulder pads.

PART TWO

2.1 IT ISN'T NATURAL(ISM)

My eureka *I want to do that!* moment came in the late 1970s when I was a teenager and went to see the production of a short play one lunchtime at the Oxford Playhouse. The play was called *Jetty* and it was about a group of teenagers hanging around on a jetty by a river (or it might have been a lake or the sea, I can't remember). I don't recall the name of the playwright, but I do remember that it was a naturalistic play about young people doing the things that young people do – experimenting with love, sex, cigarettes, alcohol. I had no idea that there were plays about people like me that could speak so directly to me. And right there and then, I thought, *I want to do that!*

Although this naturalistic play fired my desire to write, the first play that I ever finished was a bizarre, and truly awful, non-naturalistic adaptation of Mervyn Peake's book *Titus Alone* – I was going through a *Gormenghast / Lord of the Rings* phase at the time. Over the years I have written a handful of naturalistic plays, but instinctively, I always lean more in the direction of non-naturalistic drama. Don't get me wrong, I love an intense, naturalistic play, especially in a small studio space. However, I think it is important to remember that naturalism is just one of a multitude of devices that a playwright has at their disposal. And it has many dynamic theatrical applications.

First things first: let's get the difference between realism and naturalism out of the way.

Realism came first. Realism was a reaction against late eighteenth-, early nineteenth-century romanticism driven by revolution, new technology and new ideas like the positivist philosophy of Auguste Comte.[1] Naturalism evolved from realism due, at least in part, to Charles Darwin's *Origin of the Species*, published in 1859, which offered a scientific view of the natural world.[2] Realism explores real people in real situations.

Naturalism explores real people in real situations through a scientific lens. Basically, naturalism, is a more systematic, methodical form of realism. Okay? No? You disagree! I don't care. The fact is that for about the last century and a half the two terms have been interchangeable, and we've got far more important things to do than debate the terminology of these words – like write the plays that will define the next great movement in playwriting *after* naturalism. So, for the sake of this book, I am going to refer to writing that seeks to represent real speech and real actions in real time by real people as realistically as possible, as naturalism.

Naturalism has been the predominant dramatic form since the early twentieth century, sure there have been diversions, into Symbolism and Surrealism and Epic and Absurdism and other genres, but naturalism ploughs on regardless. Before the positivist philosophy of Comte and Darwin's theory of evolution inspired a generation of playwrights to put naturalism at the centre of their practice there were over two thousand years of non-naturalistic drama. For Emile Zola, naturalism was a new and exciting, ground-breaking form[3]; and, in the hands of Zola and his contemporaries – Ibsen, Ostrovsky, Turgenev, Gogol, Chekhov, Stanislavski, Shaw, Granville-Barker and others – it became the most exciting genre in the playwright's theatrical orbit. The advent of film and television took the form to even greater heights. Naturalism is wonderful. It came from a revolutionary moment in scientific, artistic and theatrical thinking and never ceases to delight. My worry is that there seems to be a disproportionate emphasis on teaching a naturalistic approach to playwriting without exploring the rich potential of complementary theatrical modes of writing. By all means, write beautifully naturalistic plays framed in beautiful naturalistic sets, all I ask is that you remember that naturalism is versatile – it can exit alongside and within all kinds of theatrical forms and genres as well as within realistic, representational worlds.

Naturalism works because it is the fastest and most effective way of recognizing ourselves on stage. Here's a character doing the ironing – I've done the ironing. Here's a character reading a book – I've read a book. Here's a character eating his own children in a pie – oh . . . maybe not that one . . .

If you want to write a 'real people, real kitchen, real cooking, linear, real-time' play, good for you, but it is possible to write naturalistically and be aesthetically non-naturalistic at the same time. I think every now and then you should challenge yourself to find a way to take naturalism to another – more theatrical – level.

How?

The simplest way to do this is with design. The theme of my real time, kitchen-cooking play, might be dysfunctional relationships, so instead of setting it in a real kitchen, how about setting it in an ever-shifting Hall of Mirrors? You don't have to leave it up to your designer to do this, you can stipulate it in your opening stage directions. Never forget, it is the whole play that tells the story, it's not just what the characters say to one another.

One use of naturalism within a non-naturalistic setting that stays with me was Ben Power's reinvention of Stefano Massini's history of the American financial institution the Lehman Brothers in *The Lehman Trilogy* at the National Theatre in 2018. This production gave us naturalistic exchanges between characters, with the three actors performing multiple roles over generations in spinning Perspex boxes. It was mesmerizing.

Or perhaps think about how you can frame your play with an idea suggested by your play. Nick Payne's *Constellations* is in essence a story about the choices we make in relationships, but it just so happens that one of the characters is a cosmologist with a passion for the multiverse, so in this play we see two characters speaking exquisite naturalistic dialogue in a narrative that follows the potential multiple permutations of the choices they either do or don't make.[4] Every scene is hardcore naturalism, but the repetition of scenes with different outcomes has more to do with the laws of probability than believability. Yet we are utterly hooked into the 'reality' of the situation. This is naturalism as theatricality. Genius.

I remember reading David Mamet's play *Oleanna* many years ago, and being struck by the idea that he had taken everyday language and heightened it to a form of poetic dialogue through his use of word choice, repetition and ellipsis.[5] Out of the 'everyday', he created something much more potent and mesmerizing than ordinary speech. Ever since then, it is something that I notice in all the best playwrights. It is ordinary speech made extraordinary. It is there in debbie tucker green, it is there in Alice Birch, it is there in Ella Hickson, it is there in Annie Baker – seemingly naturalistic speech made poetic through the playwright's diction, phrasing, use of punctuation, repetition and use of overlapping and repeating dialogue.

A while ago, an ex-student sent me a message asking me if I thought of Alice Birch as a primarily naturalistic writer. My response was to say that I think of her as a primarily non-naturalistic writer. Why? Because whilst a lot of her dialogue is naturalistic it is often the case that the form her writing takes is not. For example, *Anatomy of a Suicide* contains naturalistic dialogue, but the language overlaps, repeats, and is spoken in sync in three separate strands.[6] Her language is heightened – her word choice is carefully constructed to appear naturalistic but on closer examination will reveal a strong poetic sensibility within a non-naturalistic structure – it has a distinctive and poetic rhythm. There is a veil of naturalism behind which is a beautiful world of theatricality and exquisite language.

Perhaps we have come full circle, perhaps we do have dramatic poets today, just as they did in Ancient Greece, but we're frightened to call them that? It doesn't really matter, what does matter is that these writers transcend naturalism by writing in a way that elevates everyday language to the poetic.

We can't all write as beautifully as Alice Birch, but we can challenge ourselves to elevate our language and use naturalism in tandem with other, more theatrical ideas. Naturalism is here to stay. But we need to remember that naturalism is only one of a multitude of theatrical tools available to a playwright. The question for you is, what are you going to do with it?

Perhaps the easiest way to rupture naturalism is to break the *fourth wall* . . .

2.2 TEAR DOWN THE FOURTH WALL

I am addicted to breaking the fourth wall. My play *Reasons to be Cheerful* is set in a pub called the Red Lion, and for the purposes of the play the entire audience are regarded as being in the pub watching the performance with the cast, inviting interactions between actors and audience throughout the performance.[1] In my musical *The Big Life*, a character called Mrs Aphrodite sits in one of the boxes in the auditorium and chats to the audience between scenes.[2] My play *Bad Blood Blues* is an ostensibly naturalistic play set in the office of a drugs trial researcher, I wasn't happy about this, so I put some blues songs in between the scenes to act as a musical metaphor representing the shameful exploitation of African American participants in the racist Tuskegee Syphilis Study in 1930s USA.[3] I like plays that acknowledge the existence of the audience, I think it enables a more thrilling theatrical encounter. I also think we need to remember that the fourth wall is a relatively new theatrical innovation.

The foundations for the fourth wall were initially dug in 1758, when the Enlightenment playwright, philosopher and critic, Denis Diderot, proposed the idea of a more natural style of acting, instructing actors not to think about the spectators, to act as if they weren't there, and to imagine a wall at the edge of the stage, separating them from the auditorium.[4] It wasn't until the mid- to late nineteenth century, however, that the idea of naturalism really caught on in the theatre. So intense was the desire to portray real events on stage that French actor and theatre manager, André Antoine, went so far as to literally remove the fourth wall – rehearsing in a space with four walls and then deciding which wall to remove when the set was built so that the audience would get the best view of the 'real' events taking place in that room. Then, in the early twentieth century, Stanislavski helped to firmly establish the fourth wall for future generations by invisibly bricking up the proscenium arch of the Moscow Arts Theatre to present the plays of Anton Chekhov.

Today, the fourth wall is ubiquitous; it is one of our most commonly accepted theatrical conventions. It doesn't need to be built on a proscenium stage, constructed between the footlights and the stuccoed cherubs at the top of the proscenium arch, it can just as easily exist between the audience and the performance area in a studio, or shape-shift between actor and audience member in a non-traditional space. It might be there, like a protruding tongue on a thrust stage, or like a tunnel in a traverse configuration, or even like one long circular wrap of invisible clingfilm for a play performed in-the-round.

Yet, no matter where or what it is, the thesis remains the same: it is unseen, it is as if we, the audience, can see through it, but the actor cannot. The actors know the fourth wall is there, but they ignore it, and the audience is more than content to play along, willingly engaging in the suspension of disbelief in order to spy on the lives of the characters. It is audience as voyeur, audience as Peeping Tom. It is the transparent membrane between the private world of the characters and the public space of the auditorium.

We should perhaps remind ourselves that the idea of the fourth wall was a revolutionary innovation. In earlier forms of drama, there was no wall between actors and audience, the event itself was the world of the play. But today we seem to prefer to snoop on other worlds for a couple of hours, rather than see ourselves as part of the performance. In my experience, the majority of playwrights write with the fourth wall already securely built between their imagination and their text. I think the fourth wall was/is a brilliant idea, but it is only one of many brilliant ideas developed by theatre-makers over hundreds of years and it seems to me a great pity that we have become so obsessed with this device when there are a wealth of ideas and techniques that could potentially enrich our plays if playwrights would only take the time to remove a few bricks from the wall now and then.

In order to begin demolition, playwrights might start by asking one very simple question: why are we obsessed with pretending that the play we are watching on the stage in front of us is real? It isn't. It is a lie. It is a chimera, an invention, a figment of the playwright's imagination brought to life by the creative team, the actors, technicians and stage management, who have been working together to deceive us. It is a falsehood perpetrated by actors pretending to be hypothetical people doing things that a playwright has written for them to do. We are complicit in a deceit. So why not acknowledge that deceit? Why not enjoy it?

Breaking the fourth wall is a joy, it engages and embraces the intelligence of the audience by acknowledging that we are indulging in this gloriously duplicitous fraud together. Playwrights, your actors can communicate with your audience, either in character or as the actor performing the role, and this has the potential to bring your audience closer to your work. It will certainly make every performance genuinely unique and will make your play a simple, theatrical, celebration of the shared experience. We are all in this together, so why not celebrate that fact?

Denis Diderot was one of the great Enlightenment thinkers, but with due respect to the great man, the fourth wall has started to feel a bit like a creative prison. Playwrights, you don't need to pretend the audience isn't there in every play you write. You have options.

The time has come to think beyond invisible brick and mortar. Here are some ideas from the days before we all had to pretend that we weren't really in a theatre and from some contemporary writers who aren't afraid to try a bit of demolition when it comes to the fourth wall.

The Prologue

How about starting your next play with a prologue? You know the form: an actor comes on stage, welcomes the audience, and tells them about the play they are about to watch. Why not? The Greeks did it, the Romans did it, the Elizabethans did it. Today, very few playwrights seem to bother. It's a shame. A prologue is a great way to get all that cumbersome exposition out of the way. Just tell us what we need to know and get on with it.

In Greek tragedy, the prologue (prologos) is there to provide the audience with the information it needs to jump straight into the action of the play. It might be done by direct address, or it might be done with dialogue, but the purpose is the same – to focus the story as quickly and simply as possible. Why bother with all that painstaking exposition when you can just tell the audience what happened before the events of the play they are about to see performed?

It was a technique not lost on our medieval predecessors. Subtle exposition buried in realistic dialogue was never going to be much use in getting the attention of an audience standing in the Market Square more intent on discussing the price of sheep than watching a play. Setting the scene for a Morality Play like *Everyman* in 1510 needed considerably more gusto. Solution, bang something to get the audience's attention, get an actor to jump up on a cart, tell the audience what the play is called, tell them what it's about, and remind them that we are all going to die. No messing.

One of the most famous prologues can be found at the opening of Shakespeare's *Romeo and Juliet*:

Two households, both alike in dignity
(In fair Verona, where we lay our scene),
From ancient grudge break to new mutiny,
Where civil blood makes civil hands unclean.
From forth the fatal loins of these two foes
A pair of star-crossed lovers take their life,
Whose misadventured piteous overthrows
Doth with their death bury their parents' strife.
The fearful passage of their death-marked love
And the continuance of their parents' rage,
Which, but their children's end, naught could remove,
Is now the two hours' traffic of our stage—
The which, if you with patient ears attend,
What here shall miss, our toil shall strive to mend.[5]

In the time it takes the actor to recite a fourteen-line sonnet, we have been told where the play is set, what happens, how long it will take to perform, and to shut up and concentrate. I wouldn't mind betting that if this was a new play, it would be one of the first things a director would be likely to ask the playwright to cut. Why? Because modern convention seems to consider it a sin to give things away like this at the start of a play. But if it was good enough for Shakespeare, why isn't it good enough for us? This information doesn't kill the play, it simply shifts the focus – instead of asking ourselves what is going to happen, we ask ourselves how it is going to happen.

For a fine example of a contemporary metatheatrical prologue one need look no further than Branden Jacobs-Jenkins' play *An Octoroon*.[6] This play begins with an African American playwright (BJJ) entering and introducing himself to the audience as a 'black playwright'.[7] He then tells the audience about a recent visit to his therapist during which they discussed his depression and a Victorian playwright called Dion Boucicault who wrote a melodrama called *The Octoroon* in 1859. His therapist suggests that he write an adaptation of this play. BJJ tells us he tried, but the white guys in the cast quit so he had to play the white guy parts. Then, after playing some testosterone-fuelled rap music, BJJ confides to the audience that he doesn't really have a therapist, he can't afford one, and starts to apply whiteface. Soon after this, he is joined on stage by a character called the Playwright – a manifestation of Dion Boucicault (the writer of *The Octoroon* remember). BJJ continues his direct address – telling us about being attacked by a swarm of bees, pointing out that the ancient Greeks believed that a swarm of bees was a sign that Dionysus was present. The Playwright now starts to mock BJJ, and they have a slanging match before BJJ (now in whiteface and a blond wig) storms off. We are left with the Playwright, who is a bit drunk, looking for his assistant. His assistant then enters – a Native American actor wearing a mixture of Native American and regular clothes – and tells him his theatre has burned down. Now it is the Playwright's turn to get made up – transforming himself into the character of a Native American. Finally, we are ready for the first scene of the adaptation of Boucicault's play. Sound complicated? In truth, this is a simplification. I have written one word in the margin of my copy of the play text at the end of this prologue, that word is 'Wow!' And I mean it. 'Wow!' In performance, it is like prologue as tornado.

Duncan Macmillan begins his play *People, Places & Things* with a prologue (although he doesn't call it that).[8] As the lights fade at the beginning of the play about a young woman struggling to come to terms with years of alcohol and drug abuse, we are given a hint of the subversive nature of this drama with the stage direction that the sounds of an expectant audience build to a cacophony. We are then plunged into the final act of a naturalistic production of Chekhov's play *The Seagull*. Have we come to the wrong theatre? This is probably precisely the question the playwright wants us to be asking ourselves. As we watch the scene unfold, we realize that the actress playing Nina is having something of a breakdown, culminating in the stage manager hurrying on stage to take her arm as the set transforms into a club and we arrive in the world of the play we have come to see. The world has been turned upside down – twice. What a fantastic way to start a play.

The prologue of *The Inheritance* by Matthew Lopez, a vast play exploring the ties that link gay men from the days of E.M. Forster during the first half of the twentieth century, through the HIV pandemic of the 1980s, to the present day, starts with a group of young men sitting around writing.[9] One of the young men – Young Man 1 – tells us he has a story to tell and opens his favourite novel, looking for inspiration, and, hey-presto, E.M. Forster appears. Forster (as the character of Morgan) talks to the young men about writing and asks what it is about his novel that speaks to them. Young Man 1 tells Morgan he has a story but can't find a beginning, Morgan asks him why he needs to tell his story and the Young Man explains that he needs to tell it to understand himself. Morgan asks him who his story begins with and with this we step into the play via voicemails from this character. So, the prologue of this play consists of the writer conferring with the author of his favourite novel about what he should write, and from here we move into a play that uses the novel as inspiration and as a loose template for the story. Evidence, if it were needed, that we don't need to hide the fact of where our inspirations come from. And what a delightful way to begin a play!

In Donja R. Love's extraordinary play *One in Two*, about the earth-shattering statistic that one in two gay or bisexual black men will be diagnosed with HIV in their lifetime, the audience get to choose which of the three actors will play the lead role, #1, at the beginning of the play by seeing which of them can solicit the most applause. The roles of #2 and #3 are decided by playing rock-paper-scissors. The actors then decide to start the play by acting out a scene from when they were kids. A little way into this scene, they step out of the characters of the kids to comment on the action. Then, they get back into the scene. The opening few minutes of this play give us the theatrical vibrancy and present the ideas that will permeate the whole play.[10] The audience are immediately inside the event of the play with the actors, not stuck outside looking through an invisible wall.

The prologue of Lucy Prebble's excellent and entertaining exposé of the accounting scandal at the American energy company *Enron* is a joy to behold – three suited individuals with the heads of mice, a voice over, and direct address from a lawyer.[11]

These examples are exceptions. Most modern plays I have read or seen begin with the fourth wall firmly in place. Have we become so shy that we don't dare to send an actor on stage to welcome our audiences and tell them what they've let themselves in for anymore? The next time you are writing the opening scene of a play and struggling to get all that backstory and exposition in, when you are exhausted playing the *exposition as ammunition* game, perhaps stop trying to be an expositional smartarse and try sending one of your actors on to tell the audience where the play is set, what has just happened, and to enjoy the drama. Perhaps even use a placard or digital title or neon sign to let your audience know where they are and what's going on. It's not only Brecht who likes this kind of thing, Paula Vogel does it in *Indecent*, Alice Birch does it in *Revolt. She Said. Revolt Again.*[12]

Perhaps next time you write a play, see if you can persuade your director to come at it from a why-did-it-happen, rather than a what-happens-next perspective. Or perhaps cast yourself in your play and have some fun theatricalizing the thematic ideas that underpin your play.

The Induction

Question: what's the difference between a prologue and an induction? Answer: Not a lot. Inductions were a feature of plays written during the English Renaissance, usually a scene of some kind to set up the action of the play, or perhaps to comment on it, or to summarize it in some way. The prologue to *An Octoroon* is probably more of an induction than it is a prologue, but let's not waste time getting hung up on dramaturgical terms, the important thing is the job these things do.

My favourite induction is the glorious opening that Ben Jonson penned for his sprawling comedy about Jacobean London, *Bartholomew Fair*. It is a wonderful example of metatheatrical hijinks. It begins with the company's stage-keeper (stage manager) coming on stage and apologizing for the late running of the play due to a problem with one of the actor's costumes. He then goes on in hushed tones to confide to the audience that not only does he not like the play very much, but he also thinks the playwright doesn't know what he's writing about and that the playwright kicked him when he made suggestions for re-writes! He then goes on to tell the audience about some of his ideas for how the play could be improved before being interrupted by the book-holder (a kind of theatre administrator) and the scrivener (a legal clerk). The book-holder tells the stage-keeper to get off and informs the audience that he has been sent on in place of a prologue with the scrivener and a contract the playwright has had drawn up between himself and the audience. He then asks the scrivener to read out the contract: first, the audience have to agree to remain in their places for two and a half hours or more; they are not to take offence at anything in the play; they are only allowed to judge the play in proportion to the price they paid to get in; they agree to make up their own minds about the play and not listen to anyone else's opinion; they should not expect the play to be a throwback to earlier times at the fair – this is a modern play that gives them a picture of the present, uncouth state of the fair; next, with tongue firmly in cheek, the scrivener instructs the audience that they are not to look for any 'state decipher, or politic picklock' in the play (in other words political satire);[13] he tells them, they are not to accuse the author of profanity just because characters use the kind of oaths real people use at the fair; and he concludes by informing the audience that they have already put their seals to the agreement by paying their money to get in. He then asks for their applause and the play begins.

What an inspired induction! A playwright setting out his contract with the audience before the play begins! And a glorious example of a playwright getting their retaliation in with their critics before the play has even begun!

Let's be clear, an induction like the one in *Bartholomew Fair* wouldn't work for every play, but when the day comes that you can't work out how to begin a politically charged, contentious play, perhaps start by sending an actor on stage to talk the audience through a contract you have drawn up with them in mind.

The Chorus

The Greeks. Where would we be without the Greeks? And surely one of the greatest gifts bestowed upon us by Greek civilisation is the gift of the drama. From the Dithyramb to Thespis to the City Dionysia. From *tragedy* to *comedy* to *satyr play*. Such a rich store of theatricality. There was no fourth wall in Greek theatre, the audience sat in a semi-circle around the orchestra (the circular area where the chorus perform) in broad daylight, watching the performers; watching each other. Yes, there would be a visceral connection with the story and the characters, but no one in the audience was pretending this was really happening in real life. It was heightened, it was unapologetically theatrical.

The Greek chorus began life as dancers. Over time their role changed, they started to speak, to comment on events, as well as dance. It is a beautiful idea. A group of performers represent the general population of the drama we are watching and comment on what happens. A simple, theatrical mirror held up to proceedings on stage. They might be elderly men, they might be bacchantes, they might be the wives of soldiers, but most importantly, they represent the world of the play and get to have their say about things. All very democratic.

A big difference between audiences in fifth-century BCE Greece and today is that during the golden age of Sophocles and Euripides and Aeschylus and Aristophanes, it was considered a civic duty to attend the theatre; to laugh, to cry, to feel catharsis, but also to learn something that might benefit audience members as well as the city state they were a part of. In what type of play could a playwright be sure of hammering home a socio-political message? In their comedies, of course! Yes, their comedies. Comedies were the most political form of drama. And how could playwrights be certain that the audience heard what they wanted to say about contemporary events, tyrants, wars, famines, even when it wasn't the direct subject of their play? *Parabasis.*

Parabasis is the moment in a Greek comedy, usually about two-thirds of the way through, when the lead actors leave the stage and the chorus leader, perhaps wearing the mask of an eminent citizen sitting in the front row, takes it off, steps out of character and starts singing or chanting directly to the audience (usually in anapests – Di-di-daa, di-di-daa, di-di-daa …) about a topical issue that may or may not have anything to do with the play the audience has been watching. What could be more fabulous! I'll tell you what – when the rest of the chorus take off their masks and join in! That's what! How great is that? How theatrical is that? Arguably the first example of sung, choral, topical stand-up. Perhaps the first and last example of sung, choral, topical stand-up, but now you know about it, you can do it too!

'Me?' you ask.

'Yes, you!' I say.

What possible use could *parabasis* be to a contemporary writer? I suggest you talk to Lucy Prebble. In her play *A Very Expensive Poison*, a play about the poisoning of Russian defector Alexander Litvinenko by Russian agents in London in 2006, arguably the most poignant moment in the play comes towards the end of Act Three when the fourth wall is deconstructed not once, not twice, but three times, before being symbolically re-built for the final short scene and then being broken down again for a final comment.[14] First, the character of the murdered man's wife, Marina Litvinenko, takes a microphone and talks directly to the audience; next, she steps out of character to directly address the audience as herself – the actor – saying, 'I am obviously not Marina Litvinenko . . .'[15] Next, she hands out cards to audience members with quotes from the inquiry into Alexander Litvinenko's death and asks them to read them out loud. The fourth wall has been conclusively demolished. We are thrust into the present! And we are all listening. We are attentive. We are engaged. Because it is important. Because the device works. It is a powerful, compelling, very real, shared moment. A moment of truth and theatricality. Then we slip seamlessly back into a scene between Marina and a British government official, before the actor ends the play by stepping towards the audience, thanking us (the audience) and leaving us with a small plea not to forget: 'Please.'[16] Lucy Prebble knows how theatre should be written. Study her plays, you can learn a great deal from her.

The chorus isn't popular in contemporary drama. To some extent, the idea of the chorus has survived the cull by quietly getting on with their job in musical theatre, opera and ballet, where audiences don't tend to panic quite so much when a dozen or so men and women stride on stage in tights to perform a routine together. We might find the occasional, singular choric character commenting on events in a straight play, but a group of chanting, dancing locals is rare. What a pity.

In *How I Learned to Drive*, Paula Vogel has a three-member Greek Chorus, one to play several male roles (Male Greek Chorus), one to play several female roles (Female Greek Chorus), and a younger member to play younger girls and the grandmother (Teenage Greek Chorus). As well as playing multiple characters, the Female Chorus Member speaks four monologues (echoing the role of the Greek chorus leader); the three chorus members speak in unison, sing a Motown song, and become overlapping voices on the radio. Using a chorus to dynamically enhance your play is so simple, so theatrical.

The chorus is a glorious device. If you're ever in the position of being asked to create a large, naturalistic play, why not have a chorus figure, or, budget permitting, a full chorus of men and women enter and do a few moves before chanting a few lines about events in the play. Some people might find this suggestion risible, to them I say, invention lies in the clash of styles, innovation lies in experiment, there's nothing wrong with trying to make a straight play explode into life with a big choral interlude. Let's create a Big Bang between the old and the new.

The Narrator

An extension of the chorus role is that of the narrator. If there is a distinction between the two, it is perhaps that the narrator has more of a storytelling remit whilst the chorus is more of a commentator. The idea of having a narrator in a stage play tends to divide people into two camps: those that love it, and those that hate it. Some literary theorists might argue that the device of a narrator belongs exclusively to the novel. To them I say, no single art form owns an artistic device, they exist for us all to play with. Personally, I love it. Give me a narrator, please.

The narrator is a character of great potential and, when it works, of great beauty. No illusion. No smoke and mirrors. We are back in the wonderful world of storytelling. It is a joy to be guided through a play by a good fourth-wall busting narrator, and they don't even have to be the protagonist, in fact, it often works best when they are not. Some of theatre's greatest narrators have been bit-part players or even the story's antagonist. There is a very simple, very theatrical, storytelling trick that it is worth every playwright making a quick note of: identify an historical story with a goodie and a baddie, then get the baddie to tell the story. Simple. You want some examples? Judas in *Jesus Christ Superstar* by Andrew Lloyd Webber and Tim Rice;[17] Peter Shaffer's magnificent theatrical treat *Amadeus* – the story of Mozart, told by his arch-rival, Salieri;[18] Lin-Manuel Miranda's stunningly theatrical mega-hit musical *Hamilton* – told by Hamilton's nemesis, Aaron Burr.

My favourite narrator of all time can be found in Thornton Wilder's theatrical tour de force *Our Town* – and this narrator isn't even a character in the play (although he does play some bit-parts), it's the Stage Manager. Genius. Utter genius. If you haven't read or seen *Our Town*, do yourself a favour, get a copy and read it now. It is a work of theatrical genius. If ever there was a template for a quintessentially theatrical play, *Our Town* is it. And it all begins with the narrator ...

At the beginning of *Our Town*, the Stage Manager strolls on stage and when the lights go down on the audience, he tells them what the play is called, who it was written by, who produced and directed it, and who the actors are. And he continues, describing the people, places and events of the play as it progresses. In the final act of the play, the Stage Manager brings the attention of the audience to the graveyard outside town, all I can say is that when I first read this play, I thought I had died and gone to heaven.

Our Town is an old play now, it was first produced in 1938; it is a bit hokey, white, heteronormative, and, in some places, creaky, but the theatrical ideas are as fresh and invigorating as when Thornton Wilder first wrote it.

Perhaps we should start by asking ourselves if the play we are writing might benefit from having a narrator. Your director or dramaturg might argue that a narrator is just a vehicle for the voice of the playwright. Personally, I don't see the problem. Let's be honest, every character in your play is a voice for the playwright to some extent, so why not have a character who isn't so shy about it? In the sublime stage adaptation of Alison Bechdel's graphic novel *Fun Home* by Lisa Korn and Jeanine Tesori, the narrator is the 43-year-old incarnation of Alison Bechdel who shares the stage with two younger versions of herself. In this case, the narrator is literally the author's voice.[19] It works brilliantly.

A narrator can come on stage and tell you three years have gone by since the last scene, like they do in *Our Town;* they can tell you the interval started when it was 1530 and now it's 1532 like they do in Robert Bolt's *A Man for All Seasons*.[20] Perhaps your collaborators might claim that using a narrator like this is just a lazy expository device. No, it isn't. It's economical. It's fun. Surely, it has to be better to get information like this out of the way quickly than having to squeeze the information unnaturally from your naturalistic dialogue.

Another example of a glorious narrator is the character of Michael Evans in Brian Friel's masterpiece *Dancing at Lughnasa*.[21] Middle-aged Michael Evans narrates the play and speaks the dialogue of his seven-year-old self from outside the action of the main play while his five aunts talk to his imaginary presence. Not only does this character narrate and play himself as a child, but he also dictates the action and reveals the futures of the characters. A beautifully seamless, seemingly effortless theatrical device.

There doesn't only have to be a single narrator, any number of actors can narrate, in David Edgar's adaptation of Dickens's *Nicholas Nickleby*, a multitude of characters narrate.[22] In John Corwin's play, *Navy Pier*, four characters sit in armchairs on stage to tell the audience a story about writing a story – each of them from a slightly different perspective.[23]

A narrator can be and do almost anything. Be inspired. Try using a narrator. Try some of the ideas outlined above. Add something new. Build a monster. And if your director and dramaturg still aren't convinced, ask them if they have got a better idea. If they have – fantastic. If they haven't –

tell them that there are few more theatrical ways of framing a play than using a narrator. And if they doubt your sanity, refer them to *Amadeus*, *Hamilton*, *Our Town* and *Indecent*.

The Aside

The *aside* was beloved of Shakespeare and his contemporaries. It is a beautifully simple device: a character turns to the audience and confides in them, a brief word in their ear a confidence, a little nod, a wink, an acknowledgement that we are all (audience and actors) in this together. We are friends, or, if the character is an unpleasant one, perhaps just acquaintances.

In Greek drama, it is the chorus who do this job, turning to the audience every now and then to pass judgement on events, but by the time of Shakespeare, the *aside* had become the province of the single actor.

An *aside* is usually a brief, passing remark, or a thought spoken out loud, sometimes made by lead characters, sometimes made by minor characters. Simple. Glorious. Effortless in its theatricality.

Hamlet turns to the audience early in Shakespeare's great tragedy to tell us what he thinks of his usurping uncle, Claudius:

Hamlet (*aside*.)   A little more than kin, and less than kind.[24]

In *Julius Caesar*, the character of Trebonius has been conspiring with others to assassinate Caesar when Caesar asks them to stay close because he has something to tell them. Trebonius replies:

Trebonious Caesar, I will. (*Aside*.)   And so near will I be
That your best friends shall wish I had been further.[25]

Nasty. And we, the audience, are in on it!

Sometimes an *aside* might not even be articulated, it can be a look, an eye roll, a wink, a sigh – we (the audience) get it, we (the audience) are with the character, feeling what the character is feeling, understanding, complicit.

Isn't it thrilling when an actor on a thrust stage, playing in a Shakespeare comedy simply turns to the audience and tips them a wink? Isn't that moment of intimacy, with the actor acknowledging us, a moment for us to cherish? I'll say it again, and not for the last time, what is this obsession with pretending we are watching something we are not present at? We are in a theatre, there are people in front of us doing a job called acting, they are on the stage pretending to be people they're not while we are sitting in the auditorium in full comprehension of the pretence, having paid good money to watch them do it. Let's acknowledge it. Let's use it to make the whole shared experience more enjoyable, more memorable.

Some contemporary playwrights aren't afraid to embrace the *aside*. In *An Octoroon*, Jacobs-Jenkins revisits the technique as used by Boucicault, the Victorian playwright, in his melodrama *The Octoroon*. The characters sometimes speak their thoughts out loud, which can, if desired, be played directly to the audience or be played as a kind of subversive, oxymoronic melodramatic naturalism, in that the actor can play the line naturalistically, but there is a shared complicity with the audience because we all know that it is rare a person will actually speak their exclamations out loud.

Another thing, it isn't just in the theatre that the *aside* has a small but potent role to play. It works a treat on television. Phoebe Waller-Bridge's masterclass in writing a great part for yourself to play in *Fleabag* is an excellent example, all those little looks to camera, all those pithy remarks direct to camera, we (the viewer) become her best friend, we are her confidante. All the character needs to do is look over her shoulder at the camera, shrug, pull a face and we know exactly how she feels. It's personal.[26]

An *aside* is part of an actor's skillset, it should also be part of a playwright's toolkit. It must be the simplest theatrical magic ever invented. Let's bring it back home to the theatre.

The Soliloquy

The *soliloquy* is like the *aside's* bigger, more intense, darker sibling. It is often an inner meditation or contemplation, articulated for all the world to hear. Sometimes an actor might address a *soliloquy* directly to the audience, other times, they may choose to simply articulate the speech to the middle distance. It doesn't matter which (to the playwright, at least). The *Soliloquy* lets us into the mind of the character without having to pay homage to the gods of exposition and sub-text. To a playwright, it is a gift.

Unfortunately, many contemporary playwrights tend to overlook the gift of the *soliloquy*. Why? What's the problem? Why put yourself through some kind of Stanislavski-Meisner-Adler-Strasberg induced hell when that is the actor's job? All you need to do is get your actor to turn to the audience and tell them what's going on in their head. To hell with sub-text and the perceived wisdom of *what your character doesn't say can be more important than what they do say*. Challenge it. Let your character break the fourth wall and take us into their confidence. It's simple. It's theatrical. Bang! We are inside the character's head.

Most soliloquys happen when a character is alone on stage. A private moment. If we are left alone with our thoughts in real life, we are highly unlikely to speak them out loud, but in the theatre, we can magically hear what is going on in the mind of a character. A soliloquy turns a character inside-out. It is a poetic, theatrical alchemy that enables us to get really close to a character, to share an intimate moment with them, to enable us to hear the character's truth. In Shakespeare's *Othello*, we know Iago is up to no good because he tells us in his soliloquys! What he says to other characters would suggest that we can trust him, but we can't, and we know this because we've been inside his head!

What is the most famous speech in the history of Western theatre? It begins like this:

Hamlet   To be or not to be that is the question,
Whether 'tis nobler in the mind to suffer
The slings and arrows of outrageous fortune . . .[27]

It is the moment in *Hamlet* when the tortured Prince of Denmark tells us what he is thinking. Is he speaking his thoughts out loud? Is he confiding in us? Is he asking us what he should do? Is it a bluff – is he saying it on order for Claudius and Polonius to overhear? Are we supposed to hear it? Are we his alter-ego? Are we there? Are we somewhere else? Are we eavesdropping? Are we his friend? Does he know we are here? Who does he think we are? It doesn't matter! Well, it does, to the actor performing the speech, but for us, the contemporary playwright, willing to learn from the best, what matters is the beauty of the writing and the fact that Shakespeare invites his audience deep into the mind of this tormented individual.

In Clare Barron's feral dissection of what it means to be an adolescent female competitive dancer in the United States, *Dance Nation*, there is a wonderful soliloquy from one of the young dancers, Ashelee, in which she talks about being gorgeous, and smart, and all the burning ambition inside her.[28] There's a stunning soliloquy from the character of Cleo in Jasmine Lee-Jones' *Seven Methods of Killing Kylie Jenner* as she struggles frantically to come to terms with her identity.[29] A soliloquy is the speech that keeps on giving. Try it. You might surprise yourself.

Monologue

A monologue is usually a one-person play in which an actor plays single or multiple roles. It differs from the soliloquy in that it is more often a direct conversation with the audience, less inner-thought, more conversational, more storytelling. The actor might simply walk on stage and tell the audience their story, or perhaps they might tell their story to an unseen character (or characters), or perhaps address something that symbolically suggests another person (such as a gravestone).

I used to be a bit of a pedant about monologues. I would ask: who are they speaking to? Where are they? Why are they telling this story now? All very irritating. I don't bother anymore. Who cares? I just want to be told a story.

Seriously: who doesn't like to be told a story? Who doesn't like to listen to a great storyteller? That wonderful warm feeling we get when a good story begins, and the storyteller takes us on a journey to who knows where. That primal, around the fire after a day of hunting (work) and gathering (shopping) moment when someone starts to tell us a story.

There is the potential for great dynamism within a monologue, not just in the depth of the character portrayed, but in the glorious versatility of the actor who can, within a monologue, dive in and out of a variety of roles. A monologue doesn't have to be just one voice, an actor can slip in and out of a whole host of characters – male, female, animal, alien, tree, cardboard box, wherever the imagination might take you.

Or perhaps you might prefer to write a play with sequential monologues? One of the prime examples of this form is Brian Friel's play *Faith Healer* – four monologues telling the same story, spoken sequentially by three characters with the first and last monologue spoken by the same character.[30] It is an engrossing play.

Duncan Macmillan and Jonny Donohoe's *Every Brilliant Thing* is an excellent interactive monologue replete with audience participation.[31]

Arinze Kene's play *Misty* is a fabulous, defiant, individualistic deconstruction of the fourth wall in monologic form, he even blows himself up inside a giant orange balloon.[32] How cool is that! Roy Williams and Clint Dyer's brilliant play *Death of England* is a one-man direct address monologue complete with one actor playing several roles within the story he is telling whilst playfully interacting with the audience.[33] Yes, please! All these plays are worth investigating.

The monologue works supremely well on stage. If you haven't written a monologue before, write one, perhaps a story told by one character that includes cameos from several other characters. Experiment. Writing a monologue can make a thoroughly refreshing change from writing fragmented, slashed, dashed, CAPITALIZED, ellipsis-strewn, *italicized*, fashionable contemporary dialogue. It is a simple way to unlock a compelling theatricality.

Direct Address

Direct address infuses many of the devices discussed so far, but it is also worth looking at on its own.

I run a lot of writers' workshops for new writers, and I usually find myself confronted with a barrage of naturalistic plays. I have a theory for why this is, it goes something like this: most people grow up with television and film as their main source of drama, the vast majority of television and film drama is naturalistic, even those of us who are taken to the theatre are more likely to see a naturalistic drama than any other type of play, ergo, when someone sits down to write a play for the first time, they write a naturalistic play. To put it simply, they have very little experience and knowledge of theatricality, even if they come from a theatre-going family they are still likely have seen more soap opera than Shakespeare. The first question I often find myself prompted to ask when confronted with a new writer's naturalistic play is: why does this play demand to be produced on the stage rather than in another medium like television, radio or film? And then I might ask: would this play benefit from breaking the fourth wall? And, so, the conversation begins: What is the fourth wall? How do I break it?

There's a wonderfully simple thing a new writer can do to experiment with theatricality in the form of breaking the fourth wall, and that is *Direct Address*. Just get your characters to turn to the audience and talk to them. It is incredibly liberating. Why agonize about finding a way to reveal that a new character is the protagonist's half-sister who has lived in Nigeria for the past twelve years when she can just turn to the audience and tell them? It's easy. It's freeing. It's theatrical.

A finely tuned naturalistic scene in the kitchen is followed by a scene in the bedroom is followed by a scene in the garden is followed by a character turning to the audience and telling us that what happened in the kitchen was wrong, that what happened in the bedroom was disgusting, that what they buried in the garden was terrible, before going on to explain what they intend to do about it. In an instant, the insubstantial partition between actor and audience is blasted to pieces and we can all breathe a sigh of relief that we don't have to pretend not to be here in the same place anymore.

If you want to avoid all that clunky exposition about events off-stage, why not just tell us? Old school melodrama didn't shy away from simply having a character turn to the audience and tell them what was going on off-stage. If you're stuck trying to work out how to explain something that's happening off-stage – just get your character to turn to the audience and tell them. There is a wonderful moment at the end of Act Two in Annie Baker's play *John* – a minute after the lights come up on the audience for the second intermission of the play, the character of Genevieve comes back onto the stage and asks them to stay for five more minutes, she swears she won't take longer than five minutes, she even asks for someone to time her, she then goes into a monologue of just under five minutes.[34] It is a brilliant way to re-energize the play by pushing it in a different direction just before the interval.

Clare Barron also uses direct address to great effect in her play *Dance Nation* – characters use expositional, narrative and confessional monologues, as well as more poetically infused, reflective, soliloquys/ reveries that explore the past and the future. Lucy Prebble is another regular user.

Try it.

Audience participation . . .

. . . two words that are almost guaranteed to induce fear in the heart of almost every theatregoer. *Audience participation*. Shrink into your seat! Look away! Pray that they won't choose you! We need to talk about this . . .

I think it is probably safe to say that most of us aren't that keen on getting dragged up on stage in the middle of a show. That feeling of utter terror when a performer turns to the audience and asks for a volunteer will be familiar to many of us. That flash of terror as the performer surveys the audience, and we try to avoid eye contact and silently pray, *Please, not me!* But whether you love it or loathe it, it is a magnificent way of bringing the audience fully into the room and shattering the fourth wall.

If you do get picked (now you know why the front row seats were a bit cheaper) at least you know the audience is on your side. Not because they like you, but because most of them will be thinking, *Thank God it's not me!* The look of fear on your face will be very entertaining. Or perhaps you will put on a mask of steely bravado to get through the ordeal? Or perhaps you are an exhibitionist who loves being up on stage anyhow? Whatever the case, no matter what happens up there on that stage, you can bet those involved will never forget it.

A playwright can include an instruction for audience participation in a script, they can even provide dialogue – or optional dialogue, depending on the mayhem – but there is always going to be a quality of the unknown which unites audience and performer and blasts the fourth wall sky high. It is a unique moment, and, at its best can be a theatrical treat. And what is one of the greatest assets of live theatre? The fact that this performance will only ever happen once.

In *One Man, Two Guvnors*, Richard Bean's adaptation of Goldoni's *A Servant of Two Masters*, there is a moment when a terrified audience member joins the cast on stage and ends up getting soaked in a free-for-all at the end of Act One.[35] She is a plant, of course, but this is a fact that only starts to dawn once the 'audience member' gets soaked. Whether Richard Bean wrote this brilliant moment into his script, or it was developed in rehearsal, I don't know, but the audience plant is an old trick, and one well worth digging out now and then.

Using audience plants can be startling in its simplicity. Ella Hickson uses plants in the Q&A scene in her play *The Writer* by having them ask questions from their seats in the audience, thereby tumbling the fourth wall in another unexpected direction.[36]

My adaptation of Shawn Levy's bestselling book *Rat Pack Confidential* which toured the UK before transferring to the West End, begins with a stand-up routine that is interrupted by Frank Sinatra who is sitting in the audience.[37]

In *An Oak Tree* by Tim Crouch, one of the two characters is a hypnotist (originally played by Crouch) and the other, known as the father, is played by a different actor every night, male or female, old or young, who knows nothing about the play before going on stage.[38] The pretence is that we are at an event with a hypnotist, but this is a shared pretence because what the audience is really interested in is the fact that, like them, the second actor hasn't got a clue what is going to happen. The second actor is guided through the performance by the hypnotist, sometimes being told what to say, sometimes being fed lines through headphones, sometimes being given parts of a script to read. It is a unique event, never to be repeated, because there will never be a production of this play with the same two actors. And it is an incredible high for the audience knowing that the second actor is as clueless about what is going to happen as they are. It is such a simple, beautiful, living, breathing idea.

The audience is acknowledged and involved in *An Oak Tree*, but not to quite the same terrifying degree as in Crouch's *The Author*.[39] In this play there is no stage, just two banks of seats facing each other. The actors are members of the audience. The play focuses on the audience and audience perceptions. One of the actors greets the audience and chats to them as they arrive, finding out and using their names. One of the actors even quotes from a pre-existing preview/review of the play. How meta is that! The play contains walkouts from actors and often induces walkouts from audience members. I can't help thinking that anyone turning up to see this play without knowing what they have let themselves in for will either be totally enthralled or absolutely terrified. Whatever the case, this play is a beautiful example of what one can do in a theatre space that can never be repeated in any other dramatic medium. This play is audience as character. It is an inspiring reminder that we can still surprise. Credit is due to Crouch and his team for stretching the boundaries and removing not only the fourth wall but the entire stage!

The message for playwrights is simple: the audience is part of the performance, a fact not to be ignored but embraced. We are living, breathing creatures in the same space, experiencing the same event, don't deny it, challenge it, do something with it.

And before we end this section, a quick shout out for pantomime and the many and varied ways it seeks to interact with audiences – audience as best friend, as confidante, as booing, hissing, singalong, shouting comrade. Pantomime has a rich store of interactive joys.

Playwrights, invite your audience in, use your imagination.

When things go wrong . . .

. . . it can be a good thing.

Sometimes something might go wrong on stage, something might happen that will cause an actor to have to acknowledge the audience – a prop falls off the stage, an actor trips over a chair, the bedroom wall falls over. Don't we (the audience) love it when that happens? It often works so well that the director might decide to keep it in for the rest of the run so that every audience can have this 'unique' experience. I remember seeing a production of *Singin' in the Rain* in the West End in which the actor playing the lead seemed to forget what he was doing and had a fit of giggles, he looked out at the audience pulled an 'I don't know what's going on' face and shrugged his shoulders – it brought the house down. The audience loved it. We had all witnessed a genuinely unique performance moment. A couple of weeks later I went again (not because I thought it was the greatest show on earth, but because I was asked to accompany a group). Guess what? Exactly the same thing happened. The actor seemed to forget what he was doing, and . . . same result. The audience loved it. Playwrights, if there are going to be mistakes in your play, write them in yourself. Or be even more adventurous and invite moments of improvisation from your cast. Theatre is collaboration after all (more on this later . . .)

Exposed

I have always liked plays in which the mechanics and surroundings of the stage are visible – the lights, the ropes, the fire hydrants, the exhausted brick walls. I also like plays that not only don't seek to hide their surroundings but aren't afraid to address what is happening on stage. Bare up-stage brick walls are more exciting than hydraulic elephants for me. An in-play discussion about the play we are watching is about as exciting as life gets!

In her note at the beginning of *Revolt. She Said. Revolt Again.* Alice Birch asks her collaborators to make the off-stage visible to the audience. She then tells them there shouldn't be any set and there should be no props.[40] No smoke and mirrors, all she wants is the space and the actors. Because that is all she needs. That is all any of us need.

Act Four of Branden Jacobs-Jenkins' play *An Octoroon* begins with a dramaturgical discussion between the Playwright (Dion Boucicault – the writer of the original play) and BJJ (the writer of this explosive new version of the play) in which they debate the 'sensation scene' from Victorian melodrama – basically the most spectacular moment in the play during which the audience get the literal stage 'bang' for their monetary 'buck'. The scene then progresses through a mixture of metatheatre and melodrama, Brechtian techniques, and repetition before culminating in the ultimate 'sensation' when a boat explodes and cotton rains down on the audience! 'Or not', as Jacobs-Jenkins states directly after writing this moment.[41] From the pen of an adventurous (and pragmatic) playwright.

Expose the workings of your play, reflect the workings of your play back onto your play, then smash them up with a hammer.

The Epilogue

And finally . . .

Have you ever been at a play and been unsure if it has finished? After an embarrassing pause, someone at the back (usually the director) starts clapping and we all breathe a sigh of relief and join in. There was no such problem in Greek drama, the chorus chanted and danced an exode informing everyone the performance was over. The Elizabethans also had no problem with knowing how to end their plays – often turning directly to the audience and telling them, in verse, that the play had finished, and it was time for them to applaud. Ben Jonson ends his play *Volpone* with this address to the audience:

Volpone   The seasoning of a play is the applause.
Now, though the fox be punished by the laws,
He doth yet hope there is no suff'ring due
For any fact which he hath done 'against you.
If there be, censure him; here he doubtful stands.
If not, fare jovially, and clap your hands.[42]

In other words, the play has finished, sorry if there was anything in it that upset you, if there was you can blame me, if not, clap your hands. A conclusion, an apology, an instruction. A simple way of defending your play against criticism and sending your punters home happy.

Shakespeare ends *A Midsummer Night's Dream* with Puck's couplet:

Give me your hands if we be friends,
And Robin shall restore amends.[43]

Why are we frightened to tell the audience the play has finished?

Kudos to Jasmine Lee-Jones who pays a brilliant mini-homage to the epilogue in her play *Seven Methods of Killing Kylie Jenner*. At the end of the play, one of the characters (Cleo) turns to her friend (Kara) and confesses that she's feeling a little bit paranoid, like she's being watched, at that moment, for the first time in the play, they notice the audience. They then conclude the play with a couplet and a near rhyme instructing the audience to clap:

Cleo   They're just sat there not saying jack.

Kara   What are you going to do now . . . clap?[44]

Thank you, Jasmine.

And finally . . .

If you absolutely have to build a glass wall between your audience and the world of your plays, by all means do so, but I challenge you, every now and then, to tap it lightly with a hammer just to see what might happen.

2.3 DRAMATIC STRUCTURE IS NOT A SCIENTIFIC LAW

I was very proud of a moment towards the end of my play *Worlds Apart* when I had a character make a selfless gesture that meant another character could assume his identity and be released from an immigration holding facility. It was the best thing that could possibly happen. My coup de théâtre, however, came when this deceit was uncovered, and the wrongly released character was forced to return to the holding facility. The best thing that could possibly have happened had turned into the worst thing that could possibly have happened. How smart was I for coming up with a twist like that! Not very, is the answer. I learned soon afterwards that Aristotle had identified this technique almost two and a half thousand years earlier and had even given it a name – *peripeteia* – a structural device meaning a reversal of fortune from good to bad, or bad to good. So much for my powers of innovation.

I clearly still had a lot to learn about dramatic structure so I decided it would be a good idea to study what other writers and theorists had written about it. I always want to try something new, something different, but I also think that before you can do anything (r)evolutionary, it's a good idea to know how people have done it before you. You have to learn it to burn it down and then build it up again. The Greek tragedians did. Shakespeare did. Kane did. The more adventurous writers of recent years like Crimp and Vogel and Birch are continuing to do so. The problem is that old theories die hard. And when it comes to dramatic structure, there is a prescribed way of creating a plot that is ingrained so deeply it is hard to subvert it. And for good reason: it works! But the problem is that if we continue to use the same formulaic plots repeatedly without ever trying anything new, we run the risk of our work becoming stale. We need to learn the prevailing structural wisdom, and then ask if we can do something different, because, ultimately, dramatic structure is not a scientific law, it is a way of creating a shape for the story we want to tell, and there are as many ways to structure a story as there are stories.

Beginning-Middle-End

The extraordinary polymath Aristotle informs us that in tragedy, plot is of the *first importance*.[1] Everything else is subservient to plot. And every plot must have a beginning, a middle and an end.[2] Not only that, but the incidents in a tragedy must be placed in a precise causal order so that if any one of them is moved or omitted, the play will cease to function.[3]

Aristotle's diktat works. It works brilliantly and he did playwrights a great service in identifying the six elements of tragedy as he did – Plot, Character, Thought, Diction, Music, Spectacle, in the order – but to slavishly continue to adhere to his principles when there are so many other options available seems to me a missed opportunity.

However, we can't really move on from Aristotle until we understand his ideas and those of his subsequent apostles. So, let's begin with what you need to know about plot according to Aristotle and take it from there. What follows is a brief history of Beginning-Middle-End cause and effect structure over the past two and a half thousand years.

Around 330 BCE Aristotle wrote what were probably a series of lecture notes called *Poetics*. This short book has had an extraordinary influence on playwriting. In the book, Aristotle uses *Oedipus Rex* by Sophocles as the template for writing a great tragedy. He felt that this play was the best example of what he called a Complex Plot. For Aristotle there were two distinct types of plots, the Simple Plot – in which a unified series of actions is accompanied by a change in fortune, and the Complex Plot – in which the actions lead to a change of fortune which is then met with a reversal of fortune and recognition.[4] If we break *Oedipus Rex* down, the causal, complex Beginning-Middle-End beats of the plot look like this:

Beginning

- There is a problem – the SET-UP
- The reason for the problem is revealed – the REVELATION
- They decide to solve the problem – the GOAL

*Also known as the **Inciting Incident** – the incident that sets the story in motion. The Inciting Incident in* Oedipus Rex *is Oedipus deciding to solve the mystery of who killed Laius; the Inciting Incident in* Hamlet *is the ghost telling his son to avenge him; the Inciting Incident in* West Side Story *is Tony and Maria falling in love at first sight. It is the moment that tells the audience why this story <u>has</u> to be told.*

Middle

- Something gets in the way of solving the problem – an OBSTACLE
- Something exacerbates the attempt to solve the problem – a COMPLICATION
- There's an argument, escalating the problem – a CONFRONTATION
- It gets even more furious – into CONFLICT
- A moment of respite, perhaps things will be okay – some CALM
- Things get complicated again – another COMPLICATION
- The best thing that could possibly happen happens – REVELATION (Part 1) THE GOOD NEWS
- However – the TWIST
- The best thing that could possibly happen turns out to be the worst thing that could possibly happen – REVELATION (Part 2) BAD NEWS

    NB. This device is called *peripeteia* meaning a reversal of fortune from Good to Bad, or Bad to Good. It is a gem of a technique. If a director asks you for a TWIST do this.

- The problem has been solved, but it's the worst possible outcome for our protagonist – REALISATION

    NB. This device is called *anagnorisis* meaning a change from ignorance to knowledge.

End

- The fallout from the revelation, things get even worse – CATASTROPHE

    NB. This is the moment when we feel *catharsis* – a releasing of all the pent-up fear and pity induced by the story.

- It's over. Time to tie-up the loose ends – RESOLUTION

Someone wants something, they try to get it, they think they've got it, but they haven't got it, and their life falls apart. That's it. That's all you need to know. You can now go and write a tragedy. And it will probably be quite good, because don't we all love a good beginning, middle and end, driven by cause and effect? Of course we do. A fact backed up by multiple manifestations of this simple paradigm over millennia.

Our brains are conditioned from birth to love stories with this kind of trajectory. It is in the stories we are told as children. But it wasn't only Aristotle who got this giant story snowball rolling. Written at some point between 220 BCE and 200 CE, about 3,500 miles away in India, a Sanskrit treatise on the performing arts, *The Nāṭyaśāstra*, attributed to the sage, Bharata Muni, was being put together. This vast book covers a wide range of dramaturgical techniques including dramatic structure. One of the potential plots outlined in this treatise uses a metaphor from nature that is not too far removed from Aristotle: in the **Beginning** we have the *seed*, the desire to attain something; in the **Middle** we have the opening of the seed, the effort to attain that something; the sprouting of the seed, the possibility of success; and a moment of looking away while the seed grows, the certainty of success; at the **End** we have full fruit, the thing has been attained, success.[5]

I have always been particularly fascinated by the inclusion of the moment of looking away, which would appear to correspond to the moment of calm in *Oedipus Rex*, suggesting that a story can benefit from a moment of quiet reflection before going deeper into the dark heart of the drama.

In fourteenth-century Japan, the actor and playwright, Zeami Motokiyo identified perhaps the simplest, and most beautiful, natural metaphor for dramatic structure in one of his reputed plot formulations for Noh Theatre in his analysis of *jo-ha-kyū*: in the **Beginning** we have a small stream; in the **Middle** the stream becomes a river, that becomes a raging torrent, that becomes a crashing waterfall; and we **End** with a still pool and a return to peace.[6] What a sublime way to understand escalating cause and effect dramatic story structure!

And there's more. A lot more. We love a Beginning-Middle-End. All of us. All over the world. Perhaps the simplest explication for the formula for a Beginning-Middle-End drama that I have ever come across was set out by the prolific, philandering Spanish Golden Age playwright, Lope de Vega, in his essay, *The New Art of Writing Plays*. Lope's formula, as explained to me by director and playwright, Lawrence Boswell: **Beginning** – SET IT UP. **Middle** – COMPLICATE IT. **End** – SORT IT OUT, with a twist.[7]

Lope de Vega had a formula. It worked. And he stuck to it. He wrote somewhere in the region of 1,800 plays as well as several hundred shorter dramas. I don't know about you, but he certainly puts my work ethic to shame.

Iterations of this simple formula continue to the present day. Most mainstream television and film drama follow the same basic Aristotelian prototype via a variety paradigms, flow-charts and theoretical models, all of which are, basically, the same thing, three acts, **Beginning-Middle-End,** cause and effect, someone wants something, they either get it or they don't, SET IT UP, COMPLICATE IT, SORT IT OUT, with a twist.

It seems incredible to me that we are still using the same template that Aristotle identified in 330 BCE, a theory that the playwright Timberlake Wertenbaker once referred to as *Aristotalitarianism*. We haven't come far in 2,500 years, have we? Well, if you dig a bit deeper, we have. There are plenty of ways to structure a play that are available to the more adventurous playwright. But before we explore those options, we need to know how to use the individual building blocks used to construct a play – the acts, the scenes, the beats . . .

Making a Scene

The playwright Steve Waters relates the idea that each scene in a play is like each cell in a body.[8] Inspired by this, I started to think of each scene in a play as if it were an organ in the human body – if one of them isn't functioning properly you are in trouble. And every scene should correspond to the pulse of the overall heart of the play.

What happens in a Scene?

In a traditional narrative-driven scene, something essential to the story needs to happen. Something needs to be revealed. Something needs to shift or change. At the very least there needs to be a character or narrative movement of some kind. We need to keep an eye on cause and effect, the *effect* of the preceding scene *causes* the scene we are watching to happen, which in turn induces an *effect* that leads to the necessity (*cause*) of the following scene. And (usually) every scene will up the stakes. Higher and higher. Risk upon risk. Every scene needs to be constructed in such a way that it can serve the forward momentum of the play. I always think that a good way to judge the effectiveness of a scene is by the excitement you feel about the scene that is to follow. If you are watching your play and the audience is enjoying it and you know that the next scene is even more exciting than the scene they are watching now, you are probably on to a good thing.

And every scene needs to belong. As Aristotle pointed out: if it is not a true part of the whole it should be cut . . .

To be clear, the BASICS of narrative-driven drama are as follows:

- A scene is a single unit of dramatic structure
- A scene is a dramatic unit (usually) in continuous time (usually) in a single space in which something changes
- Each scene must have a purpose
- Each scene must drive the story on
- Each scene must tell us something we didn't know before and set up something new that we want to know about
- Each consecutive scene should (hopefully) be more compelling than the previous scene.

In many plays the structure of a scene will be a miniature version of traditional play structure. It will have a beginning, a middle and an end. It will have a (very) quick set-up, an objective, a conflict, a climax, and (perhaps) a (very) short aftermath. A character will usually want something, they will try to get it, and they will either fail or succeed, and by so-doing, cause something to happen that will have an effect they will need to deal with in the next scene.

Internal dynamics of a Scene

The positioning of the climax of the scene is just as important as the positioning of the climax of the play – again, it is play structure in miniature.

A scene will usually have a three-part structure:

i)   The moment before something happens
ii) The moment it happens (or doesn't happen)
iii) The moment after it has happened (or hasn't happened)

If the crux of the scene comes too soon and too much time is spent in the aftermath the effect may be dissipated and if nothing else happens the attention of the audience might wander.

If the crux comes too late in a long scene, the audience may have already switched off and you'll have a struggle to get them back.

Each scene needs to be managed and controlled to sustain the audience's interest and attention. If an audience doesn't care about what happens next, you've probably lost them.

The crux of each scene, then – the revelation, the conflict, the reversal – must come at the right moment. Back to play structure – the climax is probably best coming about two-thirds to seven-eighths of the way through.

As a rule (if there is such a thing) a scene should only be as long as is necessary to deliver the information it needs to deliver in the context of the trajectory of the story. However, it is worth bearing in mind that a short scene on the page may play longer in performance if it contains a big emotional moment. Similarly, a long scene on the page may play faster on stage if it is a 100 mph slanging match. And in a very long scene there may be several cruxes – such as in Chekhov where multiple character stories may be played out in sequence.

Pace

The question of pace is an interesting one – both in terms of the scene as a stand-alone unit and within the context of the play as a whole. Scenes of a similar length, one after the other, in a predictable, repeating pattern can have a soporific effect on an audience. If your second act has four long scenes, back-to-back, you might run the risk of inducing drooping eyelids. But don't make the mistake of trying a long-short-long-short repeating pattern, this too can create a predictable rhythm that can have a drowsy effect. A simple way to prevent theatrical narcolepsy is to vary scene length, you can easily break up a sequence of long scenes with a short one, interrupting the somnambulant rhythm, giving a sense of forward motion, and re-energizing the play and the audience. If you want to keep your audience invested, break up your play into scenes of different length, with different energy, and varying pace.

In writing a new scene, ask yourself: what structure is best for this scene, how does this affect the overall structure and pace of my play, AND how will this affect the audience watching my play.

An audience will get into the rhythm of a play. A four act play by Chekhov will usually have four long scenes with a number of highs and lows and shifts in pace, but an audience will know this and quickly settle into the rhythm of this structure. If this feels too comfortable for you, you could write a play with a lot of short scenes that never lets the audience settle and keeps them on an adrenaline high. Or you might want to surprise your audience with a change in scene length – a change in scene length is like a change in gear, shifting up with a short scene, or shifting down with a longer scene. Or you may wish to keep your audience on its toes by continually changing scene length so that they never get into a groove (or rut).

And it's not only length and pace you need to consider; tone is also a factor. An unremitting sequence of dark scenes can send an audience into a numbed stupor, but they can be revived with a lighter scene – and this can also give them the energy to face the dark-dark conclusion of your play. It works a treat in musical theatre where a light and amusing scene/song is sometimes used to elevate the mood of the audience before they are reduced to gibbering wrecks by the heart-breaking denouement of the show. An inspired example of this can be found in *West Side Story*, just before things get really dark, the book writer, Arthur Laurents, inserts a comic musical number, *Officer Krupke*. Interestingly, in the film version, the producers moved this scene to earlier in the musical, leading Arthur Laurents to conclude that they had completely misunderstood the structural purpose of the moment.[9]

Let your scenes do what they need to do and always keep an eye on how they slot together.

Elements to think about

The distribution of power in a scene.

The clarity of the crux/objective.

The inner conflict – the intra conflict – the extra (social) context/conflict.

The circumstances (location and situation at the start of the scene).

The shift – the change in the scene. The moment when the balance shifts.

Momentum – what is driving the scene.

Always choose the best, most fascinating, most relevant, most metaphorically ingenious, most imagistically thrilling setting for each scene ...

AND DON'T FORGET THE *SCENE CHANGES* – think about this from both a production and an audience POV. Cumbersome set changes will kill the pace of your play. Think about music. Think about light. Think about stage crew ...

You should now have a good idea of how to construct a scene, but you don't have to write scenes in the way I have outlined. Now that you know how to do it, you can deliberately experiment with doing it differently. You don't even need to call them scenes, you can call them 'scenarios' like Martin Crimp, or use dashes or dots or any other way of delineating scenes that doesn't use numbering. In terms of the internal structure of a scene, you can deliberately try to subvert the Aristotle-in-miniature structure, but be warned, it isn't easy! If in doubt, take some inspiration from the great Sarah Kane and scatter numerals all over the page like she does in *4.48 Psychosis*.[10] And scenes can be malleable, in *The Watsons* by Laura Wade, the scenes often bleed seamlessly into one another – before one scene has finished another scene has already begun. They are like interlaced fingers, it keeps the pace fast, attention focussed, and obviates the need for the constant stop-start, up and down yo-yoing of the lights and shifting of furniture in the blackout.[11]

But before you can start deconstructing and reconstructing individual scenes, you need to know how they fit into your overall structure. So, let's get back to the big picture and explore some ways to subvert the classic Aristotelian paradigm.

It is possible to structure a play differently to the one prescribed by generations of theorists and writers, but be warned, it's hard to convince other people there are other ways to do it. You are likely to be confronted by some hostility: *But that's not how to do it!* they will cry. It will be your job to convince them otherwise.

So, what are some other ways of structuring a play? Here are some **alternative structures**, starting, again, with the Greeks.

Comedy (Greek-style)

The structural template for an Aristophanean comedy usually looks something like this:

- *Prologue* – a monologue or duologue presenting the topic of the play, sometimes referred to as the 'happy idea' (usually a social/ political question)
- *Parode* – the chorus enter to set up a position for or against the idea
- *Agôn* – two characters debate the idea
- *Parabasis* – the chorus leader and chorus talk directly to the audience about the idea and/or other social/political problems
- *Episode* – a scene (or scenes) in which the actors elaborate on the outcome of the argument heard in the *Agôn*
- *Exode* – an exit song, sung in the spirit of celebration.

Not a lot of cause and effect. A contemporary version might look something like this:

Part 1 – a comedian talks to us about a contemporary issue

Part 2 – a group of singers/dancers do a song and dance about it

Part 3 – two characters have a furious row about it

Part 4 – the singers/dancers tell the audience what they think

Part 5 – the two characters have another furious row

Part 6 – everyone gets together and sings a song

Got to be worth a try, hasn't it?
Here are a few other ideas.

Fragments

A collection of scenes that can be put together in a variety of orders.

If you don't know *Woyzeck* by Georg Büchner, do yourself a favour, read it. This play, unfinished at the time of Büchner's horribly early death (he died at the age of twenty-three in 1837), was left as a series of scenes, fragments of a play, that the playwright was yet to complete. One of the great joys of this play is that because Büchner left the play unfinished and hadn't arranged the scenes in a set order, it was left to later writers, editors, translators, dramaturgs, actors and directors to order the scenes for him. It resulted in a fantastic, probably accidental, innovation – a series of scenes that can be put together in any sequence by the company producing the play. This can result in different interpretations of the content by means of different sequencing of scenes. It is also gorgeously collaborative. If the content of a play is reborn every time it is produced, this play is doubly reborn in form and content. The Beginning-Middle-End of this play are entirely at the discretion of the creative team working on the play. What a wonderful challenge for a playwright, to write a play that can be fashioned differently every time it is produced.

I have worked with several writers in recent years who have written plays which invite future collaborators to arrange the scenes in whatever order they prefer. It is a wonderful way to invite others to dig deep into the meaning and tangents of a play and present their individual interpretation for an audience.

Borrowed

A structure taken from another source.

Use the structure of a ballet, or an opera, or a novel, or another artwork to tell your story. *The Inheritance* by Matthew Lopez borrows from the novel *Howards End* by E.M. Forster. This is a story (theoretically) being written as we watch, characters appear to be creating the narrative as they tell it, sometimes they even voice displeasure with the plot. At times E.M. Forster will tell them something it might be useful for them to know about writing – such as the fact they every now and then they might want to change their mind about things as the story progresses. A writer has choices, even in the performance of a play about a play in a novelistic form, they still have choices.

You could use musical structures to structure a play – a symphony, a song, a jazz standard. Talking about her play *Anatomy of a Suicide* on the Royal Court podcast, Alice Birch explains that her play was written like a musical round – a series of overlapping, repeating musical patterns. A wonderful insight into the structure of this play.

How about using emotion to structure your play? What does a furious structure look like? What does a broken-hearted structure look like? What does a depressed structure look like?

How about using philosophy to structure your play? The writers of surrealistic drama did. The writers of absurd drama did. The writers of realism/naturalism did.

Perhaps think about the connection between content and form. Ask yourself how the content of your play can inform the form. Can the subject/idea/content suggest a shape/structure/form?

If you are writing a play about a mathematician – perhaps ask how a mathematical formula might shape your play. If you are writing a play about a politician – how can an ideology shape your play?

And don't forget the play within the play format. Brandon Jacob-Jenkins used an old play (*The Octoroon*) to propel and frame his new play (*An Octoroon*). Spread your net wide, ask what you can borrow that will allow you to innovate and think of dramatic structure in a different way.

Inside the mind

The world seen from the inside of a mind.

Our brains are very strange places, we imagine, we think, and we dream some very strange things. Our thoughts don't go through a sequential cause and effect order resulting in a climax and catharsis. Sometimes our minds go totally awry. So why not use it?

Perhaps a dream? A strange, surprising, inconsistent, unpredictable sequence of events – *A Dream Play* by August Strindberg.[12]

Or perhaps we can observe events from the inside of the protagonist's conscious mind – *After the Fall* by Arthur Miller.[13]

Or perhaps create a structure built on the experience of dementia – *The Father* by Florian Zeller.[14]

Our brains. Neurology. Psychology. Our mental health. How can we use these things to find form? Scenes that snap together like synapses. Scenes that fit together like the parts of our brains. A structure built on neuroses – a stress structure, an anxiety structure, an obsession structure. Memory can play tricks on us, use it; emotions can control us, use it; perception can be distorted, use it; a fever can make us hallucinate, use it. Use the absurd and unpredictable way our brains function to find an innovative shape for your story.

Sisyphean (or Circular)

Ending up back where you started.

Sisyphus pushes his boulder all the way to the top of the mountain and just when he is within touching distance of the top, the boulder rolls all the way back down to the bottom and he must walk back down and do it all over again. The touchstone of absurdity. But, as Camus points out, we must imagine Sisyphus happy.[15] And you must also imagine the playwright happy, because this is a wonderful device that pays great existential dividends.

Waiting for Godot by Samuel Beckett is a play in which (famously) nothing happens twice, and we end up where we began.[16] *La Ronde* by Arthur Schnitzler, contains a sequence of sexual encounters that leads back to where we started.[17]

This is a common device, but also a very satisfying one. Perhaps the best bookends for a structure ever chanced upon.

Defying expectation

Set it up – then, don't do it.

A simple idea: subvert expectation. Set up a dramatic trope, then side-step it. Lead your audience to expect one thing, then give them something completely different. Show us the **cause**; then give us an unexpected **effect**.

Modern audiences are comprised of legions of smartarses who are confident they can predict the twists and turns of a plot. And why wouldn't they be confident about it, we are fed the same story structure again and again – Beginning-Middle-End, enemies to lovers; zeroes to heroes; rags to riches. Consciously (or subconsciously) we have all been conditioned in the storytelling art of **cause** and **effect**. Challenge yourself to do something different. Give us a **cause** and then choose an unpredictable **effect**.

For example: boy meets girl, they fall in love, they don't get together (courtesy of the musical *Once*).[18]

Try to surprise your audience at every turn. Create a play in which nothing that you set up pays off in the way the audience is likely to predict.

The wheel

A theme/idea-linked plot.

Think of an old-fashioned wagon wheel – a central hub with spokes.

In Wheel Structure, the hub is the central theme or idea of your play, the spokes are the scenes, stories, vignettes, that radiate out from this hub. Your hub might be the theme of sexual exploitation, your spokes the stories of six or seven victims of sex trafficking; your hub might be the life of a small American town called Grover's Corner in *Our Town* or a Welsh fishing village called Llareggub in *Under Milk Wood*,[19] your spokes are the stories of the individual inhabitants. Your hub might be the theme of envy, your spokes seven thematically, but otherwise unrelated, stories about the green-eyed monster.

Multiple POV

An event-linked plot

The same event seen from different points of view (or different versions of the same story).

The story of the disappearance of a child, told from the POV of the mother, the father, the child, the sister, the teacher, the police officer.

Think: Event – lies, truth and memory.

The daisy-chain

A thing-linked plot.

A plot linked by a thing – an object or single location – rather than the journey of a single protagonist.

The story of a bicycle (and its four riders); the story of a guitar (and its five players); the story of a medieval manuscript and its journey to the present day; the story of a single prison cell and the cell's chain of prisoners through the ages. The story of a plot of land and the seductions and encounters that take place there over 2,000 years – Moira Buffini's *Loveplay*.[20]

Think: Thing.

Time

We can do extraordinary things with time. We can make time jump, slip and warp. We can speed it up, slow it down, and make it stop. In Thornton Wilder's play, *The Long Christmas Dinner*,[21] ninety years pass in one continuous scene of forty minutes.

Don't obsess about real time, use time as symbol, metaphor, action; distort it, run it backwards like Harold Pinter does in *Betrayal*.[22] Run it out of sequence, like Caryl Churchill does in *Top Girls*.[23]

Ask yourself if linear time is the best way to tell your story. If you can generate a stronger dramatic impact by running events out of sequence, do it. Scramble time, buckle time, go forwards and backwards at the same time, repeat time – repeat the same moment again and again with different results like Caryl Churchill does in *Heart's Desire*, part of *Blue Heart* (1997).[24]

Use time to enhance the dynamic of your play.

No conflict

Perceived wisdom: Drama is Conflict.

Challenge perceived wisdom: Try Kishōtenketsu.

Kishōtenketsu usually contains four sections: introduction, development, twist and conclusion. The story is introduced in the first part, developed in the second. But there are no major changes until the third section, in which a surprising element is introduced – this section is the equivalent of the climax in the Aristotelian paradigm, but different in that it doesn't obviously follow on from preceding events. It is left for the fourth section to pull the strands together, to recontextualize events, to wrap up the story.

One: A girl goes shopping.

Two: She buys a hammer.

Three: We see an elderly man sitting in an old rowing boat on a beach.

Four: The elderly man watches as the girl repairs a hole in the bottom of the boat.

Meandering

Go for a long walk.

A meandering structure is a story that follows a winding path or a winding river without apparent direction. It is usually episodic. You are more likely to find a meandering structure in a novel than on the stage. Good examples are *Alice in Wonderland* (Lewis Carroll), *Don Quixote* (Miguel Cervantes).

Branching

Climb a tree.

A variation on the Meandering Structure is Branching Structure. This structure consists of a system of branches that extend from a trunk by adding new branches. Once again, this is more of a novelistic structure that can be found in books like *Game of Thrones* (George R. R. Martin). It also forms a fundamental part of many gaming structures.[25]

Parallel

This structure has dual or multiple storylines that mirror and reflect each other.

Stories can include different protagonists or a single protagonist living different 'lives' or the same protagonists in different worlds. *Constellations*, by Nick Payne, shows two characters living in parallel manifestations – brilliantly showing the effects of the choices we make in life (more on this below – in Science). A play can offer a single character in multiple personalities – in a play of mine called *Lush Life*, directed by Max Roberts and originally produced by Live Theatre in Newcastle in 2008, I had five actors playing one part.

Think in parallel.

Science

A dramatic structure built from a scientific theory.

Evolution – a play that changes slowly over time.

The Big Bang – a play that expands.

The Multiverse – make one of your characters a scientist who is researching the multiverse and use parallel universes to shape your play. This is what Nick Payne does in his magnificent play, *Constellations* – a play that shows scenes between the same couple informed by what might be happening in parallel existences. *Constellations* is a brilliant play and contains what has to be my favourite ever writer's note at the beginning of the play:

An indented rule indicates a change in universe.[26]

That's it. That's all he has to say. Because he doesn't need to say anything else. That single line does all the work for him. I can't imagine a universe where a playwright could come up with a better note. In the Big Bang of Twenty-First-Century writer's notes, Nick is my winner.

Planetary Motion – scenes/planets that orbit a central scene/sun.

Universal Law of Gravitation – scenes that keep pulling in the same direction.

Thermodynamics – you can't win, you can't break even, you can't quit the game.

The Uncertainty Principle – Simon Stephens alludes to this principle in his play *Heisenberg* in which the unpredictability relates to the relationship between his two characters.[27] It is an excellent starting point for a play, and I can't help thinking that much more can be excavated from this theory.

Chaos theory – anything can happen.

Let form tell the story

In drama, it will often be the content that drives the story and suggests the form and structure of the play, but it is possible to reverse the dynamic and let the form tell the story. In *Happy Days* by Samuel Beckett, while the character of Win takes us through the detail of her daily existence she is swallowed up by a mound of earth – the form tells us that her life is passing her by as she obsesses about the contents of her handbag.[28] Like the vast majority of us, she is fixated by the trivial things in life (her handbag) while she is in the process of dying (the enveloping mound). It isn't what she tells us that shapes the story, it is the mound that is swallowing her up.

Reverse the paradigm: think about how the form of your play can tell your story rather than the content.

Postdramatic structure

Structure after drama. Structure without drama. Structure as chaos. Structure as individual audience member interpretation. Structure as whatever it will be according to the performance. More on this in the chapter 2.10 *Write a Postdramatic Play*.

When you have alighted upon a new structure, you can begin to think about how the individual scenes will work within that structure. My advice is to first identify the beast, then go full Frankenstein and start to transplant the organs you need to make it function.

And . . .

If you can't avoid (or resist) a traditional structure, how about doing what Seneca did and putting a musical interlude between each of the acts? Seriously. Have you ever been watching a play and noticed that the energy in the room is beginning to sag? It feels like the momentum has been lost. There is a simple solution. Put a song in! I'm being serious. If you want to re-energize your audience, take them to a different place with a different energy, what better way to do it than with a song. In Golden Age Broadway musical theatre, they would often insert a blockbuster of a song to wake the audience up when the energy in the room was sagging. So why shouldn't we do it in a play? Paula Vogel wasn't worried about inserting a song or two into *Indecent*. She uses a song to stir the audience after setting up the world of her play; she uses a song to show the process of immigration and assimilation; she uses a song interleaved with dialogue to show the rising tide of genocide. This is a play with performance at its heart, in which the performers of the play it was inspired by were ultimately banned from performing plays and were only allowed to perform songs, dances and skits. But your play doesn't need to be about a performance troupe for you to include songs. Shakespeare did it. We are working in the medium of live performance. Music is live performance. I have sometimes found myself bored to tears at a new play wishing silently to myself for the characters to burst into song to break the tedium. So, why not? Serious playwrights: songs are not the enemy; they are your allies.

How are **contemporary writers** using structure? Below are some examples from a selection of what I believe to be some of the best modern plays.

Dance Nation

In *Dance Nation* Clare Barron basically uses a classical Aristotelian complex plot – it is a play about entering a dance competition and like many sport/competition stories the shape of the story is dictated by progress in the competition. What is interesting about her structure is the way that she successfully fuses the narrative (the competition) and the thematic (the story about growing up). These elements co-exist and the arc of the old-school competition plot is given a visceral new life in the way that it simultaneously tells the rights of passage story of the adolescent characters. Inspired crafts(wo)manship.

Seven Methods of Killing Kylie Jenner

Jasmine Lee Jones bookends her play *Seven Methods of Killing Kylie Jenner* with what she terms a 'Pre-meditation' which foreshadows the end of the play and a 'Post-Mortem' that takes us back to and then beyond the moment we saw at the start of the play. The opening is a great teaser for what is to come. Other than this, the play uses a solid cause and effect narrative with the parallel escalation of events in the real world and in the Twittersphere.

An Octoroon

In the original version of *The Octoroon* by Dion Boucicault, each act ends with a tableau, at the end of the first act of Branden Jacob-Jenkins' *An Octoroon*, the actors attempt a tableau, but then the contemporary playwright adds a couple of extra (very modern sounding) pages of dialogue. Then we get the tableau. He has given us a false ending and then a modern addendum, then another ending. Neat trick.

An Octoroon has a dual structure – the complex Aristotelian melodramatic original and the metatheatrical devices of the new play that constantly interrupt and break the structure of the original play. Jacobs-Jenkins also ends his version of the original play early, denying the audience the 'Bad Thing–Good Thing–Bad Thing' twist and catharsis of Boucicault's melodrama.

Revolt. She Said. Revolt Again

In many ways *Revolt* is a revolutionary play – how could it be anything else? But Alice Birch does give some structural elements for us to cling onto because it is basically a four act play with a discernible shape – a first act of fragments; a second act that is, in essence, a one act play; a third act that (arguably) has a climax in the form of a cacophonous postdramatic avalanche of words; and a short fourth act as resolution. So, it does kind of behave (in a revolutionary sort of way).

How I Learned to Drive

Paul Vogel's *How I Learned to Drive* is structured around a series of driving lessons, told sometimes in reverse, sometimes shifting from first to second gear, sometimes breaking down, making left turns, and ending with a talk about driving in today's world (except it's more than driving, of course, it is also sex). The play is structured so that the first story/ chronological episode of abuse comes at the end of the play, we don't see the escalation of abuse, we go backwards to see when it started. It is a beautifully put together play by a playwright who has theatricality in her DNA (or should that be engine?)

Indecent

Time is yours to manipulate on the page. There are no laws. You are in charge of the temporal universe. As Paula Vogel writes in the introduction of her wonderful play 'Indecent', working with her collaborators helped her to realize that 'I could write a tour of Europe in a page.'[29] And she does – almost (in the published script it takes two pages, but the text is generously spaced, and she does manage to travel from Germany to Russia to Turkey to Slovakia in this very short time). And this isn't the only time-bending Paula achieves in this play. 'Indecent' is a play about a play – and she manages to give us the entire original play in less than three pages. Kudos.

Don't be afraid to speed things up or slow then down when you need to. Don't labour to give us real events in real time when you don't need to, even in a predominantly naturalistic play.

The Writer

I was always told that it is essential to establish your contract with the audience in the first five minutes of your play. In other words, the first few minutes need to outline the precise nature of the suspension of disbelief required of your audience to engage with the performance. But you don't have to do this. You can set up one type of play and then pull the rug out completely from under the audience's feet, like Ella Hickson does in *The Writer*. The opening of this play is sublime – a play has just finished; a young woman and an older man enter and discuss the play they have just seen. She is a writer; he is a director. In the following scene, the writer and director of the scene we have just watched (in which they played a slightly more attractive versions of their 'real' selves) enter for an audience Q&A about the scene we have just watched. What started as one thing has become something else. What a great metatheatrical twist and how gloriously disorientating for the audience. And it doesn't stop there. *The Writer* is a complex play about writing, performance, the nature of representation, the staging of the female experience, confrontation, probability, myth, sex, sexuality, feminism, and its structure mirrors this complexity. After a disorientating, metatheatrical first half of the play in which the playwright sets up the story of a writer and director and actor (boyfriend), she then takes us somewhere totally unexpected with a provocation – a piece of direct address storytelling which, in Ella Hickson's words, 'should be an attempt at staging the female experience,'[30] complete with photographic landscapes, drawings, dance and celebration. Weren't expecting that were you, director? What are you going to do with it? And after all this, we come back to the world of the play as it was, with the characters (the writer and the director) trying to work out how to finish the play they have started.

Story

Before we move on, we need to think about that thing they call STORY.

There are, allegedly, seven basic stories: Overcoming the monster, Rags to riches, The quest, Voyage and return, Comedy, Tragedy, Rebirth.[31]

Or, if you prefer: Cinderella, Achilles, Faust, Tristan and Isolde, Circe, Romeo and Juliet, Orpheus.[32]

Or, if you prefer: Love, Money, Power, Revenge, Survival, Glory, and Self-awareness.[33]

There are many books and essays on the subject of story, but I don't think it is essential for a playwright to spend hours of their valuable time debating the number and types of plots, let's leave that to the theorists and get on with writing our plays. The only time I have found referring to these story types vaguely useful was when I got a bit stuck and needed the storytelling equivalent of a *Get out of Jail Free* card by experimenting with where my story might go if I laid an *Achilles* story type over it or a *Circe* story type. It was an interesting process, but I quickly discarded the result.

If you want to challenge yourself to write your own archetypal *Orpheus* story, good luck to you. My concern is that you might force yourself into a story straitjacket or start to worry when your *Faust* veers into *Cinderella*. If you can use these basic story types to help you write, use them, but don't waste precious time analysing whether you're writing a *Romeo and Juliet* or *Tristan and Isolde*, just write your play. Besides, I recently discovered that there is only actually one basic story. I was teaching a class on story and structure when one of my students informed me that according to one of his tutors at his previous college, there are only three stories: **Love**, **Money** and **War**. Which prompted another student to suggest that surely the category of money can be subsumed into war and that, therefore, there are only two stories: **Love** and **War**. To which another student suggested that surely love can be subsumed into war, which gives us one story: **War**. It would appear that every story ever written is about **War**. So now you know that you can write all your plays content in the knowledge that you have their archetypal story type totally nailed.

Knowing how dramatic structure works you can now begin to play with it. But this is only one part of your dramatic art. You also need to create characters and get them to talk . . .

2.4 YOU DO NOT NEED TO KNOW EVERYTHING ABOUT YOUR CHARACTERS

When I wrote my play *Bad Blood Blues* for *Theatrescience* in 2006, I decided to try something I had never done before – I wrote character backstories. This play is a two-hander, and I went into minute detail about character traits, opinions, idiosyncrasies, timelines and all kinds of likes and dislikes until I had several pages of bullet points for each of the characters. Then, I sat down to write the play ... and I ignored almost every single one of them. At this point I remembered why I never usually bothered with detailed character backstories before I started to write: my characters much prefer to reveal themselves to me as I write them. In the act of writing a scene in this play I discovered that one of my characters had polio as a child, there was nothing about this in my backstory, just a lot of useless information about the music she liked and her favourite holiday destination. Useless. Basically, for me, writing backstories can be a bit of a waste of time.

We expect our characters to be hyperreal these days and some writers go into painstaking detail about their characters, but I'm not convinced we need to do this, and it certainly hasn't always been this way. Aristotle considered plot to be more important than character and this continued to be the perceived wisdom until about 200 years ago. Arguably, the first challenge to the primacy of plot came in the form of the psychologically complex characters of William Shakespeare. During the centuries that followed, the idea of character and character development grew in importance to the point where, with the advent of naturalism, it started to rival plot in importance. Today, it is rare to discuss a play without talking about the arc of a character. Today, it is often the case that a story is driven more by how a character changes than it is by plot. Nowadays, it seems that what happens is less important than what a character experiences.

Is character more important than plot? That's for you to decide. But it doesn't have to be. As a playwright you have a rich store of options as well as three-dimensional character development. There are other ways of creating character. There are other things an actor can do. But you might struggle to find much written about it in the late twentieth- to early twenty-first-century crop of 'How to' books. I am complicit in this myself. I went through my teaching notes stretching back many years to find out what I had to say about characterization and soon discovered that I had said very little about alternatives to representational characterization and had been singing from the same character hymn sheet as the vast majority of other playwrights, dramaturgs and teachers from the last 100 years.

The dominant model in today's dramaturgy is to create a fully fleshed out, three-dimensional, true-to-life, consistent representation of an individual, with fully mapped out inner conflicts, a spider diagram of intra-personal relationships, and carefully identified extra-personal worldviews, complete with a full backstory and/or psychological profile complete with good and bad qualities and idiosyncratic character traits. They must want and/or need something – a goal or intention or (super) objective – and undergo change as a result of trying to get it. And all this before you even start to write your dialogue.

There are a lot of variations and spin-offs from the above advice, but it usually boils down to *believability*, *wants* and *change*. Reviewing this information today, I have two questions:

1 Do *all* characters need to be believable?
2 Isn't at least some of this work the actor's job?

It seems to me that most of the above advice on creating a character comes from the development of acting techniques of the last 120 years or so. Stanislavski to Strasberg to Adler to a multitude of acolytes. Phenomenal, wonderful, extraordinary work. But, as far as the playwright is concerned, isn't all this just acting technique?

As David Edgar so insightfully deduced, 'What characters do is pursue objectives, an insight which was codified by the Russian director

Stanislavski into a theory of acting which implies a theory of writing.'[1] Stanislavski took characters from the plays he was directing and challenged his actors to find the truth in their characters, a corollary of which was to push writers to develop more naturalistic characters to enable the actors to create ever more believable characters. A radical development in theatre that continues to resonate well over a century later. Brilliant. Brilliant. Brilliant. But my worry is that we, as playwrights, have become slaves to what is basically a method of acting.

Shakespeare's characters – for example, Hamlet, Ophelia, Macbeth, Juliet – all have psychological depth, but I doubt if Shakespeare ever sat down to work out what they had for breakfast. I would like to suggest that we leave the minutiae of backstory to our actors. I think it's a waste of our valuable time. And, after all, out artform is about collaboration, isn't it? I think we should concentrate on writing our plays rather than building exhaustive character biographies with information that will force itself into our plays unnecessarily or be of no use whatsoever. If we choose, we can spend a bit of time getting to know our characters before we start to write, but we also need to allow our characters to create and re-create themselves as we write them. Let them tell us what they like, let them tell us where they want to go, let them tell us what they want to eat. I think Harold Pinter might have agreed, he said 'When a writer sets out the blueprint for his characters and keeps them rigidly to it, where they do not at any time upset his applecart, when he has mastered them he has also killed or rather terminated their births.'[2]

Creating characters should be a two-way street. You approach them; they approach you. They are a stranger walking towards you. When you first see them, you know nothing about them. As they get closer, you might be able to discern things from the way they walk, their expression, the clothes they wear. If you force them to walk a certain way, or make an expression that is alien to them, or wear clothes that don't fit, you will never get to know them properly. You need to let them show you these things. And sometimes they might refuse. It is a battle of wills. And the best plays are the ones in which the characters get their own way. If you cast a character in bronze and never allow them to re-cast themselves, you are in trouble. A character will reveal things to you just as a new acquaintance will, and that revelation could fundamentally shift your perception of them. Let it happen. If you are lucky, your characters will reveal to you who they are, you shouldn't seek to impose things upon them.

There is one word that I think all playwrights need to remember when creating a character: flexibility.

The only thing a playwright needs to know when creating a character for a naturalistic cause and effect drama, is what they want. The only thing a playwright needs to provide for their collaborators are the words on the page – the things the character does and the things the character says. The director and the actors will do the rest. For most playwrights, spending precious hours developing a backstory when they could be writing their script will be a waste of time, a displacement activity, a method of procrastination.

But that doesn't mean that knowing absolutely nothing about your characters before you write is necessarily the best approach for everyone. Most writers, I believe, will probably do a little bit of character development and then find out the rest as they write. And – importantly – they will be prepared to change their character as they discover more about them. Like many other aspects of dramatic writing, the solution often lies in finding the balance between extremes. It's the old, Thesis – Antithesis – Synthesis paradigm.

Thesis – you must know everything about your character before you write!

Antithesis – you don't need to know anything about your character before you write!

Synthesis – know a bit and discover the rest as you go . . .

Beyond which approach suits you best, I want to remind you that there are other options. A character can be an archetype, a character can be a cypher, a lampshade can be a character. And what happens if the character the writer has created is interpreted entirely differently by the actor? Is that a problem or just one of the joyous variables of collaboration?

To get a better understanding of the many ways in which character can work on the stage, other than the true-to-life, representational model, let's take a look at how playwrights have used character in the past and what some of the more innovative playwrights are doing today. As ever, these techniques are there for us to use, abuse and revise with our own additions. Let's try to think differently about character. Think laterally.

The Greek tragic hero

Write a tragedy! Go on! You know you want to! Okay, but where to begin? You need a *tragic hero*.

Aristotle would probably suggest that there are four basic things you need to aim for in your hero:

- they should be **good**
- your portrayal of them should be **appropriate**
- they should be **lifelike**
- and they should be **consistent** (or if they are inconsistent, they should be consistently inconsistent)[3]

It all sounds quite familiar, doesn't it? We might not put the emphasis on a character being 'good' in the same way anymore, but all the other elements – being appropriate, lifelike, consistent – are basic naturalistic character requirements. The path from Aristotle's advocacy of lifelike characters to the snot and excrement of today's hyperrealism would seem to be quite a short one, except, there have been some considerable deviations from that path and there are some fundamental differences between the kind of good-appropriate-lifelike-consistent character Aristotle advocates and the type of character you are likely to find in a naturalistic play today.

In Aristotle's day the *tragic hero* was likely to be an historical-mythological character, so they weren't literally likely to be *like us*, they would most likely be a virtuous, capable and powerful noble. However, the character would most definitely be *like us* in the way that we associatively feel and suffer their pity and fear. Never underestimate the power of fear and pity in your audience, it's what they need! We all need a good emotional purge from time to time and what better way to do it than through fear and pity of unmerited misfortune, the two emotions fundamental to the experience of catharsis – the process of sluicing pent-up emotions through drama.

Next, you need perhaps the most essential *tragic hero* character trait: the fatal flaw or *hamartia*. This is a tragic human quality, like hubris that will ultimately lead to your hero's downfall. And it is as a result of this fatal flaw that your hero will suffer a reversal of fortune that will lead them to a new understanding of their predicament.

In brief: a *tragic hero* is a character of noble birth with heroic qualities whose fortunes change due to a fatal flaw that brings about their downfall.

Thankfully, we have moved on from the idea that only nobles are worthy of dramatic interpretation, but the fundamentals of this paradigm can be found in a vast number of characters. Perhaps the best twentieth-century version of the *tragic hero* can be found in the plays of Arthur Miller. Who is Eddie Carbone if not a classical Greek *tragic hero*?[4]

It isn't hard to create a *tragic hero*, but there is more to the Greek *tragic hero* than meets the eye. Today, if a playwright were to set about creating a *tragic hero*, they would probably illuminate that *hero* in a glaring fluorescent naturalistic light and expect the part to be performed by an actor, face streaked with tears, their clothes purchased from the online shops that the writer's backstory stipulates they like to buy from, their words fractured and scattered like the fluttering dialogue of everyday life. And we would probably feel a great deal of fear and pity along with them, but this wasn't how the Greeks did it.

I am indebted to the great Thornton Wilder (again) for the observation that during the first production of Euripides' *Medea* – specifically, the passage where Medea contemplates the murder of her own children to get revenge on her philandering husband, Jason – the audience was so shaken that a major disturbance took place. (Quite where Thornton Wilder heard this anecdote, he doesn't say, but I believe him, because he is Thornton Wilder after all . . .)

Let's break this moment down into Aristotelian pre-requisites: a fundamentally good character, appropriately personified, with a lifelike personality, consistent in her characterization, informs us that she is contemplating the murder of her own children as revenge for abandonment by her errant husband, Jason. But there is a big difference between the way a Greek audience would have met this character and the way we might meet a character in a similar predicament today. As Wilder points out:

> Firstly, Medea was played by a man.
>
> Secondly, the actor wore a mask on his face, and shoes with six-inch platforms.
>
> Thirdly, the costume symbolized that this character was a woman of royal birth.
>
> Fourthly, the dialogue was written in poetic meter and performed in a kind of musical recitative.[5]

Not exactly naturalistic. Yet we still feel the fear and pity. We feel the character's pain, but we don't need to pretend this is the real Medea in front of us – it isn't. Instead, we get to use our imagination and feel her pain through the evocation of language, movement and symbol. And it is just as effective as a fully-fledged, dribble and mucus-fuelled, naturalistic, emotional breakdown.

In classical Greek drama all actors were men, all actors wore masks, all actors (after Aeschylus) played more than one role, much of the dialogue was sung, and dance was a part of many scenes. I am not advocating that men should play women's roles (unless women, trans and non-binary actors get to play all the men's roles as well). However, I am suggesting that the next time you are tempted to create a hyperreal tragic character, why not consider putting her in a mask with giant heels and writing her lines in iambic trimeter (or trochaic tetrameter, if you're feeling really adventurous), and having her do a song and dance? Just a thought.

Stock characters

A stock character is a character that relies heavily on stereotypical traits that mark them out as a specific character type. Basically, they are an expositional short-cut relying on cliché and parody. Surely no great contemporary dramatist would stoop so low as to write a stock character into their new play, would they? To which I say, why not? Why not have a two-dimensional stock character in your play? Let your 'real' characters bump up against 'unreal' ones. Play with the idea of stock traits. Tease. Don't dismiss the idea of stock characters simply because it is not fashionable, use them to create something new.

Aristophanes gave us boastful imposters, ironic adversaries, and buffoons with very specific accents, costumes and props. The moment they appeared, the audience knew who they were and what they represented. Here comes a character with a truncheon, must be a parasite! That one's got a crook, must be a shepherd! That one's got a sceptre, must be a royal!

Similarly, a character walks on stage in a Roman comedy by Plautus and the audience know immediately who that character is; his mask, his costume, his posture, his gait, tell us immediately that this is an old miser, a young lover, a cunning slave, a flatterer, a braggart. Nothing needs to be explained.

Aristotle's student, Theophrastus, even went so far as write a book called *The Characters* introducing the idea of character sketches, thirty-two of them, from *The Ironical Man* to *The Avaricious Man* by way of *The Gossip*, *The Grumbler* and *The Oligarch*. How about sitting down to write a play with no other information than that you have three characters called *The Gossip*, *The Grumbler* and *The Oligarch*? No character development, just jump straight in.

How about bringing the prototypical characters of the Medieval English Mystery, Morality and Miracle plays back to life? Characters with names like Death, or Vice or Everyman. Is the character of Everyman a simple, symbolic representation of every one of us? Yes! Of course he is! He's called Everyman! Does the character of Vice encourage immoral behaviour? You bet! Has Death come to claim our living form? Absolutely! Cut to the chase, name your characters for what they symbolize!

And then there's *commedia dell'arte*, replete with its troop of stock characters and variations thereof. The young lovers, the masters, the servants. In *commedia dell'arte* the young lovers – the *innamorati* – were unmasked roles, while the masters and the servants were masked roles. It is rare to read or see a contemporary play in the context of new writing with masked roles; and as for a play with a mixture of masked and unmasked roles – those plays would appear to be almost extinct. What a pity. A mixture of masked and unmasked roles could create a potentially fascinating theatrical dynamic – the real and the unreal; the natural and the unnatural; the three-dimensional and the two-dimensional; empathy and distance. There is so much to play with here.

I wish playwrights weren't so afraid of masked characters. I wish we were more willing to engage with the kind of physical theatre that masked characters demand. Ask yourself what a mask can do for a character. Think for a moment about one of your own plays – what would happen if one of the characters wore a mask? What would happen if all of the characters apart from your main character(s) wore a mask? Perhaps try to write a play with one or more masked characters – see what this does to your writing. Will it make the character bigger, louder, more stereotypical? Is that a problem or is it a theatrical blessing? Embrace the theatricality of playing with character in mask. It is such a rich theatrical tool it seems insane not to use it.

Perhaps we can experiment with reinventing *commedia dell'arte* for the twenty-first century. Take the stock characters and re-stock them, so to speak . . .

We could start with the masters – Pantalone, Dottore, Capitano.

Pantalone: an old merchant, very fond of proverbs, pretends he is younger than his years, attempts to court younger women. A contemporary Pantalone could become a contemporary captain of industry, reliant on soundbites, all hair dye and fashionable footwear in a pathetic attempt to attract a young lover.

Dottore: Pantalone's acquaintance and rival, an academic, or lawyer or medical doctor, a pedant, credulous, prone to pretentious use of Latin phrases. He could become an online autodidactic academic – spouting half-learned theories from a lectern in the corner of his living room in a vain attempt to get likes on YouTube.

Capitano: a windbag, a coward, full of how brave and clever he is. Capitano could become a narcissistic, prolix politician, in love with being seen to be important whilst not giving a damn about the actual work that needs to be done?

And the servants, the *zanni* – Arleccino (Harlequin), Scapino (Brighella), Pulcinello (Punch).

Arleccino: a mixture of cunning and stupidity, a dancer, an acrobat, carries a wooden sword (aka a 'slapstick'), becomes a Deliveroo rider, loves going to festivals, never goes anywhere without a selfie stick.

Scapino: Arleccino's mate, cynical, funny, lustful, becomes a prank-playing, sardonic barista whose life swipes by before him on a vast range of dating apps.

Pulcinello: idiotic and shrewd, nasty and nice, villainous and loving, becomes a very mixed-up intern working for a political think-tank.

And while we are at it, we can change all these male stock characters for female stock characters.

Alternatively, we can create a whole host of new stock characters for the twenty-first century. The Influencer. The Populist Politician. The Conspiracy Theorist.

Then, we should ask ourselves what their mask might look like.

The great thing about a mask (and an easily identifiable costume for that matter) is that the audience will immediately jump to a conclusion – and we can play with that, twist it, subvert it. No one would ever mistake an Arleccino for a Pantalone because of their mask, their costume, their physicality. Why are playwrights so frightened of using these elements in contemporary theatre? Why are we so frightened of masks and stock characters? I think part of the problem is that these practices are perceived as belonging to the past – but I don't see any reason why playwrights can't re-engage with them for the present and take them into the future. I also think that we are so obsessed with putting things into neat boxes that reinventing something like *commedia dell'arte* for today or, shock-horror, mixing it with another genre like naturalism might make audiences' brains burst. It wouldn't, of course. However, I do think that our love affair with naturalism has led to a fear of breaking the fourth wall in a naturalistic play with such devices. I think our theatres would be a much more exciting places if we mixed things up a bit more. Perhaps put a stock character wearing a mask in your next play. I dare you. And I'm not just talking about putting them in a comedy. Write a blistering critique of contemporary capitalism with men and women in power suits and then, at the start of Act Two, have your leading entrepreneurial demigod enter wearing a mask and do a dance whilst going around hitting people over the head with a wooden sword. Why not? It's THEATRE! It's (a) PLAY!

The satyr

A satyr is a half-beast, half-human, drunk, lustful follower of Dionysus with a large phallus and, if you're lucky, a mask with horns! Sadly, you won't see a lot of satyrs on the contemporary stage.

The tragedians of ancient Greece weren't just expected to write tragedies, they also had to master the art of the *satyr play*. A *satyr play* was a ribald, burlesque of mythology, usually in a bucolic setting served up after the playwright's trilogy of tragedies – a moment or puerile filth and comic relief to send the audience home in high spirits.[6] Perhaps we should consider adding a short play like this to the bill after a searing modern tragedy? A production of Sarah Kane's *Blasted* followed by a ten-minute slapstick routine replete with custard pies and fart cushions.[7] It might cheer some people up.

There is only one fully extant *satyr play* – *Cyclops* by Euripides. It is a dreadful, misogynistic, fatuous play. I don't recommend reading it, unless you need evidence that people were just as puerile two and a half thousand years ago as they are today. However, we do have fragments of one other – *Trackers* by Sophocles. And it was the fragments of this play that inspired Tony Harrison to write his utterly brilliant play, *The Trackers of Oxyrhynchus*.[8] This play is remarkable, not only for its glorious poetic language and theatrical sensibility, but for the reintroduction of the satyr onto the modern stage when a group of clog-dancing satyrs emerge from packing cases and tap dance their way around the stage.

Strange mythical beasts. Where are they on the modern stage? In *Enron* Lucy Prebble not only gives us mice-headed businesspeople, but also cannibalistic Raptors. She creates potent, literal monsters of the financial commodities and unethical practices, bringing the stage to spectacular life with colourful manifestations of the themes of her play. Why aren't more playwrights doing this? Why not put a half-human, half-beast in your next play? Perhaps as a representation of your character's dark side. Perhaps as comic relief. Not every character on stage has to be in human form.

A one-actor multiplicity

Get one actor to play a cast of thousands. A slight tilt of the head, a cough, a slouch – it is so simple for a single actor to change character. Write a play with multiple parts and then, on the title page, write: A Play for One Actor. Job done.

In *Random* debbie tucker green has one actor play a family – a sister, a brother, a mother, a father.[9] Having just one actor embody her entire family spins the centrifugal familial force that drives this play and takes us deep into the heart-wrenching bereavement at the centre of their story. Embodying the family in one body, using direct address monologues and dialogue between characters, all spoken by a single actor, enables a simultaneous connection and objectivity that allows us to grieve with the characters and, at the same time, think deeply about the story. A masterclass.

And it can work in other ways, multiple actors can play the same character at different ages, they can play different versions of the same character at the same age. And perhaps try enrichening access-led theatrical solutions like having a D/deaf actor playing the same part as a hearing actor, thereby creating multiple layers of further interpretation (more on this in the chapter 2.11 *Write Accessibly*).

Let's think harder about the one actor per character paradigm.

Inanimate objects

Any object can become a character.

The extraordinary theatre company, Forced Entertainment, produced a series called *Table-Top Shakespeare*: Shakespeare's plays told by a single actor, on a table-top, using an array of household items for their cast, a salt and pepper pot for a king and queen, a matchbox for a servant, a toilet roll tube for an innkeeper. Everyday items magically transformed into characters. So simple. So effective.

Did you ever use a broom as a horse or a rifle when you were a kid? It's called 'play' for a reason. Things don't always have to be what they appear to be. A thing can represent another thing. Playwrights, you don't have to be literal.

The cast for Lawrence Boswell's, fantastic stage adaptation of *Beauty and the Beast*, includes a Wardrobe, Vanity Table and Screen.[10] In Kushner and Tesori's *Caroline, or Change*, there's a great part for a Washing Machine.[11]

Let your furniture talk! Let it dance! Let it fall in love! It's a lot of fun, ask any actor who has played the character of Snout in the play within the play in Shakespeare's *A Midsummer Night's Dream* how much they enjoyed playing a wall separating two lovers . . .

Be an animal

And it's not only furniture that can talk; animals can. Anthropomorphise! You know you want to!

Or simply make a human character like an animal. Have a quick look at Ben Jonson's 1606 city comedy *Volpone*. In this play the wily, eponymous Volpone, 'the Fox', is helped by his parasitical servant, Mosca, 'the Fly', who buzzes around the ears of the three greedy legacy-hunters, Voltore, 'the Vulture', Corvino, 'the Crow', and Corbaccio, 'the Raven'.

Sometimes a simple animal metaphor will serve your play a lot more interestingly than knowing your character's New Year's resolution was to give up smoking.

Puppets

Puppets? Yes please! And I don't just mean puppeteers in black manipulating a proportionally precise horse puppet. I mean fully fledged human characters played by puppets in a play with flesh and blood actors. Why not? The next time one of your actors needs to have a conversation with her deceased Mother, give her a glove puppet.

Many years ago, I saw a production of *Hamlet* performed by the utterly magnificent Footsbarn Theatre, in which Gertrude and Claudius were played as Punch and Judy-type puppets in a puppet booth – it was glorious.

Paula Vogel refers to her play, *The Long Christmas Ride Home*, as 'a puppet play with actors.'[12] In this play, three children are played by Bunraku-style puppets that should ideally be manipulated by three actors who then play the adult versions of the children when they are grown up.[13] The play is a beautiful theatrical nexus between Thornton Wilder-inspired dramaturgy and Japanese Bunraku puppet theatre. Do we feel any less connected to the children because they are played by puppets? On the contrary, we feel an incredibly strong pull from them, they are the slightly distorted memory of who the adults were as children, and, as Paula Vogel points out, they might also be a bit spooky too.[14]

We should not be frightened of puppets as writers. Lucy Prebble isn't. in *A Very Expensive Poison* three oversized caricatured puppets of Gorbachev, Yeltsin and Brezhnev appear from the world of the TV.[15] Puppets explode the imagination. Seek out a puppet-maker, seek out an expert puppeteer, ask their advice, go on an adventure with some string and papier mâché! And if you are not convinced about 3D puppets how about some shadow puppets, it is amazing what you can bring to life with a light, an old sheet and some cardboard cut-outs. It's like ancient television without all the scenes set in kitchens with people shouting at each other in strong regional accents. Go inside your character's head with shadow puppets. Experiment. Be brave. Mix it up.

Psychological truth

Several of the most relatable, potent, psychologically complex, multi-dimensional characters ever created by a playwright talk in blank verse and rhymed couplets; they engage in punning wordplay and talk directly to the audience; they use little in the way of props or specific character costume; and they perform on a stage with little or no set. I am, of course, referring to the characters created by William Shakespeare.

Shakespeare's characters are 'real', but they also have the (theatrical) ability to stand outside themselves, to try to understand themselves. They articulate their inner thoughts and learn from them. We don't tend to think our thoughts out loud, but we do (sometimes) learn from them (I hope). By theatricalizing the thought process Shakespeare takes us deep into the psyche of the character, a non-naturalistic technique that enhances rather than diminishes empathy.

If Shakespeare can give his characters such extraordinary psychological depth using so few naturalistic, representational tools, shouldn't we at least begin to reassess our Gloucester-like blind devotion to creating 'real' characters all the time? Can we start to think of the psychological truth of a character as being contained in heightened presentational language and behaviour rather than obsessing about which brand of toothpaste they might prefer?

It is always satisfying to observe a believable character going on a journey of self-discovery and to empathize with the challenges and changes this provokes, but it isn't the only way to do it. Brecht didn't want empathy, he believed that if the audience developed an emotional attachment to the characters, they would not be able to evaluate the social message of the play.

In the Theatre of the Absurd sometimes characters are stereotypes; sometimes there is an absence of character development; sometimes there is a distinct lack of the motivation that is found in characters in naturalistic drama; sometimes character identity is blurred; sometimes characters are unsure about who or where or even what they are.

Here is something I believe to be true: a playwright can spend years developing a sublimely wrought protagonist, then a great actor can come along, interpret the part in a totally different way and create a far better character.

Of course, sometimes an actor might come along, get it horribly wrong and produce a dreadful misinterpretation of a character, but isn't one of the joys of our profession to be found in that messy symbiosis between writer and actor?

There is a story I once heard about a much-admired playwright, who, when asked by an actor what the motivation of his character might be, was told in no uncertain terms that there is no such thing as character or motivation and that he should just say the words that he (the writer) had written and get on with it – that was what he had trained for, wasn't it? That was what he was being paid to do, wasn't it? How much does a writer need to know about their character? Enough to make them an exciting prospect for an actor to interpret. How much does an actor need to know about their character? Enough to make them live and breathe in the context of the play. That's all.

Modern character

Here's an interesting question: To what extent should a contemporary dramatist get involved in casting?

In Clare Barron's note on casting at the beginning of her play *Dance Nation*, she explains that all characters, other than two adult roles, are between eleven and fourteen years old. However, she asserts that these adolescent characters should mostly be played by adults ranging in age from twelve to seventy-five plus. And she goes on to explain why – she wants us to 'Think of it as a ghost play: the actors' older bodies are haunting these 13-year-olds characters ... And these 13-year-old characters are haunted by the specters of what they will become.'[16] What a simple and, at the same time, beautiful way to express the idea of growing up – adolescent characters played by the adults they will become. By doing this Clare Barron enables us to see the present and the future and the past at the same time. And, importantly, this does nothing to diminish our empathy with these characters, in fact, it enhances it because we know where they are going. Wonderful.

Dance Nation is a play about young people more than it is a play about dance, with this in mind Clare Barron also includes a note about dance at the start of her play, explaining that the presentational essence of dance is more important than literal dance talent. She follows this up with a wonderful idea in an audition sequence early on in her play, when she suggests that the audition pieces are delivered as a 'ballet of the face' – instead of physical leaps and turns, we get facially exaggerated deep breaths, furrowed brows, open mouths.[17] Casting isn't dependent upon the ability to dance, it is more important to find actors who can embody the idea of dance, the actor's presence is more important than being able to do the splits – and the audience loses nothing in this choice, in fact, they are much more likely to see themselves in the characters by this choice. And all this, at the playwright's instigation.

Does the age of a character need to be set? Not always. In fact, not setting a specific age can add a further dynamic to your play. In Paula

Vogel's *How I Learned to Drive*, the character of Li'l Bit ages from forty-something to eleven years old and Paula Vogel suggests that although the part was originally written for an actor in their forties, her age, and that of the other characters, is flexible, with the only caveat being that at the end of the play when Li'l Bit states her adult age, it is given to reflect the age of the actor playing her.[18] There is also a potent moment of character displacement towards the end of this play, while Li'l Bit's lines are spoken by the Teenage Greek Chorus member while Li'l Bit sits mute in the front seat of her uncle's car as he abuses her. This simple displacement is both devastating and profound, proving that a step away from a realistic, representational encounter can feel even more intense than the pretence that the event is really happening.

Casting yourself

How about putting yourself in your play? I have never been entirely convinced by navel-gazing plays about being a playwright, but I love it when writers put versions of themselves in plays about writing the play we are watching. Gregory Burke does this to great effect in his excellent play *Black Watch* by showing a nervous playwright researching his play about an elite Scottish army infantry battalion.[19]

Arguably one of the most ambitious plays about a playwright writing a play is Branden Jacobs-Jenkins' play *An Octoroon* – a play about a playwright writing a play about a play written by another playwright who is also in the play. In Act Four of this play, the two characters representing the respective playwrights of the two plays stop to discuss the dramaturgy of the play they are now appearing in – could life get any more exciting that this? Not for me it doesn't! Then, there is the part of Br'er Rabbit, a character from the oral storytelling traditions of African Americans who is to be 'played by the actual playwright, or another artist involved in the production.'[20] Br'er Rabbit is sometimes perceived as a trickster provoking and bending social norms, in this play the character becomes a trickster provoking us by bending theatrical norms. Lesson: bend the rules, include a scene in which you discuss how and why you are bending the rules, and while you're at it give yourself a part in your own play. Why not?

There are ten young men sitting around writing at the beginning of *The Inheritance* by Matthew Lopez. Perhaps they are all versions of the playwright? Sometimes, in this play, the young men morph into other characters. Sometimes characters in the present talk to characters in the past. Sometimes the younger and older versions of the same character speak at the same time. Sometimes two characters played by the same actor are in a scene together. Sometimes there is a reaction to what is happening in a scene from characters not even in the scene. Sometimes characters deliver third person narration – and why not, it is a play inspired by a novel that inspires someone to write – which is why long passages of prose, and third person narrative finds a rightful place alongside the dialogue. Sometimes the narration is delivered by one character, sometimes by a group of characters, sometimes an actor even steps out of character to deliver narration.

I think it is probably relatively safe to bet that Laura Wade was quite pleased when she was commissioned to write a play based on an unfinished novel by Jane Austen. Jane Austen had done all the hard work, all Laura had to do was finish it off. How hard could it be? Answer: very hard. Whatever actually happened during the adaptation process, at some point Laura Wade stopped writing the adaptation and started to write a play about writing the adaptation. The resulting play, *The Watsons*, is an utter joy – with the playwright entering the play herself in the guise of a servant after the opening scenes and the rest of the play given over to working with her fractious cast of characters in an effort to get the best out of the adaptation. It is like Pinter's battles with writing his characters put directly into a play. Wonderful.

In *The Writer* by Ella Hickson, the characters are the people making the play – the writer, the director, the female actor, the male actor – sometimes they are inside the play, sometimes they stand outside the play, sometimes they talk about the play and how to write it. The actors are asked to play with the very fabric of the nature of writing, representation and performance. All of it initiated by . . . the writer.

Doubling

And don't forget to fully exploit the idea of multi-roling – perhaps tie it to the thematic vision of your play, make a virtue of it. In Paula Vogel's play *Indecent*, a play about a group of itinerant Jewish actors, she has seven actors playing thirty-six roles – and why wouldn't she, they are actors playing actors after all! It is totally in keeping with the vision of the play – as well as being a pragmatic solution to the potential cost of staging a play with thirty-six parts. As playwrights we need to consider these things – and it's not exactly a new strategy, in Thomas Preston's blockbuster play of 1561 with, perhaps, one of the longest titles in the theatrical canon – *A Lamentable Tragedy Mixed Full of Pleasant Mirth, Containing the Life of Cambises, King of Persia, from the beginning of his Kingdom, Unto his Death, His One Good Deed of Execution, after that Many Wicked Deeds and Tyrannous Murders, Committed by and through him, and Last of All, His Odious Death by God's Justice Appointed* – there are eight actors playing thirty-eight roles.[21] On a count of roles per actor, Paula wins.

And doubling shouldn't be limited to saving money on the production budget. Think creatively! Doubling can be utilized to enhance the ideas behind the play. Doubling as symbol; doubling as metaphor. Have fun with it. Like debbie tucker green does in *Random* (see the earlier section on *A one-actor multiplicity*). Like Duncan Macmillan does in *People, Places & Things*, a play in which the actor playing the mum of a recovering addict, called Emma, also plays her doctor and her therapist, not only blurring the lines between the authority roles in Emma's life, but also engaging with her struggle to know what is real and what is false. In a memorable moment when Emma first goes for group therapy and is greeted by the Therapist (played by the actor who plays her mum, remember) she says: 'God, you all look like my mother.'[22] Funny, poignant, painful. Expert use of doubling.

Naming your characters (or not)

Finding the right name for a character is essential. Sometimes (in my experience) a character can't even function properly until you've got the right name for them. But how about not naming them and perhaps using a dash (–) instead of a character name, and how about blurring the line between character and actor?

Amidst the literary papyri of the British Museum is a second century CE fragmented papyrus scroll of a previously mentioned *satyr play*, *Trackers* by Sophocles. It is remarkable for many reasons, not least the fact that these fragments, along with the text of *Cyclops* by Euripides, are the only remaining examples of satyr plays that have survived from the days of ancient Greece. I mention it here because of a remark made by Professor Mark Joyal in which he notes that the text of *Trackers* has 'short horizontal strokes on the left-hand side of some lines to indicate changes of speaker.'[23] In recent years, playwrights have begun to use this simple delineation of speaker as a creative tool.

- – How?
- – Keep reading and you'll find out.

One of the great playwriting innovators of the last thirty years in British theatre is Martin Crimp. His plays have been hugely influential on the more adventurous British playwrights of recent years. In his play *Attempts on her Life*, there are no designated characters, the speaker is designated by a dash (–) and it is up to the creative team to decide who speaks which lines. He also offers the creatives the option of having a character speak in an African or Eastern European language and, most interestingly to me, he plays with the idea of blurring the line between actor and character. He does this in Scene 16 by introducing stage directions suggesting that the actor may have forgotten her lines and is looking for a prompt. Later in the scene he informs us that she seems to dry completely, and, after a moment of confusion, another speaker takes over her lines. Crimp doesn't want us to know if this is stage fright or genuine distress. Subsequently, she tentatively joins back in.[24] What is the implication of this blurring? Does Martin Crimp want us to question the nature of performance? Does he want to remind us (the audience) that we are watching a play? Is he playing with the idea of verbatim theatre and experimenting with verisimilitude? Is this supposed to be a metaphysical comment on the nature of performance? Is it real? Is it false? Is this some kind of new performative formulation? Is this postdramatic text in action? It is up to the director and actors to decide how they want to interpret this. True collaboration between the playwright and the interpreters of their work.

These days I read a lot of plays which use a dash (–) instead of a character name, it has become one of the hallmarks of those playwrights who wish to invite collaboration and set a challenge to the creative teams making their plays. I also read a lot of plays in which playwrights use a dash (–) instead of a character name for absolutely no good reason whatsoever – please don't do it unless it serves your play. A good guide on when (and when not) to use a dash (–) is in Alice Birch's play *Revolt. She Said. Revolt Again*. There is no cast list included with the published text of this play. In three of the four acts, characters are designated with a dash (–) but in Act Two the characters are named. Why? Because in this act the designation of lines needs to be absolute, so the use of a dash (–) is unnecessary and, in fact, would be counterproductive. If you want to give the decision about the attribution of lines to your interpreters and it will serve the dynamic and repeated re-interpretation of your play, do it. If you are doing it because it looks cool, don't do it – use names.

A stage direction in Act Two of Alice Birch's *Revolt. She Said. Revolt Again.*, informs us that it doesn't matter if the character of Grandma looks very young – we are not pretending the actor *is* the grandmother, this is a play, an actor can be anyone or anything.[25] And Alice Birch also plays with the idea of blurring the line between actor and character. At the start of Act Three, she tells us that the line between actor and character can be paper thin and that the actors will need to be in more than one scene at a time. Not only that; she also tells us that it's okay to find that difficult.[26] What a delight to find a play that invites the actors and audience to engage in the nature of the pretence. What a delight that this is included in the playwright's text. Techniques like these play with the very nature of performance, they ask the creatives and the audience to engage with the fact that we are watching a performance whilst still embracing the lie. In the hands of an expert playwright and expert creative team, this can have a profound effect.

Sometimes, writers like Ella Hickson, for example, don't even bother with a dash (–) to delineate character, they just put their dialogue on consecutively spaced lines.[27]

You mean like this?

Yes.

Not even a dash?

No.

Does it work?

You tell me . . .

In *One In Two* by Donja R. Love, after the audience has helped to select which actor plays which role (see Chapter 2.2, *Tear Down the Fourth Wall*), they step in and out of numerous further roles. Then, towards the end of the performance, one of the actors decides he doesn't want to carry on with the play and the actors (not the characters) get into a fight, one of them gets stabbed and leaves, and the other two actors conclude the play. It is a brilliant, pyrotechnic, meta-characterful treat, enlivened by the fact that the actors are playing themselves as actors, which is basically another character and offers another level of interpretation.

Character can be so much more than age, gender and occupation.

We all love a beautifully rounded, believable character, but we don't always need to write them as Stanislavski and his adherents might ask actors to explore them. There are a multitude of options available to us, and not all your characters need to be created from the same three-dimensional template. Explore, invent and create some monsters.

2.5 YOU ARE A DRAMATIC POET

My play *Lush Life* is about a singer obsessed with Ella Fitzgerald. I wanted to show the different faces this character presented to the world, so I divided her up and had five actors playing different aspects of a single character. I did this because I wanted to play with the different voices of this one character: her rational voice, her ambitious voice, her romantic voice, her self-loathing voice, and her angry voice. I also did this to focus on each voice as and when it became dominant, to juxtapose voices in unison and repeated patterns of speech, and to fuse them and create a climactic vocal cacophony when they spoke over each other. Each voice had subtle differences in vocabulary and articulacy. Choosing the right words for each voice and playing with the way the voices interacted was challenging and rewarding. It was the most consciously lyrical way I had ever written. I ended up thinking in terms of the play being a *word song*. I had always known the value of words, but writing this play really confirmed for me the importance of understanding that language is our principal tool and that every single word we write needs to be chosen for weight, balance, rhythm, sound and meaning – language is not disposable.

There is a surprising lack of focus on the use of language in modern playwriting books. We should perhaps remind ourselves that we started out as DRAMATIC POETS. The term 'playwright' was originally coined by the irascible bricklayer's son Ben Jonson as an insult in the early 1600s. Jonson modelled himself of the Roman lyrical poet Horace and was not impressed with those he considered to be mere artisan writers cobbling together plays for a few shillings. Hence his conflation of the word 'play' and the word 'wright' – as in shipwright (a maker of ships) or cartwright (a maker of carts). As far as Jonson was concerned, a great writer was a *dramatic poet*, not a wright, a mere maker of plays.

What a pity that so many playwrights seem to have forgotten that they can also be poets. What a pity that so many of us seem to prefer naturalistic dialogue over dramatic poetry. What a pity that words have become functional rather than magical.

I think the problem is probably down to our dramaturgical education. Most contemporary dramatists receive their writing education from naturalistic television drama. Most TV and film drama uses a regulated version of broken, stilted, repetitive, tangential everyday speech – regulated in a way that makes it slightly less messy, so that we can understand it whilst still playing lip service (pun intended) to the fact that we don't speak in perfectly formed sentences, and we sometimes don't say what we really mean (sub-text). It is essential for a dramatist to master these skills and I love a great TV drama but regulated naturalistic speech isn't the only way to write dialogue. There are plenty of other options available to a playwright beyond the representation of everyday conversation.

Far too many of us seem to have forgotten the versatility and beauty of words. Worryingly, we seem to have forgotten that it is not just the choice of words but the sound they make that is central to our writing. We seem to have forgotten the sensory power of sound – let's not forget that language originated in sound. Today, we seem to focus our efforts on how best to replicate everyday speech without thinking about how we can elevate language to something new; to something (brace yourself) more poetic. We have forgotten how to move beyond the literal, to use language as emotion, as colour, as time, as travel, as violence, as dance, as repression, as chaos. Language as an abstract device that illuminates a feeling more brightly than anything directly stated ever can. We seem embarrassed to think of dialogue as poetic. Why?

I am not suggesting that you need to become an expert in prosody, just that you need to become acutely aware of the power of words. You do not need to obsess about the metrical rhythm of a line but to learn to respect the fact that it will have a rhythm. You need to understand that great dramatic writing comes from working a bit harder with language – the use of language, understanding language. Why do people love Shakespeare? Because we can come back to his plays time and time again and find new things in them every time. The harder you work to understand Shakespeare the better his writing becomes. The more you internalize the joy of language, the more you will respect the colour and flow of language in your own writing.

There were no words for anything until Homo sapiens started to make them up. Point at something and make a noise that sounds something like 'stone' and eventually it will become known as a 'stone'. We invented language. People like us. And we continue to invent, reinterpret, evolve, break and bend language. It is not a fixed thing. Words come and words go. The meaning of words changes, usage, punctuation, grammar, all are in a constant state of flux. Who gave 420 new words to the English language? Shakespeare. Shakespeare codified, constructed and concocted words. Not all them were neologisms, many of them were words that were already in use, but what a wonderful contribution to the English language.

Words begin as a small stream of communication that becomes a river of interaction that becomes an ocean of connection into which we continue to empty our philological effluent. And, if you'll forgive me for extending that rather gross metaphor, it is an ocean that will never stop rising. Words come and go in popularity; they can mean a different thing at different times in history. I'm not suggesting that you spend your time inventing new words, nor that you must write densely poetic text, but I am suggesting that you take a bit of extra care over the words you choose and how you choose to use them because it just might make a world of difference to your writing. Language is ours to do with as we please. Let us always remember that language is a living thing, not a corpse.

Because I believe in standing on shoulders, I am going to indulge in a quick history lesson in the use of language in the Western theatre tradition. This isn't just for the sake of linguistic cheerleading; it is because I believe that if you explore where our use of dramatic language comes from you might just be amazed at what you can take from it and how it can inform your own writing. Use every bit of information that follows to ask yourself how you might use these techniques. Ask yourself if there is anything you can build on, or subvert, or fracture. Challenge yourself to take these ideas somewhere new. Let's learn to treasure the words we use today like they used to and then do something with those words to make the giants of the past green with envy.

Greek (& Roman) drama

Diction

In Aristotle's *Poetics*, diction is the fourth element of tragedy coming after plot, character and thought. When it comes to this element the important thing to remember is that diction is the choice of words, *and* the sound they make. This is far too often overlooked! Lesson: A playwright will often learn more about their dialogue when they hear it read out loud than they will by just reading it to back themselves in their own head. Our words are written to be spoken – it is the spoken word we need to pay attention to, not the prettiness or realness of the word on the page.

Don't bloat your play with padding, consider your words, choose them carefully. Try different words. Different word orders. Some words and juxtapositions of words can trip an actor up. You won't know which ones until you hear them. Some words won't work well when wound with witticisms in wilful alliteration.

Rhythm of words

To find the right rhythm of words, Aristotle recommends the use of **iambic verse** '. . . *which as far as possible models itself on speech* . . .'[1]

Back to basics. Forget English Literature, this isn't about writing essays it's about understanding your craft. A lack of knowledge about the way words work together is like a musician not learning scales – you might get away with it for a while, but there will come a time when you need to know it if you are going to take your work to the next level. What is an iamb? A short unstressed syllable followed by a stressed syllable.

- IAMB: di-DUM

Why is this important? Rhythm! Language has a rhythm. You either work with the rhythm of your language or against it. Every writer has a rhythm to their language – in the plays of the best writers there is what appears to be a magical quality to the flow of their language. It isn't magic, it is an understanding or words, how they fit together and the rhythm and sound of language – as they use it. If you want to fracture your use of language into short staccato phrases, you need to understand that this will have an effect on the rhythm of your play. This will mean that the feel of language will be different for an audience. I love scattered, staccato language, it can sound fantastic, the problem is that some writers aren't listening to the sound and rhythm of their words, they are too busy just enjoying scattering them across the page.

I am not asking you to map out your plays in **di-DUMS** – all I want to do is emphasize that words have rhythm, and the rhythm of your dialogue is there for you to use as one of your primary devices.

Sound of words

Speak your words out loud. Keep your ear open for verbal trip hazards and tongue twisters. Enjoy the sound that words make together. Aristotle gives ample space to the study of how words sound in his *Poetics*, not a great deal of use to those of us who don't speak Greek but an appreciation of the importance of sound in pronunciation, stress and inflection is essential. Don't overlook it.

Choice of words

Aristotle also gives plenty of room to the selection of words for meaning in the chapters on diction in his *Poetics* and in his *Rhetoric*. The right words for the right characters. The most effective metaphors. Your words are in your gift. They are yours to choose as you see fit. Your choice of words is what will make you unique. Your vocabulary, your syntax – these things belong exclusively to you in the context of where, when and who you grew up with. No one else has that. Use YOUR words. Play with them in the mouths of the characters you create. But remember this: finding your voice as a writer doesn't mean writing every character with the same voice. And try to avoid characters speaking in cliches unless that is what you want your character very specifically to do.

One of the reasons we can tell that an Elizabethan play had more than one author is because of the difference in vocabulary and rhythm of the language. Language is our common denominator and our most individual tool. And we can learn so much from how the great playwrights like Shakespeare used language.

Shakespeare

Why do actors like to speak Shakespeare? Because he took the time to write poetically. He cared about the words on the page. AND he knew they would be thrilling to speak. He knew they would sound good. If you've only ever read Shakespeare in your head or seen his plays in performance, there is a very simple exercise you can do: pick up one of his plays and speak it out loud. How about this – read it out loud, read it slowly . . .

> Tomorrow, and tomorrow, and tomorrow,
> Creeps in this petty pace from day to day
> To the last syllable of recorded time,
> And all our yesterdays have lighted fools
> The way to dusty death. Out, out, brief candle!
> Life's but a walking shadow, a poor player
> That struts and frets his hour upon the stage
> And then is heard no more: it is a tale
> Told by an idiot, full of sound and fury,
> Signifying nothing.[2]

If you didn't find all those percussive, alliterative p's and d's and t's, and that sublime sounding sibilance thrilling to speak, you are in the wrong profession. You need to think about the words, the character, the context, AND the sound the words make. Please don't throw away your words, they are the most important tool you have – without them there is no play text. Use every word as if your life depended upon it.

We don't have to try to write like Shakespeare but knowing just a little about how he did what he did with words is like opening the best present any playwright ever received. If you want to refresh your writing and start thinking about it in different ways, the best place to start is with Shakespeare. If you take a moment to understand, read and speak Shakespeare's words, a whole new world of dramatic language will open up before you. Understand what Shakespeare did and take it to new places. If there's one giant upon whose shoulders we should all seek to stand it is William Shakespeare.

Shakespeare wrote in Blank Verse – unrhymed lines usually in iambic pentameter (five iambic feet):

> But **soft** what **light** from **yon**-der   **win**-dow   **breaks**
> di- DUM di- DUM di- DUM di- DUM di- DUM

And it wasn't just the Greeks and English Renaissance dramatic poets who thrilled to the use of the iambic foot. Spanish Golden Age dramatists used a verse form known as the *Quintilla* – an eight-syllable iambic line [Four Feet – Iambic Tetrameter]. French Neoclassical dramatists of the seventeenth century (Racine, Corneille, Moliere) usually used a six-footed iambic line – the Alexandrine [Iambic Hexameter].

However, Shakespeare's Blank Verse is much looser in terms of meter and rhyme than the French or Spanish forms. The thing to bear in mind is that Shakespeare, being Shakespeare, was a rule-breaker. He liked to take the regularity of the meter and break it with irregularities and cross rhythms, producing a tension that keeps the actor and audience on their toes, and he keep his use of rhyme to a minimum.

Peter Hall wrote that Shakespeare's language is like 'a complex score that demands to be read as a piece of music.'[3]

If only more contemporary playwrights treated their text as a note-by-note score in which every note, rest and change of rhythm were carefully composed. I think playwrights could benefit immensely from thinking of their text as a score – just as a score is the composers detailed instruction to the conductor and musicians, the play text should serve as the playwright's detailed instruction to the director and actors.

A quick note about dramatic punctuation – the grammar, dots, dashes and slashes of a playwright's script are phenomenally important. Why? Because they set the rhythm for your play and serve as your direct instruction about pace, rhythm and tone to your collaborators. More on this later in this chapter in the section on the *Modern Era*, but I raise it here, in the context of Shakespeare, because you need to be aware that editors of Shakespeare's plays sometimes punctuated the plays for reading NOT for speaking. Even their use of upper- and lower-case letters varies significantly. THE TEXT NEEDS TO BE SPOKEN. We can go back to the quartos and first folio or simply make up our own minds about the punctuation, but the best way to understand the language is to speak it out loud and find the best rhythms that way.

I remember being taught about Shakespeare's use of iambic pentameter at school and then trying to apply the meter to arguably the most famous speech in the entire Shakespearian canon:

To be or not to be that is the question
Whether tis nobler in the mind to suffer
The slings and arrows of outrageous fortune
Or to take arms against a sea of troubles[4]

I couldn't do it. It didn't make sense. No one had told me about the eleven-syllable line!

To be or not to be that is the **ques(tion)**
Whether tis nobler in the mind to **suf(fer)**
The slings and arrows of outrageous **for(tune)**
Or to take arms against a sea of **trou(bles)**

The eleven-syllable line has what is called a 'feminine ending' – the idea being that the softer unstressed syllable frees the verse from being colloquial, common speech and highlights certain important words. The end of the line is usually where the primary meaning is often found: **question, suffer, fortune, troubles** – and it helps to express hesitation, self-doubt, insecurity by softening the last syllable of the line. This also helps to move the listener away from the regular rhythms in verse which can become predictable and monotonous.

Often, Shakespeare will mix them up – a line of ten syllables followed by a line of eleven syllables. Sometimes he uses fewer than ten syllables – it is up to the actor to work out why. It might mean that the playwright anticipates a pause here or that he wants to break the rhythm for dramatic effect. Or he might use a caesura in a line, a break, perhaps indicating a slight pause, perhaps indicating the line should be slowed before the cesura? In other words, the words might be Shakespeare's instruction to the actor on how to play the line.

Sometimes one character will have half an iambic line, and this will be followed by another character who completes the iambic line, thus keeping the iambic rhythm. Sometimes he might use a string of ten monosyllables. During the 1990s there was a short-lived fashion for beginning plays with interactions of single syllables between characters often suggesting a hesitancy and uncertain quality to the relationships, e.g., *Blackbird* by David Harrower,[5] *The York Realist* by Peter Gill.[6] It works a treat.

Shakespeare has been continually staged for hundreds of years. Why? Well, he's a great writer, yes, but what else can we learn from his example? Perhaps that a play written in a style that invites multiple interpretations, that embraces ambiguity, that is *poetic* – whatever that means to you – will have greater longevity than a play that seeks to imitate the precise speaking patterns of a specific era or location. Should the human race survive another 400 years, it will be interesting to guess which contemporary plays will continue to be produced alongside Shakespeare.

Modern era

Dramatic language has become more naturalistic since the turn of the twentieth century. Modern theatrical diction is very different to what it was in classical Athens or Renaissance London, but contemporary playwrights are doing some incredible things. The use of language and dramatic punctuation is potent today. Let's look at some of the techniques that contemporary playwrights are using and ask ourselves where we might go with it.

Because the use of what we might call dramatic punctuation (the dots, dashes, slashes and commas, etc.) isn't standardized, many playwrights include a brief note at the start of their play explaining their use of these devices. For some writers a comma (,) on its own on a line might indicate a pause, for others a line break might mean a pause, for others a full stop (.) on a line on its own might mean a pause. There are no fixed rules, although some things have become semi-standardized, but it's a good idea to let your reader/collaborator in on what these things mean for you. A basic guide (that not everyone will agree with) to common usage, might look like this:

,	pause
. . .	a change in train of thought, a pause
/	overlapping speech begins here[7]
–	a dash at the end of a line indicates an interruption
[ ]	words in square brackets are not spoken
Italics	*for emphasis*
CAPS	FOR EMPHASIS
.	after each word in a sentence Gives. The. Words. Equal. Weight.

In my play *Lush Life* about a jazz singer, mentioned at the start of this chapter, I was faced with the challenge of writing five actors playing the same role using overlapping and sometimes simultaneous speech. It was driving me crazy trying to manage all the intersecting dialogue – until I hit upon the solution of setting out the dialogue in five rows like a musical stave. On the page, it looks brazenly pretentious, but it works a treat.

The great thing about all this is that you can make up your own system of punctuation – so long as you explain it at the start of your play! A play does not need to be grammatically correct, but it does need a coherent and consistent use of dramatic punctuation.

Make your words dance and explode

In *Dance Nation* by Clare Barron there is a moment when the group of young dancers are waiting for their teacher to announce the casting for their next performance, the dancers chant in unison as they wait, performing a choric dance of words mirroring the idea of dance in their unison chanting. By doing this the writer shifts the idea of dance from the physical to the verbal, it is a simple but beautiful way to bring to the fore the physical core of the play in the spoken word.

In her Bruntwood Award winning play, *Shed: Exploded View*, Phoebe Éclair-Powell glories in the use of the spoken word – utilizing synchronized speech, overlapping speech and parallel storytelling, climaxing in an explosion of words *and* an exploded shed. Like many of the best writers she also glories in the use of repetition.[8] Clare Barron uses repetition at the end of *Dance Nation* where it turns into a feral chant. Shakespeare used it – *Fie. Fie. Fie. Fie. Fie.* Repetition for emphasis, repetition for colour, repetition for texture, repetition for effect. Use it. Use it. Use it. When asked about the use of repetition in her plays in an interview in *The Independent* debbie tucker green said, 'That's how people speak. Listen to a group of kids – just repeat and repeat and repeat.'[9] debbie takes this simple fact of communication and turns it into dynamic, lyrical dialogue. Listen to the way people speak. Use it. Use it. Use it.

Use your font

Clare Barron loves to play with words on the page. In *Dance Nation* she uses increasing font size, CAPS and repeat letters to suggest how an actor might interpret emphasis in the increasing excitement of a line. Perhaps you should try it YOURSELF, NEXT TIME YOU WANT TO SHOW EUPHORIAAAAAA!!!

At the end of *Dance Nation* there is a huge choral chant utilizing Barron's trademark increasing font size that grows until one word fills the whole page.

At other points in this play, she uses small font to indicate that the words might be spoken quietly or are more introspective or that small font should literally be performed in a 'small' way.

Jasmine Lee-Jones is another playwright who likes to play with font size, sometimes using it to suggest a crescendo in the delivery.

Use your dots, dashes, exclamation marks, etc.

Sometimes Clare Barron uses a short sequence of descending, diagonal double-dots to suggest how an actor might play a pause. Sometimes she uses dots decreasing in number – from 3 to 2 to 1 – in the centre of the page to suggest a kind of fade out.[10] Sometimes she uses an ellipsis to suggest a pause in a character's speech and she even uses them in her stage directions, when the characters are waiting for someone, there are six consecutive ellipses, one on each line – suggesting that it is quite

. . .

. . .

. . .

. . .

. . .

. . .

a long wait.[11]

My favourite use of punctuation in *Dance Nation* comes when the playwright wants to suggest a shocked/surprised reaction in a group of characters – she doesn't write 'They are shocked and surprised', she gives us four exclamation marks '!!!!'[12]

In her writer's note at the beginning of *Revolt. She Said. Revolt Again.* Alice Birch gives us a quick run-down of her specific use of dramatic punctuation. A dash indicates a change of speaker; a forward slash, overlapping speech; words in square brackets are not spoken, etc.[13]

Duncan Macmillan often uses a comma (,) instead of writing 'Beat' or 'Pause'. Lucy Kirkwood uses a comma (,) to indicate a 'Beat'. She also uses the word 'Pause'. For Lucy, a 'Beat' is shorter than a 'Pause'. In *Chimerica* she points out that 'A beat doesn't always mean a pause but can also denote a shift in thought or energy.' She goes on to suggest that when a line is broken by a comma or there is a line break 'it's generally to convey, a breath, hesitation, a grasping for words' concluding that 'Actors are welcome to ignore this.'[14] Collaboration. It's good to collaborate. And as for punctuation, again, the fact is, there are no rules. So, set your own. It's your play. It's your punctuation. Use it to get the way you hear your text across. Then allow your actors to interpret it. Actors are smart. Give them the freedom to use their intelligence.

How long do you want your pause to be? A short *beat*? A long *pause*? Why not do what a lot of writers do and just leave a gap on the page that reflects the length of the pause you want?

Annie Baker even goes so far as to use an asterisk (*) to indicate a scene change. In the note at the start of her play *The Antipodes*, she writers: '* indicates a leap forward in time. This leap forward should be indicated by subtle shifts in actor behavior and movement without lights or sound.'[15] Not using scene breaks seems to me a glorious way of encouraging the momentum she wants for her play.

Lesson: Dramatic text does not obey the rules of punctuation or grammar. As Lucy Kirkwood points out in her writer's note at the beginning of her play *Mosquitoes* – 'The text has been punctuated to serve the music of the play, not grammatical convention.'[16] Use punctuation and grammar to musicalize your play, not constrain it. Think hard about how you can use the dots, dashes, gaps and slashes of our craft. Ask yourself how you can you use the language tools at our disposal in a way that has never been conceived off before. Not for the sake of it, but because it serves your play . . .//--- or perhaps leave out punctuation altogether thereby inviting total interpretation from your collaborators if you want to set them a real challenge because it's quite hard to read something without any punctuation but it works a lot better in drama than it does in prose where it can drive you nuts yes no really it can have you tried to read the last episode yes of Ulysses yes no I said yes I will . . .//---

Use your alignment

Most of the text in *Dance Nation* is left-aligned, but sometimes it is right-aligned, sometimes centred. This alignment challenges the director and actors to ask themselves how to interpret the different alignments. Perhaps left-aligned is regular dialogue. Right-aligned, interior thought. Centre, prayer. It is an invitation to interpretation and collaboration.

In *Anatomy of a Suicide* Alice Birch sets her text out in three columns using landscape page orientation to accommodate the fact that she is engaging with three contiguous narratives. The layout enhances the musicality of the text on the page in the way it enables the reader/collaborator to see the repetitions and poetic juxtapositions. It's quite hard work to read three columns at the same time, but well worth the effort.

In the seminal *Attempts On Her Life* Martin Crimp aligns most of his text to the left in the traditional way, but some commentary and more poetic segments he aligns right. Poets play with alignment, why shouldn't playwrights? Playwrights, you have the whole page to work with, do something with it! You are a Dramatic Poet!

Use different literary styles

Sometimes in *Dance Nation* a character will turn and talk directly to us, the audience; at one point a character's words metamorphose from verse to prose as the character herself transforms into a pagan god and back in front of us.[17] How's that for ambition?

In *Seven Methods of Killing Kylie Jenner* when one of the characters enters the warped Twittersphere, Jasmine Lee-Jones gives her a speech that moves from a brilliantly written contemporary monologue that is left-aligned to a furious poetic section about an abused African woman that she moves to the centre of the page. An incredibly effective way of giving the second half of the speech a different focus and weight.[18]

Alice Birch, like many of the best contemporary playwrights, loves to play with language, breaking and fracturing her dialogue, turning the ordinary into poetry, playing word games. Act Three of *Revolt* becomes an avalanche of text, a storm, a deluge, building to a crescendo, a cacophony. Words. Words. Words, as Shakespeare might say. It is a verbal climax. A linguistic catharsis.[19] If only all playwrights understood the value of words like Alice Birch does and were prepared to put the time and effort into prioritizing the use of language.

Tarell Alvin McCraney's play *The Brothers Size* contains dramatic language at its best – an innovative poetic-dramatic hybrid, a mixture of poetry and pragmatism, complete with stark, spoken stage directions, internal monologues, invocation and lyrics. The text has a beautiful musicality, there are some lines, which the playwright indicates by using *italics*, that are sung, but there is also a musicality to the dialogue, and where there is a character name without text, the playwright explains that these are silent actions that hold a rhythm. Music. Pulse. Rhythm. The writer's vision of the lives of the characters in this play is made manifest in the language.[20]

Some writers even have the nerve (and talent) to write plays in Blank Verse – Mike Bartlett's *King Charles III*, for example. How else was he going to write it? It's a play about the accession of a King to the British throne. It has to be in iambic pentameter![21]

Expose your exposition

Why bother to hide exposition? Why not play with it? Branden Jacobs-Jenkins has great fun with the clunky exposition of Victorian melodrama in *An Octoroon*, making the over explanation of plot great fun and mixing it with some very contemporary idiomatic American-English creating a linguistic clash that reflects the cultural clash at the heart of the play. Great idea: actualize your theme in your dialogue.

Manifest metaphor

In *How I Learned to Drive* Paula Vogel shows us how the character of Li'l Bit was abused using the metaphor of learning to drive – neutral gear, first to second, etc. But, being Paula Vogel, she also not only uses driving as a metaphor for sex she uses it as a metaphor for time, life skills, and, literally, as what it is, driving. She also gives the abuser (Uncle Peck) a speech which uses fishing as a metaphor for grooming and abuse.[22] *How I Learned to Drive* is a play rich in ideas and should be at the top of every ambitious playwright's 'To Read' list.

Monolingual translation

How do you speak in different languages on stage whilst keeping the play in one language? Ask Paula Vogel. In *Indecent* when characters speak Yiddish, they speak in perfect English, when they speak English as their second language, they speak with a slightly broken accent. It works. Ask Brian Friel. In *Translations* some characters speak Irish, some characters speak English, but the whole play (apart from some Latin and Greek) is spoken in English. How? Through the rhythm of Irish-English and idiomatic differences spoken by the Irish characters, and the neater English of the English characters. It works. Don't believe me? Read the play, it is superb.[23]

Be a poet

Don't be frightened by the idea of poetry. All you need to do is take everyday speech and heighten it. Listen very, very carefully to the way people speak and then play with the irregularities, repetitions, digressions, hesitancies. There is a world of dramatic prosody in everyday speech pattens.

Talking about her early work in a rare interview in *The Guardian* debbie tucker green said, 'I was just messing about, writing stuff down and throwing it away or keeping it if it interested me. Then the writing started to get longer. I didn't know whether it was a poem, the lyrics to a song or a play. It is all much of a muchness to me. It's all words, ain't it?'[24] Perhaps this is why debbie is such a great writer? She keeps the words that interest her and throws away the ones that don't. Word by word, line by line, page by page, debbie's writing is always lean and beautifully expressive. Her influences are poets and songwriters, and it shows – every word is weighed and balanced, chosen for meaning, effect, sound, and because the word resonates. debbie does her own thing, we could all learn so much from the way she channels her individuality onto the page.

Finally

4.48 Psychosis by Sarah Kane is an extraordinary play. A play that is extraordinary on the stage (in the right hands) and extraordinary on the page. A play with no cast list, no indication of how many actors are required, no indication of set, no indication (other than in the spoken text) of where or when anything in the play takes place, fragments of dialogue, indented speech, lists of pain, scattered numbers, poetic wordplay, repetition, space, and more pain, so much pain. If you haven't read it, do yourself a favour and buy a copy. You will not be disappointed. And if you are, you're definitely in the wrong job.

Language is our lifeblood, it is our vital fluid, it is our gore. The pulse of our words is essential for the life of our plays. Think about the words you use. Think with more adventure, more ambition, more beauty. Respect words. Cherish them. Love them. Then give them away.

2.6 GET MUSICAL

Many of the new writing practitioners I worked with in the 1990s had a purist steak that dictated that musical theatre was to be avoided at all costs. But I had a dark secret, I wanted to write a musical. Most of my plays have music or musicians at the centre of them, largely because I love music and that was the world I lived in and knew better than any other, but they weren't musicals. For years, I had been trying to work up the courage to suggest to the Theatre Royal Stratford East that I should write a musical for them, but I had never quite been brave enough. Then something happened that was like a synchronistic thunderbolt from the gods. I don't believe in synchronicity or gods for that matter, but it was just what I needed to give me a little bit of a push in the direction of musical theatre.

This is what happened.

In 1999, I was working as Literary Manager at Soho Theatre Company, and at this point Soho was in a state of limbo between the company's most recent home at the Cockpit Theatre in Marylebone and the synagogue in Dean Street that was to become the company's new home. At this moment in time Soho consisted of a handful of employees working from a small office in Mortimer Street in the West End. We had been based at the office for about eighteen months when I left work one evening and passed a cardboard box that had been left outside a building a couple of doors down the street. The contents of the box caught my eye, they looked a bit like dog-eared scripts, but I'm not a natural scavenger so I kept on walking. However, my curiosity got the better of me and I doubled back to take a closer look. I was right, they were scripts. Looking around to make sure no one was watching, because, although I'm not Catholic, I live my life in an almost permanent state of guilt, I leant down and took one of the scripts out of the box. It was an exhausted copy of the libretto for *West Side Story* – which just happens to be my favourite musical of all time.[1] There were two or three more exhausted copies of the *West Side Story* in the box with their orange covers hanging on by the slenderest of publisher's threads, but underneath these was a libretto with a yellow cover, it was a copy of *Guys & Dolls* – which just happens to be my second favourite musical of all time.[2] I continued to dig through the box and found a third musical, *Carousel*, which, at the time, I didn't know.[3] How on earth did these librettos, which are incredibly hard to get hold of, find their way into a box, a couple of doors down from Soho's office, where I would find them? Perhaps there was a god after all, I thought. But looking up at the small sign jutting out above the door of the office outside which the box had been dumped, I read the name *Josef Weinberger* and suddenly it all made sense. Josef Weinberger Ltd is a licensing agent for musicals and these were obviously copies of some of the musicals they licensed that they considered to be too worn out to be hired out anymore. They were going to be pulped. So, I did what any decent-minded citizen would do, I stealthily picked out the librettos in best condition and looking around to make sure Stephen Sondheim or Rogers and Hammerstein weren't watching, shoved them in my bag and walked swiftly to the tube station.

Over the next few months, I studied the librettos intensely, then, out of the blue, I got a phone call from Philip Hedley, the Artistic Director at Stratford East, who wanted to know if I had any ideas for a musical. I did.

I have never been able to work out why so many contemporary playwrights seem so frightened to include music or songs their plays. What are they frightened of? Is mixing the text of a new play with a song a crime? Is it considered to be in bad taste? Get over yourselves! Music has phenomenal potential for a playwright. I'm not suggesting you need to put a torch song and tap routine in every play you write, I'm just pointing out that to turn your back on such potent performative potential is a bit blinkered.

We tend to forget that music was an integral ingredient of Greek drama. The text of a Greek tragedy is rhythmical, it was written to be sung or performed as a kind of recitative (a form of musical declamation in the rhythm of ordinary/iambic speech) and, accompanied by the flute and sometimes the lyre, it was a fundamental a part of the delivery of the text. Music was at the heart of all great Greek drama.

If you visited the theatre in seventeenth-century London (not during the plague or Civil War or during the years of Cromwell's reign when plays were banned, though) you might have been entertained with a short concert before the play began.[4] What a wonderful idea! How about a band playing songs as you take your seats for the play?

Characters quite regularly burst into song in Elizabethan dramas, but we rarely if ever give our characters permission to do so. Why? As far as I am aware, there is no law against it. Open your hearts! Open your lungs! Sing us a song!

At the beginning of Scene Four in Lucy Prebble's *Enron*, we get the stage direction, 'Magical music'. How's that for an invitation to the play's composer? But that's not all, because she adds that the sound of singing builds to 'an atonal babble of commodity process and bids'.[5] Schoenberg meets the New York Stock Exchange meets Lucy Prebble. Divine chemistry. And if that isn't enough to get your musical juices flowing, how about the stage direction in the same play that a group of financial analysts form a barbershop quartet and sing a song about the energy and commodities company at the centre of the drama![6] What a wonderful, inventive and economical way to reach into the dark thematic heart of the play. Use music!

In *The Long Christmas Ride Home* Paula Vogel makes suggestions for all kinds of music that can be used, but whatever the creative team decides, she makes it clear that she wants 'music and sound effects' to 'run under the entire play'.[7]

And, before we continue, a little plea for the musicians in your plays. Firstly, please use live music, not pre-recorded music – theatre is LIVE performance. Secondly, please don't hide your musicians. I want to see them. It is a joy to hear AND see a musician perform live. Why hide them somewhere we can't see them? (And, yes, I'm also a musician, but you know this makes sense . . .) Music can open the theatrical soul of a play, the Elizabethans didn't hide their drummers, the Greeks didn't hide their flautists, they put them front and centre because the music spoke to the essence of the play. Music is important in film because it unlocks the emotion of the drama. In the theatre, we can have the bonus of the musicians actually being present, so don't stick them in the pit or squeeze them next to the props table off-stage, show them, celebrate them. Your musicians are part of your performance, they are part of the live experience, their musicianship is there to serve your play, their physical presence is another link between audience and performance that celebrates the present moment – this music, played like this, in this play, by these people, here, now. Hiding your musicians is an unnecessary pretence that is once again driven by the desire to pretend we aren't really here. Don't do it. Show them. Don't apologize for having music in your play by concealing your musicians, let your audience enjoy every aspect of your production, make it a totally inclusive live event with everything in full view.

Have you ever considered writing the book (meaning the dialogue, the script, the spoken word) for a musical? Chances are, you are probably reading this book because you are serious about writing serious plays and that very simple question about writing the book for a musical may already have brought you out in a cold sweat. But you are missing a golden opportunity to expand your theatrical imagination. Writing the book for a musical is a glorious, challenging and hugely rewarding experience. You might even learn something, and, if you're lucky, earn something.

Musical theatre tears down the fourth wall from the moment the show begins. These characters may scream and cry real tears, they may take us deep into the human psyche, we may associate with them as keenly as any character in a naturalistic play, but the major difference is, that sooner or later, and for no apparently realistic reason, they are going to burst into song. And probably dance a bit as well.

In the UK there is a noticeable divide between adherents of new writing and fans of musical theatre. I have always found this partisan division somewhat ridiculous. It is even reflected in audiences – I rarely see the same people at musicals and new plays, it is as if they are hewn from different human stock. For some (not all) 'serious' theatre makers, musical theatre (such as the big shows on Broadway and in the West End) is often viewed as tacky and lightweight. For some (not all) musical theatre aficionados, serious new plays (such as the plays produced at the Royal Court and Manhattan Theatre Club) are seen as pretentious and boring. Well, now and then, it could be argued that both camps are right. But not always. And the two forms can learn a huge amount from each other. How about more theatrical miscegenation?

Musical theatre is crying out for good book writers. Sometimes the dearth of first-rate book writers will mean that producers will turn to established playwrights to write the book for a new musical. Quite often it doesn't work. Why? Because whilst it is still basically a job entailing dramatic structure, character and dialogue, it requires a different sensibility – a musical sensibility – a sensibility that has to be learned, the skills aren't immediately, automatically transferrable. And if you are now thinking, but I'm not very musical, you are not listening, this isn't about knowing the difference between a crotchet and a quaver, it's about the musicality of text.

What exactly does writing the book for a musical entail? It is the same as writing a play in that it requires all the knowledge required of a playwright, but it is different in that it requires the playwright to prioritize economy and make room for their collaborators. You are likely to be the creative in charge of the architecture of the story – the overall shape – but you will also be expected to sacrifice your genius on the altar of collaboration. Collaboration with a lyricist and a composer. Or collaboration with a composer who is also a lyricist (see chapter 3.2 *Theatre is Collaboration* for a more detailed examination of the process of collaboration).

It might be that you are also collaborating on writing the lyrics, or working as the book writer and lyricist, but let's not get carried away just yet, let's start by taking a closer look at what it means to write the book for a musical.

Someone has had an idea for a musical! Hooray! (Perhaps even you?)

You have been asked to write the book! Hooray!

But you've never written the book for a musical before and your technical knowledge and experience of music consists of half a dozen squeals from a recorder at the age of seven. What are you going to do?

Instead of keeping your fingers crossed and hoping that your skills as a playwright will transfer seamlessly into the musical theatre arena, how about taking a quick look at one of musical theatre's book-writing giants – Arthur Laurents. Heard of him? You should have, the man was a genius! He wrote the book for *West Side Story* AND *Gypsy*.[8] If you don't know those shows, don't do what I did and wait to find copies of some libretti dumped in the street, buy them and study them until they are seared into your creative brain.

Key advice from Arthur: 'A good plot depends on character. Then, economy . . .'[9] In the plot versus character primacy debate, Arthur's Number One is Character. This is important as Arthur's approach to musical theatre (he began his writing career as a radio/audio dramatist and playwright before he switched to book writing) is to take characterization VERY seriously. Prior to the Era of Arthur (1950s) the books for musicals were often dire, botched, excuses for a string of popular tunes. The book was not important, the book was not taken seriously, the book was there to serve the genius of the composer. Then, along came Arthur, and the book took an exponential creative leap forward. Arthur took his characters seriously, he constructed excellent plots, he wrote superb dialogue. He put emotion instead of wit at the centre of his work. He had learned his craft. Arthur Laurents took his work very seriously; he brought a serious sensibility to book writing. When asked to write the book for a musical about the stripper Gypsy Rose Lee, he turned it down, it sounded like an awful idea. Then he had the idea of writing a show not about Gypsy Rose Lee but about her showbiz mom, Rose, and the show *Gypsy* was born. Arthur Laurents was a great writer, but he was also a pragmatist, which is why he was able to collaborate. He elevated the quality of dialogue, and the better the dialogue, the better the book, the better the musical, but he also understood that the song would always be King.

As a book writer your will need to learn to live with the possibility of the lyricist or composer/lyricist being 'inspired' by your text for their lyrics. That fantastic speech you wrote about heartbreak might just end up as fragments of lyric in a song instead. The only way to really deal with this is to enter into the process in the full knowledge that there is likely be a song in the scene you are writing, and it may be that what you write spawns that song. Writing a speech that you know might be turned into a song is sometimes referred to as a dummy lyric; you need to learn to live with it. Or you might get lucky, talking about one of the perceived innovations of *West Side Story*, that the last three scenes of this musical don't have a musical number, Arthur Laurents explained that this was an accident. The musical was supposed to end with an aria sung by Maria, so he wrote a speech for her as a dummy lyric. But the composer, Leonard Bernstein, 'never found music that satisfied him and so to this day, West Side Story innovatively ends with a speech that is a dummy lyric.'[10] Happy creative accidents, people!

I can't remember who told me that the book in a musical should be the shortest distance between songs, but I don't believe that this necessarily has to be a negative thing, learning the joy of economy is a very important lesson for every playwright – it's not how much you say, it's how you say it.

Quite often in musicals it will be the songs that do the heavy emotional lifting. You need to accept that music and dance can tell the story just as well as that big, blistering row you just wrote. Laurents remarked that in musical theatre everything needs to be integrated, every technique needs to be taken as far as it can be taken, every element needs to be seamlessly combined.[11]

Nothing exists in isolation. Text sparks; song reveals; dance illuminates. And our job as book writer is to understand this. Especially in terms of dialogue and song. A song is not a static thing. A song is not there to simply reflect what has just happened. A song should be dynamic. It should move the story forward, not stand to one side and simply comment on it. A song is also an expositional gift, enabling you to move through time and deliver a lot of information in just a few minutes. Lin-Manuel Miranda remarked that the technique he used to get through the vast amount of exposition required in *Hamilton*, was inspired by Stephen Sondheim and his character of the Witch in *Into the Woods* who relates her backstory at the start of that musical, as Mr Miranda said, 'It's an attempt to delight the ear while filling it full of information.'[12] In the right hands a song lyric can be emotional, narrative and expositional dynamite.

One of the aspects of craft you will need to master quickly if you are to write the book for a musical is the juncture between dialogue and song. This isn't as easy as you might think. Do you sneak the music in early and let the dialogue evolve into a song? Do you clear the stage, give us a moment of reflection, and then ignite into song? Does your character just turn around and start singing? Sometimes, when done badly, the dialogue can feel like a short run up a steep ramp before leaping off into song – try to avoid that.

And then there is the wonderful world of diegesis. Do your characters know they are singing or don't they? Are they singing in the 'real' world of the drama or are they singing outside the 'real' world? If the characters know they are singing, for example, *Let Me Entertain You* at the start of *Gypsy*, it is a diegetic number. If they don't know they are singing, for example, *America* in *West Side Story*, it is non-diegetic. The relevance of this for you, the book writer, is that knowing or not knowing will need a different approach in your script. If someone is going to sing a song in the 'real' world, it will more than likely be acknowledged – 'I think I'm gonna sing a song now!' If a song is non-diegetic it may be a form of monologue (or dialogue) in song, in which case you will need to tread lightly into the lyric.

And talking of lyrics . . .

Have you ever written a lyric for a song? If the answer is, no, I challenge you to give it a go. Choose one of your favourite songs and re-write the lyrics. In other words, write new lyrics to fit the same melodic, syllabic pattern as the original. This is a great way to learn about the sound of words and how some syllables are stressed while others are unstressed. A syllable that is unnaturally stressed is the hallmark of the amateur lyricist. A quick example, if you try to replace a word like *heaven* which has the stress on the first syllable hea*ven*, with a word like *embrace*, which has the stress on the second syllable *em*brace, it will sound lopsided and forced. Have a go. You might be surprised at how satisfying it can be.

Have you ever written a poem? I bet you have. Well, sorry, but a poem isn't the same thing as a lyric. A poem is written to be read or spoken aloud, it has its own rhythms, the words themselves are the music, adding music is like adding another layer of chocolate to a chocolate cake, it can make it sickly and indigestible. Music enlarges words and can impose unintended meaning. It is possible to set a poem to music of course, but as Stephen Sondheim points out, it can distort the poet's phrasing and can sometimes render the language unintelligible. For Sondheim, 'Music straightjackets a poem and prevents it from breathing on its own, whereas it liberates a lyric. Poetry doesn't need music; lyrics do.'[13] A poem doesn't need the oxygen of music. A good lyric, on the other hand, cannot live without it.

A good lyric is clear, concise, contains detail rather than generalizations, includes innovative rhyme, is appropriate for the drama, and is a good fit for the character(s). It can do the expositional and emotional heavy lifting, move the story forward and, when appropriate, have its own narrative arc, for example, when a wronged character moves from feeling pity for themselves at the start of a song to deciding to take action by the end of it.

And as with all writing, the most important thing is the words, which in a theatrical context takes us back to the Greeks and means not only word selection but also the sound of the words. The great American composer George Gershwin would seem to agree with Aristotle, he said that 'in song lyric writing, sound is one of the most important things . . .'[14]

Lyric writing isn't about a word looking pretty on the page, it is about the sound it makes in the singer's mouth. And it isn't easy. George's brother, Ira, the lyricist in the family, talked about the art of lyric writing as being something that 'requires a certain dexterity with words and a feeling for music on the one hand, and, on the other, the infinite patience of the gem-setter.'[15] What a wonderful way to think about writing a lyric – you need to mine and set gems. A good lyric is like a gold necklace set with gems here and there that shine, shimmer and sparkle.

And you need to be pragmatic. You need to think about the voices you are writing for. Different characters will have different personalities, different voices, different vocabularies. What type of singer are you writing for? What range will they need? What kind of timbre? These are two-heads-are-better-than-one questions. Talk to your composer.

Lyrics work in different ways for different writers, if you want to have a go at writing lyrics seek out the lyricists that you like, study them, work out how they did it, then add *essence of you*. For playwrights who understand and prioritize the use of language, playwrights who elevate language, Alice Birch and debbie tucker green, for example, the transition to lyric would be, I believe, not such a great leap, the lyricism is already present in their text. For others, it will take a longer run up and the challenge will be not to diminish characterization by switching from idiomatic speech into a different style of expression in a lyric.

What happens when book and lyric blur into one and the characters sing all the way through? I'll tell you what happens – it becomes a libretto. The book for a musical is sometimes referred to as a libretto but for the sake of simplicity, let's go with the idea that if a show is sung-through, if the whole show is set to music, consisting of recitative and aria, or sung dialogue and song, we'll call it a libretto. The original home of the libretto is opera, but before we get too operatic, let's stay with musical theatre and the idea of you, the playwright, writing a libretto. How would that work?

When *Hamilton* was in its infancy and Lin-Manuel Miranda had written the first few songs his plan was to get a playwright in to write the book. It didn't work. The problem was that 'everyday speech couldn't sustain the energy of rapped lyrics.'[16] What Lin and his collaborators realized was that what they needed was recitative, or, as they might put it, rapped speech. So, *Hamilton* is a kind of rapped-through musical – marrying Lin-Manuel's twin passions of popular music (hip-hop, R&B) and musical theatre.

Oscar Eustis, Artistic Director of the Public Theatre in New York where *Hamilton* was developed referred to the musical as 'a perfect example of verse drama,' pointing out that 'until about 200 years ago, virtually every playwright in the Western tradition wrote in verse.' All of which takes us back, again, to the Greeks, and to Shakespeare, because as Eustis points out, 'Lin does exactly what Shakespeare does . . . He takes the language of the people, and heightens it by making it verse.' Verse has longevity because it transcends everyday speech. Verse 'demands and rewards your attention.'[17] Sometimes you need to work hard to find the meaning in verse but there are such rich returns for that effort.

Like Shakespeare, Lin-Manuel Miranda is a rule-breaker. In most musical theatre the perceived wisdom is that the content of the story should determine form of the lyric. *Hamilton* is the story of one of the founding fathers of the United States who was responsible for setting up the nation's financial systems in the late eighteenth century. If the content were to dictate the lyrics, the characters should have been singing exclusively in a late-eighteenth-century American-English vernacular infused with the lyricism of constitutional debate, but Lin-Manuel Miranda adds another element, very un-eighteenth-century rap. He should never have been able to get away with it, but he does, and it is this miscreant rule-breaking that is one of the things that makes *Hamilton* so incredibly special.

Writing recitative, whether rapped-through or sung-through, requires that the playwright tune in to the rhythms of the language they choose even more acutely than they might do in a play. It could be that you are writing to music that is already written, it could be that you submit your text to your composer, and they fit it to music. It could be that your composer will need to change some of your text to fit the music they write, you need to learn to live with that. The basic hope is that you can inspire each other.

And remember not to overwrite, economy beats prolixity, jewels are more important than ballast.

What about rhyme? For Sondheim, 'A perfect rhyme snaps the word, and with it the thought, vigorously into place, rendering it easily intelligible.'[18] Rhyme can help to make the meaning of a lyric more intelligible by pinging the synapses of association. Why do students sometimes make up little ditties as a way to remember information for exams? Because rhymes help to make the information stick, they help to focus attention on meaning.

And it's a good idea to vary the type of rhyme and the positioning of rhyme in a lyric. You can use internal rhyme, near-rhyme, assonance rhyme, consonance rhyme – and if you don't know what they are, look them up! But beware of killing the audience with constant rhyming couplets or repeating ABAB patterns. Mix it up. Or perhaps just have fun and go for a crazy rap rhyme scheme like Lin-Manuel Miranda where rhyme is constantly popping up in wild ways in unexpected places. The libretto for *Hamilton* is a masterclass in having a good time with rhyme.

The trick is to write a lyric that is incredibly smart, without it ever seeming smart. So don't be obscure, over-elaborate or overtly ornamental. Tell it like it is. Again, a lyric is not a poem, your audience will only get one chance to hear it, it needs to be comprehensible, they don't have the luxury of reading it again like a poem to find the hidden gems, the gems need to be on the surface. And don't forget the sound different words make, vowel sounds, percussive consonants, slightly sibilant sentences. Enjoy the challenge of writing solos, duets, trios and chorus pieces. Most importantly, make every word count.

The best piece of advice I can offer to anyone wanting to write lyrics is this: Study Ira Gershwin, Stephen Sondheim, Lin-Manuel Miranda. Their lyrics are a treasure chest.

By the way, writing a musical isn't fast – average five years development – so get ready for the long haul.

My first musical, *The Big Life*, took twenty-five years to reach the stage. The process began when I was at school. The Shakespeare comedy I studied for my 'A' Level in English Literature was *Love's Labour's Lost*. I remember thinking to myself at the time that the story of four men who decide to give up relationships with women for three years to improve themselves with study would make a great plot for a musical. Twenty years later, when Philip Hedley asked me if I had any ideas for a musical, the idea of adapting *Love's Labour's Lost* popped back into my head. I proposed it, Philip liked it, suggested that I work with the great reggae musician, Paul Joseph, and we were up and running.

I did a scene-by-scene breakdown of the play, laid my story over the top, wrote the book and lyrics, gave them to Paul Joseph to write the music, and, hey-presto, we had the beginnings of a musical. We were lucky to be in the very capable dramaturgical hands of the multi-talented actor-director-writer Clint Dyer to develop the musical and the show grew from there. Subsequent rewrites led us further and further away from the plot of *Love's Labour's Lost* as our musical found its own narrative imperatives, but I always knew the original play was there to guide us if we came unstuck. It took just over five years to write it and get it produced, but it was worth the wait.

Using a Shakespeare play as the basis for a new musical is an old trick – *Romeo and Juliet* as *West Side Story; Taming of the Shrew* as *Kiss Me Kate;*[19] *Comedy of Errors* as *The Boys from Syracuse*[20] – so it wasn't exactly an original idea, but it was an accidentally brilliant way to begin to learn how to write a musical.

Many of the best musicals are adaptations of one kind or another. The reason for this is that plotting a musical is fiendishly difficult and an adaptation gives the writer not only a bag of ideas to play with but also a structural safety net. I would strongly recommend to any playwright wanting to embark upon an adventure in musical theatre to begin by adapting an out of copyright text, it is a fantastic way to find your feet. Just write a scene-by-scene breakdown, lay your story over the top and write. Rewrites are likely to lead you away from your original source material, but that's all part of the process, go with it.

A playwright will need to immerse themself in musical theatre before they make the crossover. It is inadvisable to try to step across from one to the other with no understanding of the different requirements, when a playwright tries this, it can create an awful lot of work for the musical theatre dramaturg! The same is true of opera. Opera needs good playwrights, but playwrights need to listen and appreciate the total dramatic form of opera before they attempt to write an opera libretto.

Opera

I was asked by one of my peers to write something about writing an opera in this book. I agreed it was important to include the opera librettist's art, but, unfortunately, although I have come close on a couple of occasions, I have yet to write a libretto for an opera, so I felt like a bit of a fraud. However, I am fortunate enough to know the brilliant Cecil Castellucci and Emma Muir-Smith. Cecil is an author of books, graphic novels and libretti, based in the USA, and Emma is a singer, librettist and opera director in Australia. So, I asked them if they could give me a few tips.

Cecil was keen to point out that she has no formal training in writing libretti and that she is more in the new-opera-for-all-make-it-less-stuffy camp. That sounded perfect to me. This is what Cecil wrote:

In my process I collaborate closely with the composer. I write out the sentiments and feelings in a script format that tells the story. But I am very aware that the two pages could very well be too long and eat up all the time that there is allotted for the opera. In the collaboration, the composers that I work with grab the phrases that excites them and use them. I have made a commitment to not be precious about my words; but be the caretaker of the story. (I feel like this in comics, often throwing out a lot of captions and dialogue.)

Sometimes I use a rhyming scheme. Sometimes not.

An aria is different than a spoken monologue. A duet is different than two people talking. A chorale is different than chorus.

It is extra important to read the text out loud, even if half of it might get thrown away. If it is difficult to speak, it's going to be too difficult to sing.

I also sometimes sing my text aloud with little melodies that spring into my head before it even goes to the composer. In that way I can kind of feel if it is musical at all. This music I sing is never what the composer is thinking and that's fine by me. It's just a way to feel if it's got a musical vibe to it.

Sometimes feeling doesn't need words. It can be a sound.

I have to think about syllables a lot. If I need to tweak something in the story but the music is set, I have to make sure that any word I swap out feels like the same shape as the one I removed.

In the operas that I've written, I've been told how many singers and what their voices are. So, often I am constructing the story to make do with the bodies I have. This may be different with other people. For me it has forced me to be creative.

Thinking poetically is your friend here.[21]

You can tell that both Cecil and I used to be in bands – I also make up melodies for the lyrics I write for my musicals, even when I'm not the composer. It is imperative to know that your words can be sung, so what better way to find out than by singing them to yourself. Thank you, Cecil.

Emma is steeped in opera and offered these five fantastic top tips:

1 Familiarize yourself with the art form and learn to listen.
   Puccini's *La Bohème* is my favourite example of music and drama working together.[22] Watch it first – in person or online, and *then* listen to it several times. You'll be amazed at the layers you pick up each time, both structurally and in the orchestral detail – the recurring themes, musical motifs, the way certain instruments can evoke mood, and the ways singers can emote with their voices. The bustling Act 2 Christmas market scene is also a stunning masterclass in chorus writing.

2   Keep your structure watertight and be economical with your words. Clear structure provides scaffolding for your composer around which to develop their music, and being economical with your words leaves space for the music to bring its half of the drama. Get rid of any words – particularly small joining words – that aren't absolutely crucial for meaning or character, learn to love a brutal edit, and enjoy discovering your characters through their music as you work with your composer, which brings me to . . .

3   Develop a close working relationship with your composer, and make sure you're on the same page about music serving the drama. That's not to say that the libretto is more important than the music, but rather that all musical choices should be dramatically-motivated. There should always be a reason for a particular chord, rhythm or texture. Your composer should be able to explain to you why they've done something – if they can't, see if you can find the motivation together. Remember, composers are musically trained, but they often need a helping hand on the dramatic side of things. Be patient, and add notes throughout your libretto indicating how a section or moment feels to you, or what emotion a character is experiencing.

4   Leave your composer motivic and thematic gifts. For example, a character might say the exact same words at three different points in the opera: once in ambivalence, once in anguish, once in euphoria. Repeating the same sentence thrice in a play could be strange (depending on your play), but in opera, this is a gift to your composer. They can illustrate each iteration of this motif with completely different musical colours and orchestration, revealing change or development in your character throughout the opera.

5   Give the gift of onomatopoeia to your singers: think about how the sounds of words can evoke their meaning. For example: 'shimmering' with its 'sh' and 'mm', when sung, might be more evocative than 'sparkling', which has effectively the same meaning, but has a different energy due to its hard 'sp' and 'k' consonants. Think about the mood you're trying to evoke, say your words out loud, and select them carefully. Google 'word painting' and think about it when writing – it's your new best friend.[23]

Brilliant tips and she's right about 'word painting'! Thank you, Emma.

And just in case you're wondering if there is one tip that I think trumps them all. There is. And it's, always work with a great composer.

If all the above seems a bit much for your playwriting sensibilities to deal with, how about writing a play with original songs? Usually diegetic, these plays simply feature characters picking up an instrument and playing and singing a song.[24] Or you can use songs (performed live, please) as an interlude between scenes. Or just stop the play and sing a song. Just don't overlook the power a song can bring to a play.

Alternatively, there is the much-maligned Juke Box or back-catalogue musical. Write a show that slots together the songs of your favourite bands. Don't sneer. It's fun. And it's a challenge – you need to do a lot of lateral thinking that can take you to some very interesting places and lead to innovative solutions. Just because it's a Juke Box musical is not an excuse for a bad script, let it stretch you, find a way of doing things that is new. And if you're still sneering, spare a moment to think of the playwright Catherine Johnson who, with no previous experience, wrote the book for *Mamma Mia* – didn't do her any harm, did it? And at the very least it's a fantastic excuse to listen to lots of songs by your favourite songwriters all day and do what we are supposed to like doing – making up stories.

As ever, I would like to challenge you to learn all you can about writing a musical or an opera, and then do it differently. Bring who you are to the game. Like Lin-Manuel Miranda did. And at this point, I would like to sing a familiar tune – it is called *Standing on the Shoulders of Giants* and this time it is going to be sung by Lin-Manuel Miranda. Lin stood on the shoulders of his rap heroes and his musical theatre heroes, but arguably no one more so than the great Jonathan Larson, the writer of the ground-breaking, rule-bending musical *Rent*.[25]

Lin-Manuel Miranda was hugely influenced by *Rent*, and it is easy to understand why. *Rent* is a re-working of Giacomo Puccini's 1896 opera *La Bohème*, but at the same time it is also one of the most innovative pieces of theatre of the late twentieth century.[26] Larson was one of a kind, a unique character who channelled his ambitious, iconoclastic worldview into his work. Tragically, Larson died just before the first performance of *Rent* in 1996, but what an incredible musical legacy he left us. *Rent* might be thirty years old, but it is still as potent on a personal, political, psychological level today as it was when it was first produced. Larson's struggle to survive in New York is mirrored by the stories of the characters in this musical. The rock music, the urban setting, the use of a chorus, the head-on confrontation with AIDS and sex and drugs, the radically diverse and inclusive cast made for a musical bursting with originality and energy. It was an urban story told in the way that only someone who had experienced it could tell it. Which, along with his specific cultural perspective and musical tastes, was precisely what Lin-Manuel Miranda brought to his musical *In the Heights*. Larson stood on the shoulders of Puccini, Rogers and Hammerstein, Sondheim, he added his late-twentieth-century personality and tastes and wrote the show he wanted to see. Lin-Manuel Miranda did something similar. Find the writers that inspire you, climb onto their shoulders and then bring yourself to your work.

Finally, some words of wisdom for anyone currently slogging through the writing of a new musical or libretto. As the character of Rose in *Gypsy* says, 'If you have a good strong finish, they'll forgive you for anything.'[27]

2.7 GET PHYSICAL

A few years ago, John Rwothomack, a young Ugandan-British actor and director, got in touch with me to ask if he could direct a new production of my play *Bad Blood Blues* for Theatre Deli in Sheffield. I was more than happy to give him the go ahead. I didn't get to see the production because on the day I was due to travel to Sheffield from London, England was gripped by icy weather that made travelling anywhere virtually impossible. But I heard great things about it and was very impressed with John's work when I watched the video he kindly sent to me after the production had closed. A little while later, John got in touch to say he had a proposition. We met in London and he told me that when he was a boy in Uganda he had narrowly avoided being recruited as a child soldier and he was looking for a playwright to write a one-man play for him to perform on the subject of the abduction and coercion of children into armed militias. He asked if I would be interested in writing it. I was flattered, but I said no. I think John was a little surprised. When he asked me why I didn't want to write it, I told him that he should write it. John was taken aback; he had never written anything before. I told him that if he had a go, I would work with him as his dramaturg to help him knock it into shape. John did have a go, and a few months later after a couple of drafts he had a script called *Far Gone* ready to workshop with the director Moji Kareem and movement directors Akeim Toussaint Buck and Lilac Yosiphon.

John had proved that he could write, but it was only when we started to work on the play in the room that the full potential of the piece started to become evident. The magic ingredient was John's physicality. In the play, the character of Okumu – the child played by John – is abducted by members of Joseph Kony's Lord's Resistance Army (LRA) and a stage direction explains that Okumu is made to go on a long march along with a group of other new recruits. As Okumu marches onwards, the stage directions specify that 'we should see the effects of the long walk, a fly might land on him, the thickness of the forest, and awareness of everyone around him, etc . . .The march continues for as long as is appropriate.'[1] In performance, this simple stage direction transformed into an extraordinary physical sequence which, through movement alone, demonstrated the fear, exhaustion and dehumanization of John's character on his four-week long march to the LRA base in Sudan. What struck me most was the power of John's non-verbal physical communication; the movement said so much more than any amount of text could ever have done.

I asked John if he could tell me something about his writing process. This is what he had to say:

My approach to writing has always been to use as little speech as possible and rather be guided by movement and improvisation. When writing Far Gone, *and creating its physical language, I started by researching the physical language of daily life in a Northern Ugandan village and then that of guerrilla rebel life. Having decided what characters I needed to tell the story, I then researched and detailed every character. To find my characters voices I needed to physicalize them in a rehearsal room before putting pen to paper. Having understood in my own body how they moved and spoke, the words followed.*

Plays are written to be staged, not read.[2]

I agree with John, we are writing for an audience not a reader. We can also learn a lot from John's physical approach to creating character. I wonder how many playwrights try to get to grips with what it physically feels like to be a character before they write them. I wonder how much more potent our characters might be if we could physically feel more like them, like an actor, as we write them. By feeling the character in our bodies, by sensing them from the inside-out, rather than imposing on them from the outside-in, perhaps we might create more dynamic characters.

Playwrights, you need to remember that actors have bodies as well as heads. Bodies that breathe, bodies that move, bodies that can tell stories without a single word ever being uttered. Actors aren't just talking heads. I think we all need to use the physical aspect of performance more. Perhaps you are worried that you don't know how to write it. Perhaps we all spend too much of our time sitting down on our backsides. Whatever the case, it's a missed opportunity. You don't have to have studied choreography or learn a new lexicon to introduce dance or movement into your play, you just need to remember that movement can also tell your story and include a simple stage direction, like John does, to indicate that you want a specific moment to be physicalized – a movement director or choreographer can do the rest. Lucy Prebble knows how to do it. In *Enron* she writes:

> *Physical sequence. The company at work. The Traders dance. As they do they create a round table. Skilling holds meetings around it. People come and go. Meetings end and begin. The table is removed. Fast, ordered fluidity. Numbers fly through the air. The stock price throbs, but never alters much, gradually edging up in comforting, rhythmic pulses. Lay plays golf somewhere in bright sunlight. Time passes. Days and nights. Gradually a slowing. Computer lights over faces. A calm.*[3]

What a fantastic gift to a movement director, and not a box step, heel turn, arabesque or cha-cha in sight! All you need to do is think about the kind of movement sequence you would like and leave the rest up to your collaborators.

Incorporating movement is not a new concept. Movement was an essential part of Greek drama; for individual actors and chorus members, it was part of the delivery and interpretation of a text. Most of the movement was expressive of character or situation, similar to the way that symbolic movement and gesture is outlined in the Sanskrit treatise on dramaturgy, the *Nāṭyaśāstra*. In the case of the individual actor, the movement would be singular and in rhythm with their dialogue, status and situation; for the chorus, it was more likely to be a unison moment symbolizing the meaning of their text. The thrill of movement, dance theatre, physical theatre, call it what you will, is immense. We need to break down the barriers between the physical and the text. We need to explore and understand the joy and potential of physical performance and we need to put it into our plays.

We are not afraid to let dance do some storytelling in musical theatre, so why are we frightened to experiment with more movement in our dramas?

Dance illuminates. Movement can colour speech, it can be used instead of speech, to physicalize the sub-text, and to say with movement what cannot be said with words. Movement is a universal language that we can all understand. There is no need for translation. Metaphor is central to the language of the body. You can find truth in physical as well as verbal communication. Movement and text are beautiful together. They don't have to be antithetical. You don't have to put a tap number in your next play but why not think about the way an actor might breathe – breathing is a matter of life and death! Emotion is physical. Revulsion is physical. Elation is physical. Everything from the curl of a solo performer's wrist to a grand multi-performer gestural unison dance can speak to us.

Movement has been codified in a multitude of performative ways over millennia, but what does movement mean to a contemporary playwright? Sadly, it would appear, very little. USE IT! Use physical language to show lust, hate, joy, sadness, hunger, cold, and more and more and more and more. Make the movement fit the mood – enhance the tragic moments with big, sweeping gestures, enjoy the funny moments with ridiculous and wild interactions, explore grief with the pain of the slightest movement.

Playwrights, look at the extraordinary work of dance companies like Ballet Rambert and London Contemporary Dance Theatre. It's wonderful, beautiful, extraordinary. You should be screaming, *I want some of that!* And if the work of these companies is a bit too much for you, take a look at the amazing work of physical theatre companies like Gecko, DV8 and Frantic Assembly. There is so much we, as playwrights, can learn about expression and emotion from physical theatre companies.

We don't have to live in hermetically sealed little generic boxes. Playwrights over here; dancers over there. We are all making theatre. Let's work together. Characters aren't just what they say, they are also what they do AND how they do it. And they can manifest what they do in all kinds of physical, non-literal ways. They are movement, and gesture, and symbol. In the same way that a word can become absurd upon repetition, the repetition of a movement can draw attention to the absurdity of an action. Think of character as movement, think of character as physicality, think of character as a whole living, pulsing, bleeding, belching, broken, beautiful physical entity. We should try to marry the cerebral with the physical. Make the cerebral physical. Try saying what we want to say with a body instead of a mouth. Or both. Tell our stories with the whole body.

We should set up more links with physical theatre companies. Perhaps we should all pull on some loose clothing and go to a workshop? If that idea terrifies you, perhaps get in touch and ask if you can be a fly on the wall. See how they put a show together. Observe how they physicalize a theme or idea or emotion. See how they record sequences in notes and scripts for performance.

Thankfully, Frantic Assembly have regularly commissioned and collaborated with playwrights over the years, writers like Anna Jordan, Mark Ravenhill, Abi Morgan and Bryony Lavery. Frantic's distinctive approach has had a huge impact on theatre in the UK. New writing companies are now much more likely to employ a movement director for the production of a new play than they were twenty years ago. That is a wonderful thing. But many playwrights still seem oblivious to the potential of movement. It shouldn't be a production add-on; it should be part of our playwriting arsenal. We need to embrace the techniques of physical theatre and work with the practitioners of physical theatre to create a symbiosis that enables us to take theatre to new, exciting and ever-more *theatrical* places.

2.8 THINK BIG

My first play at Stratford East required eleven actors; my second play there also required eleven actors; my third, required eight. It never occurred to me, at the time, that these were big casts. It was only when I moved to the other side of the production fence and started to work as a dramaturg for various theatre companies, that I realized most new writers start off by writing for companies of two or three or four actors. By having these three plays produced I had learned how to write for a big cast without really knowing it. Most playwrights don't get the same opportunity, a corollary of which is that when a writer gets the chance to write a large-scale play, some of them struggle to come to terms with the opportunity.

I still love to write for big casts, but opportunities are few. I recently wrote a play inspired by Ben Jonson's *Bartholomew Fair*. Jonson's original has thirty-three named parts, as well as puppets and extras. It can be mind-boggling dealing with such a huge number of parts, but at the same time, what a wonderful learning curve. I ended up with a cast of twenty-two – with a couple of parts doubled. This play eventually found its way onto BBC Radio courtesy of a Naked Productions and Graeae Theatre Company collaboration directed by Polly Thomas and Jenny Sealey, with eight actors playing eight parts. By today's standards, eight is still quite a lot, but I think it's safe to conclude that cast sizes have shrunk considerably since the 1600s.

Thinking big isn't just about cast size, it is also about ambition. My play *Bad Blood Blues* is a small play with two actors and one musician, but the ambition of the play – confronting the ethics of Big Pharma – is big. Small can be BIG. As a concept, the idea of the big must, therefore, be approached from two perspectives: large-scale plays with a big cast and small-scale plays with BIG ambition. I will begin by *thinking big* about the former.

Over the last sixty years, new plays by new writers have shrunk. They have withered into little, predominantly naturalistic nuggets of drama with two or three characters. We have escaped the refined upper-middle-class drawing room for the shabby working-class sitting room. As far as I am aware, our imaginations haven't become smaller, so why have our plays? What happened?

Part of the problem, I believe, is that today wannabe playwrights are weaned on a diet of small cast plays. If you live in the UK and want to write plays, you are likely to be drawn to the great new writing theatres in London and Edinburgh, places like the Royal Court, the Bush, the Traverse. More often than not the plays produced in venues like these will have a small cast – not because the people programming these theatres only want to produce small-scale plays, but because the economics of production make it almost inevitable. Every now and then a slightly bigger play will come along – for example, *Jerusalem* by Jez Butterworth[1] – but often these plays come with potential West End transfer money already attached. The vast majority of plays don't, so they need to fit the *new play paradigm* – a small cast, and (usually) one set.

Ambitious, aspirant playwrights study the early, successful, small-scale plays of great contemporary writers like Alice Birch and Ella Hickson and think to themselves, *if I want to be the next Birch or Hickson, I have to write small plays too!* They watch small-scale plays at the Royal Court and the Bush and the Traverse, they are inspired by these small plays, and they are encouraged to write small plays.

New playwrights get little or no encouragement to write their big new play because they rarely see one performed. They get little or no education in how to write big plays because they are soon discouraged by the paucity of production opportunities. Budding playwrights struggle to write plays on a larger scale – plays like *King Lear* or *Bartholomew Fair* that ran for three-plus hours, had huge casts, a multitude of locations and even sub-plots(!) – for a number of reasons. The most pressing of which is that, today, if a playwright writes a large-scale, big-cast play, complete with a sub-plot(!) the chances of production at a new writing theatre are incredibly slim. In the UK today, there are basically three options: the National Theatre, the RSC, or a drama school. A cast of six will make most producers at a new writing theatre company break out in a cold sweat. A cast of eight in a new play by a new writer is likely to be dismissed immediately.

I believe the root problem lies in that most sensible of all nouns: pragmatism; and that most pernicious of all human inventions: money.

Example: a producer has two plays and one slot to fill. One play, the best one, needs six actors. The other play, a quite good one, requires two actors. It's the end of the financial year and money is tight. What does the producer do? They produce the two-hander, of course. What does the playwright who wrote the play for six characters do? They go home and write a two-hander so that next time something like this happens, they will be ready. Result: the producer produces the small-scale play; the playwright writes a small-scale play.

Every writer needs to know how to handle a big play for that moment when the opportunity to write one finally comes along. Some playwrights score a string of fringe successes, the National Theatre take notice, they are commissioned to write a big play for the Olivier stage, and they haven't got a clue how to do it. Why? Because they don't know how. They haven't seen many big new plays written by their contemporaries. They have never tried to write one – what would be the point, no one would do it. Suddenly they have twenty to thirty actors, but they can only manage to get two of them speaking at the same time. Result: massive stage, thirty actors running around climbing moving staircases to fill the space, and a sequence of duologues downstage centre. And that's if they get that far, most times, the play will already have been rejected.

How do we solve this? Firstly, we can study the plays of writers like Shakespeare to excavate the methodology behind writing large cast, large-scale plays (with sub-plots). Secondly, we can study how some of our contemporary writers are doing it. Let's get up on those shoulders again. That should get us started.

You've got a big story, it's going to be a big play, it needs a big cast ... Where do you start?

Let's take the deductive Shakespearean route and make a plan. *NB. Any resemblance to King Lear is entirely intentional . . .*

Let's say you've got a story about an ageing entrepreneur who wants to pass his business empire onto one of his three daughters, but before making his choice he wants to find out who loves him the most (it's a story about *succession* . . .) Our story ends with the entrepreneur going mad and dying along with the daughter who loves him the most – who he thought loved him the least!

You've got thirty actors.

Where do you start?

Well, you've got your story arc, so let's make a list of characters:

Entrepreneur
Daughter #1
Daughter #1's husband
Daughter #1's loyal PA
Daughter #2
Daughter #2's husband
Daughter #3
Daughter #3's friend – a doctor
Businessman in love with Daughter #3
Another businessman in love with Daughter #3
Entrepreneur's Right-hand man
Right-hand man's son #1 (also an employee)
Right-hand man's son #2 (also an employee)
Right-hand man's son #2's friend
Right-hand man's right-hand man
Old man that lives in one of Right-hand man's properties
Loyal Executive
Funny guy who works for the entrepreneur
Journalist
Motorcycle Messenger
Employees
Other businessmen and women

Let's see how Shakespeare might manage a cast this size:

Act 1 Scene 1
The Board Room
Part 1. The Entrepreneur's Right-hand man, his son #2, and the Loyal
    Executive discuss the impending division of the Entrepreneur's
    family business.

Technique: Basically, a Greek-style prologue, with three characters, setting up the action of the play – the main plot, the Entrepreneur is going to announce his successor from amongst his three daughters; the sub-plot, the Entrepreneur's Right-hand man's intentions with regards to the inheritance of his two sons.

Part 2. The Entrepreneur, colleagues and family enter. This is a big multi-
character scene in which they talk business, climaxing with the
entrepreneur handing the business over to his two older daughters.

*Technique: One character leads the exchanges – this character is the
fulcrum of the scene, many characters speak, but the action revolves
around the scene's lead character, he is the centrifugal force of the scene
with several other characters contributing to the conversation. This is a
useful device that prevents the sequential duologues that the novice
playwright might write in their first big play. When the centrifuge of the
scene leaves, a handful of characters are left for a short time to discuss
the fall-out.*

Act 1 Scene 2
An Office
Right-hand man's son #2 is annoyed that he might miss out on his
promotion in favour of Right-hand man's son #1. He decides to
take matters into his own hands. He tells Right-hand man that he
has seen an incriminating email from Right-hand man's son #1.
Then he tells Right-hand man's son #1 that he's got his back.

*Technique: A small-scale sub-plot scene with just three characters
focussed on the actions of a single character.*

Act 1 Scene 3
Daughter #1's House
Now that Daughter #1 has power, she turns cold on her father.

Technique: A small-scale scene focussing on the main plot.

Act 1 Scene 4
Daughter #1's House
Entrepreneur and his retinue arrive for a visit. They laugh and drink,
they are in high spirits. Daughter #1 gives Entrepreneur the cold
shoulder. He leaves for Daughter #2's house.

*Technique: multi-character main plot scene around the centrifugal force
of the protagonist, with other characters left to summarize the fall-out
from the scene after he leaves.*

Act 1 Scene 5

Outside Daughter #1's House

The Funny guy who works for the Entrepreneur makes some jokes about what has happened. The Entrepreneur is disturbed, is he losing his mind?

Technique: a small, tightly focussed scene foreshadowing the main plot.

I could go on. But I don't need to because you get the gist, and you can stand on this giant's shoulders just as well as I can. If we break the first act of *King Lear* down into its most basic beats, we have:

Act 1 Scene 1 (Part 1) Small scene – three characters – set up main plot and sub-plot

Act 1 Scene 1 (Part 2) Big scene – multiple characters – protagonist as centrifugal force for dialogue

Act 1 Scene 2 Small scene – three characters – sub-plot

Act 1 Scene 3 Small scene – two characters – main plot

Act 1 Scene 4 Big scene – multiple characters – protagonist as centrifugal force for dialogue

Act 1 Scene 5 Small scene – three characters – main plot

Easy enough, isn't it? Move between large-scale scenes where the lead character is at the centre of the action and smaller ones with a tighter focus.

Just because you can write a good play with four characters doesn't automatically translate into writing a play with a bigger cast. If you want to learn how to do it, take any play by Shakespeare, Lope de Vega, Ben Jonson and a host of others, and do a similar analysis. Don't be lazy. Don't think that because someone said you write good dialogue, you automatically know how to write a scene with twelve characters in it. Study.

Take a look at *The Antipodes* by Annie Baker – look at how she manages the group dialogue, look at how she avoids the dominance of sequential duologues, look at how the characters take it in turns to assume focus (to become the centrifuge). This is a play about stories, about *who* creates stories, about what *we* – as playwrights – do; and there couldn't be a more important conversation for us, or for our audiences, to have. It is about corporate storytelling versus the individual vision. Annie Baker's play is a masterclass in exploring the big idea of who tells stories and managing multiple character dialogue – and a must for anyone intent on entering a writers' room to create a new TV drama one day . . .

Don't ignore the idea of sub-plot just because it isn't fashionable. Surely we can still cope with sub-plots, can't we? Have our brains grown so small in their capacity to concentrate that we can only deal with one plot per play? How wonderful to have a secondary plot that not only mirrors, refracts and contrasts the primary plot, but also provides another window onto the theme and vision of the play. Sub-plots can move in the same direction; they can move in the opposite direction; they can join together at the end of the play; they can diverge in totally different directions. The best sub-plots not only reflect the main plot, but they also add something to it by complementing it and critiquing it. Surely it is time to revive this wonderful device. What might you do with a sub-plot? What could you do that no one else has done before? How can you spin the idea of a sub-plot into a new twenty-first-century dramatic innovation?

Thinking big might also mean embracing the use of music, movement, dynamic shifts in language from prose to poetry, and bigger sets (or empty stages). It will involve a scene structure that acknowledges the length of the play by breaking the action up into larger (longer) and smaller (shorter) scenes – just as in the example from *King Lear*, above. You might need two intervals instead of one, or none. In recent years plays have not only got smaller they have got shorter. The fashion seems to be for new plays to be about 70–90 minutes with no interval. The reason for this would appear to be quite simple, this is about the same length as a film. Have we become so indoctrinated by the length of films that our plays need to copy them? Why not write a huge, seven-hour epic, instead! Have you ever been to one of those plays that lasts all day? Fantastic, isn't it! Long plays don't need to be boring if the audience know what to expect and know there will be adequate comfort breaks.

If your Olivier commission is still some time in the future, there's no reason why you can't practise now. We need to learn to practise our art and not just sit around waiting to get struck by the lightning bolt of genius. And it needn't be a purely academic exercise. You can always write a big play with a huge number of characters with a small cast if you are clever with doubling. And you don't need huge sets – in *Indecent*, Paula Vogel requests a few suitcases and some planks.[2] A bare stage, suitcases, planks and imagination. That's all. Shakespeare didn't need a scene change form Sicily to Bohemia. He just told us where we were. We can do that.

I love big plays in small spaces. London's tiny pub theatres are wonderful places to see giant plays. At the other end of the scale, I love small (cast) plays in big spaces. Seeing Robert Lepage perform his one-man show *The Far Side of the Moon* on the stage of the Olivier was extraordinary, not least for the fact that he alone – one actor, accompanied by a small astronaut puppet, a large mirror and an ironing board – could fill that giant space with the play's big ideas.[3]

What constitutes a big play? Big ideas, big ambitions, big casts, big concepts, big questions, big scale, big story . . . all of which, apart from cast size, should be relevant to *all* plays. Every play should have the ambition to be big in some way.

A small cast play can be big thematically and it can be big in terms of what you, very specifically you, have to say. Roy Williams and Clint Dyer's *Death of England* is a play for one actor about a working-class, white man, growing up in London, but it is also a play that confronts the huge question of race and identity. Nick Payne's *Constellations* is a play for two actors about a woman and a man falling in love, but it is also a play about life choices, parallel universes and metaphysics. Suzie Miller's *Prima Face* is a one-woman play about a brilliant young barrister who has worked her way to the top, but it is also a theatrical *cri de coeur* about class and sexual abuse that packs a fierce and authentic punch.[4] *Top Dog/Underdog* by Suzan Lori-Parks is a play about two African-American brothers living together in a single room, but it is also a play about the whole of humanity, what it means to be connected to another human being and the struggle to come to terms with the expectations of the world we live in.[5] *Copenhagen* by Michael Frayn is a play for three actors about why we do the things we do, but it is also about nuclear physics and saving the world from total destruction.[6] If you think about the plays you love, you will probably soon see that they are about so much more than what is visible on the surface. Small plays can be immense.

If you want to know how to handle a large-scale play with a large cast, start playing with ideas now. If you like the idea of going large, go large now. Tony Kushner went large with *Angels in America*;[7] Matthew Lopez went large with *The Inheritance*. Brilliant playwrights, taking big chances to write big plays. If it needs to be big, write it big. But even if you don't want to go big in terms of scale, never settle for less than big in the idea behind your play. By all means write small for a small cast, but always try to say something important, big, colossal even. *Think big.*

2.9 SHOCK, BREAK AND PROVOKE

I have only ever been shocked in the theatre once. It wasn't sex, it wasn't gore, it was two words spoken directly to me from the stage.

In 2001, I went to see a production called *First Night* by Forced Entertainment at Toynbee Studios in London. *First Night* was a seedy variety show in which nothing quite goes to plan. It wasn't the most ground-breaking Forced Entertainment show I'd seen, but it had one moment that seared itself into my memory for all time. This was when a mind-reading act took to the stage and – very slowly and very deliberately – pointed to each member of the audience in turn, and, told them how they were going to die. It was one of those moments when you prayed your seat would swallow you up and disgorge you somewhere into the bowels of the London Underground deep below. I don't know how many people there were in the audience that night, probably about two hundred, and I was hoping (along with most people in the audience, I assume) that the mind-reader might stop their grisly predictions before they got to me. Surely they wouldn't predict the death of every single person in the audience, would they? Yes, they would. On and on they went, pointing randomly to each audience member and predicting death from cancer, death from heart attack. On and on. They didn't seem to care how long it was going to take. Finally, they got to me, pointed, and said, 'Car crash'. And I thought: *Fuck you, I'm not going to die in a car crash!* I have, however, never forgotten that moment, and every now and then when I get into a car I remember those two words like a theatrical curse. After I had the accident in Russell Square that nearly killed me, one of the first thoughts I had was that if I had died at least Forced Entertainment would have been proved wrong! Yes, I had been hit by a car, but it wasn't a car crash. If Forced Entertainment had set out to shock, as far as I was concerned, they had succeeded monstrously.

I don't think l have ever set out to deliberately shock audiences with anything I've written. There isn't a lot of sex and bloodletting in my plays. There is some. There are a series of murders in *Lush Life*, but none of them on stage. There is a death in *Reasons to be Cheerful*, but it is represented symbolically. There is on-stage sex in *Bad Blood Blues*, but the plot demands it. There is a lot of filth in *Reasons to be Cheerful*, but I would argue that you can't write a show with the songs of Ian Dury without a lot of filth as that was pretty much his trademark.[1] In this show there are also a lot of what my disabled collaborators refer to as 'crip jokes' – jokes about disability, but, again, disability is at the heart of the show, and I regularly heard these affronts bandied about in the rehearsal room, so I always felt they were justified. I suppose what I'm saying is that I have never used shock to get attention. But perhaps I've missed a trick? You never know what you might unleash by daring to step out of your comfort zone . . .

The shock of the (not so) new

Playwrights have used shock tactics to get noticed ever since the beginning of this thing called *theatre*. From Greek and Roman dramatists – Aeschylus describing the sensational murder of Agamemnon, Sophocles giving us the blind Oedipus, Euripides' Medea murdering her own children and Seneca's Thyestes eating his own children – all the way through to the blowjobs, rapes and drug overdoses of *In-yer-face* theatre. Take for example Edward Bond showing us a baby being stoned to death in a pram,[2] or the anal rape in Howard Brenton's *The Romans in Britain*.[3] Playwrights have been shocking their audiences for millennia. It's a great way to make a name for yourself. Write something outrageous, get someone to perform it, provoke a storm of protest and *Hey Presto!* Instant fame! It's not as simple as that, of course, and I'm not convinced it is the most desirable way to begin a career, let alone sustain it, but playwrights have been doing it for a very long time.

Greek tragedy is bursting at the seams with shock. Euripides wrote several plays with sensational content – something that was apparently frowned upon by the good people of Athens but didn't stop them going to the theatre to see his plays anyway. They lapped it up. And we still go to see his plays. People love a bit of gore and incest and cannibalism and bestiality. People love to squirm and avert their eyes. Make 'em laugh, make 'em cry, make 'em faint.

When Sarah Kane's *Cleansed* was revived at the National Theatre in 2016, five people fainted and forty people walked out in the first week due to the violence depicted in the play.[4] The main cause of the walkouts came about twenty minutes into the play when one of the characters has their tongue ripped out. It's not surprising that such a graphic moment would cause audience members to faint or walk out, except it is. Firstly, we've been cutting one another's tongues out on stage for years (in Shakespeare's *Titus Andronicus*, Lavinia gets her tongue cut out and her hands chopped off – and all this after she has endured the horror of being raped). Secondly, it's not real, it's pretend. Mind you, people still faint when it isn't done realistically, if stories of audiences fainting at the sight of a blinded Oedipus in Ancient Greece are to be believed. Personally, after an on-stage eye-gouging or stabbing, I've always preferred seeing a length of red ribbon being pulled from the victim's wound rather than a gush of theatrical blood from an imagined severed artery, but that's because I prefer to see theatre as a presentational art rather than a faithful reproduction of the real thing.

Notoriety

There was a time during the 1990's when it felt like almost every play I read or saw had buckets of blood, a blowjob, rape, or someone shooting up in it. But the shock had gone. I can remember watching a young man being bent over a sofa and anally raped by another man; I can remember another young man getting a blowjob about two feet in front of me; I can remember the front row of an audience I was in being handed a sheet of polythene to protect us from the splatters of blood that were coming our way, but I felt nothing. *In-yer-face* theatre had shocked me into numb disinterest in the shocking. It felt like it had become a game of puerile one-upmanship.

You could argue that Euripides made a name for himself by writing plays with sensational content. You could argue that Shakespeare enhanced his name with the gore of *Titus Andronicus*, one of his earliest plays. You could argue that the bloodthirsty revenge and incest tragedies of playwrights like Webster and Ford – that were doing the rounds after Shakespeare called it a day – were written with a deliberate agenda to shock.[5] You could argue that Royal Court writers like Edward Bond, Sarah Kane and Mark Ravenhill used shock to launch their careers. But let's not overlook the fact that all of these individuals happen to be very fine playwrights. The shock came with the play. The sensation was integral to the play. The trauma was what the play was about.

When Tim Crouch was commissioned to write a play for the Royal Court Upstairs, he wrote *The Author*, a play about writing a shocking play that is produced at the Royal Court Upstairs. It explores and analyses the type of 'shocking' play that the Royal Court is famous for and seeks to trump the shock of the play that the author writes with the shock of what he subsequently does. It's ... shocking ...

But writing to shock is not for the faint hearted. If you are going to set out to really shock, be prepared to be slaughtered on the altar of the popular media. Could you cope with the vicious backlash that Sarah Kane had to endure? Sarah Kane was an incredible, ground-breaking playwright, but she was hounded and hurt and never recovered. What great plays we might have had if she had been celebrated as her work deserved.

Future shock

What is the most shocking thing you have ever seen on stage? Did it make the play better? Did it make the play worse? Does shock work? Let's be honest: it does. Shock was why Grand Guignol worked.[6] It is why people still pay to go to the London Dungeon. It may be why people who never usually go to the theatre queue for plays with sex and mutilation in them. We love gore. We love sex. And we love it most when people are pretending to do it in front of us. So, why not write a play in which someone eats a dead baby, or thrusts a knitting needle deep into someone else's ear, or severs their own penis, or eats their lover's eyeballs mid-coitus? Actually, don't do any of that because it's already been done.[7] Think of something even more shocking! Go on, I know you can do it! Put it in your next play and really shock people! But only if it serves the play. Gratuitous shock is pathetic. If sex, drugs or cannibalism are a central part of your play, its theme, its vision, the BIG idea behind the play, put them in. I love shocking stuff just as much as anyone else when the shock has earned its right to be there. But I don't think a playwright should ever set out to shock for the sake of shock. If all you want to do is shock, don't write plays, write horror.

The interracial sex scenes in the first act of *Slave Play* by Jeremy O. Harris are strategically shocking.[8] We see what appear to be a sequence of time-warped antebellum sexual encounters between three black slaves and a white mistress, slave overseer, and indentured servant respectively.

It is only when one of the characters cries out the safe word, 'Starbucks' towards the end of one of the scenes and the role-play is revealed that things fall into place – these men and women have signed up for modern day *Antebellum Sexual Performance Therapy*. It is a brilliant conceit and totally, justifiably shocking.

For me, the greatest example of a play that shocks without being gratuitous is *How I Learned to Drive* by Paula Vogel. This is a play about abuse. It is a play about the grooming of an adolescent girl by her uncle. It was written in 1997 and although it won the Pulitzer Prize for drama, it has taken almost twenty-five years for the play to make its way to Broadway. Why? Because the subject matter is shocking. However, the treatment of the subject matter is anything but shocking, it is measured, it is honest, and it is theatrical. Paula Vogel tells the story of the abused girl, Li'l Bit, backwards, from the perspective of the woman who was that girl, now in her forties. For most of the play the abuse is suggested, not shown, as the characters do not touch. Only when we get towards the end of the play, to Li'l Bit's first driving lesson at the age of twelve, and the moment when the uncle initiated the abuse, do the girl and the uncle come into physical contact with one another. Even in this moment, the action is disembodied by having a chorus member speak the girl's lines.[9] It is a shocking scene, beautifully and theatrically realized without any unnecessary sensation. This sublime play delivers its punch so much more powerfully than any gratuitous, literal shock.

Shock is a tactic to be used constructively and theatrically. It should grow out of what you are writing, and never be imposed upon it.

Breakages

If the whole idea of shock is an anathema to you, I would suggest you ask yourself how you can break things instead.

Here's a quote from Tim Etchells, the Artistic Director of the theatre company that so effectively messed with my head when they predicted how I would die, relating theatre to a child's elemental relation to a toy:

How can I break this?
 Meaning:
 What kind of stresses and strains reversals, upendings, speedings up, slowings down, shatterings, dissections, refractions, distortions,

simplifications, complexifications, pairings down, new disciplines, hybridisations, cross-cuttings, re-mixings, and re-wirings can I subject this form to? And what might be produced in the process?

If I break it, will it maybe still function? Might it function in some new way? Might it do something new? Or might it do something old and worth returning to? Or produce some unexpected combination of affects old and new?

How can I break this? What kind of fun can I have with the rules of this game, this form? Or How can I modify, expose, weaken or otherwise intervene so that it can do something that I might really need to do?

How can I break this?[10]

This is wonderful. And so much more exciting than working out how to make people faint. If only every playwright asked themselves these questions at the start of each new play. What happens if I write this scene backwards, or speed it up, or slow it down, or break it into a dozen pieces, or mirror it, or distort it, or cut it to the bone, or play it as farce, as melodrama, as surrealism, or all of those at the same time. What might that do to my play? Will it still work? Will it now work but in an entirely different way?

Lucy Prebble isn't frightened to mix things up. She has very eclectic theatrical tastes and she isn't afraid to use them: mask, a ventriloquist's dummy, anthropomorphic symbolism, music, songs, *and* physical movement/dance sequences in the same play.[11] Why this obsession with hermetically sealed forms like New Plays and Musical Theatre and Dance Theatre and Physical Theatre and Mime when you can put them all in the same play! Stop pigeon-holing drama and throw it all on the stage at the same time. You know you want to.

Ask yourself: What are the rules? And then work out how you can have fun with them, change them, break them.

Paul a Vogel once said:

I always ask myself, 'What are the rules right now?' And then I break them. For years, it was believed that linear storytelling was the way to write a play. None of my plays are linear. I'm not interested in business as usual. Now that non-linear playwriting is common, I might consider writing a linear play.[12]

What a beautiful, simple, contrarian attitude. Take a look around you, observe what the current trend in playwriting is, then do the opposite. I often tell playwrights that once we spot the thematic zeitgeist, it's time to run in the opposite direction, so why shouldn't the same apply to the current, fashionable rules of the game?

Playwrighting has not stopped growing for 2,500 years, and one of the reasons for that is that we like to break the rules. Thespis broke the rules when he decided to speak lines to the leader of the dithyrambic chorus as a solo performer. Aeschylus broke the rules when he introduced a second actor and dialogue was born. Sophocles broke the rules when he introduced a third actor and all sorts of possibilities presented themselves. And on and on we go. The theatre would be a very dull place if we all agreed that there was only one way to do things. So, let's keep breaking things.

One word of warning: don't break it if you don't know what you are breaking. There can sometimes be a tendency amongst new writers to reinvent the wheel without actually knowing what the wheel is. It's like creating abstract art before you learn how to draw. You need to know what you are doing to undo it. There might, now and then, be a few happy accidents, but they are rare. Study it, try it, play with it, and when you know what it is, shatter it.

Ionesco knew how to create solid, middle class, socially conditioned, characters who took themselves very seriously. They were conventional people. But the joy of Ionesco (one of the joys) is observing how he exaggerates the world around his characters, taking it to almost comic extremes, pushing his characters to the edge of absurdity. For me, this is an example of a playwright, lovingly smashing his toys.

Sarah Kane constructively breaches the rules in *Blasted* – a naturalistic opening followed by escalating symbol and shock, first inviting her audience to passively observe proceedings on stage and them provoking them to endure and viscerally engage with mutilation, death, masturbation and cannibalism. It is Beckett meets Brecht meets Barker meets Büchner, filleted, and served up as only Sarah Kane knew how. She knew what she was doing.

As writer and director Lisa Goldman writes in *The No Rules Handbook for Writers*, 'Successful rule-breaking also requires mastery.'[13]

Don't throw your toys out of the pram, break them, constructively.

The impossible

How about setting yourself the challenge of writing something that it would be impossible to stage? This is what Paula Vogel sometimes gets her students to do in an effort to explode their imaginations. It might not result in the best play you have ever written, but it might teach you that, in fact, nothing is impossible on stage.

Antoine Artaud's short play, *Jet of Blood*, includes a hurricane, colliding stars, living human body parts, eating eyeballs during sex, and scorpions crawling out of a nurse's vagina. None of it impossible to stage. Mind you, I'm glad I'm a writer when it comes to challenges like this so that my collaborators can get on with the job of working out precisely how to do it.

Provocations

Finally, if I haven't annoyed you enough in this chapter, here are some provocations to wind you up just a little more.

Devil's Advocate

- Let's ban all plays that don't strategically shock
- Let's ban all plays that don't seek to break things
- Let's ban all plays that don't have a least one moment that is impossible to stage
- Let's ban all plays that don't question what theatre is and how theatre works
- Let's ban all naturalistic plays without at least one non-naturalistic element
- Let's ban all plays written in a single genre
- Let's ban all serious plays that don't have at least one funny moment, and all comedies that don't have something serious to say
- Let's ban all plays that don't have at least one song and/or dance and/or physical sequence in it
- Let's ban plays that don't acknowledge the audience
- Let's ban all plays that don't force the audience to engage with it
- Let's ban plays that don't use live musicians
- Let's ban the use of film, video, projected images and computer graphics in our theatres

- In fact, lets ban all technology
- And let's ban all characterization and pretence of psychological truth
- And while we're at it, let's ban all plays that don't have at least one scene in which the characters stop the action of the play to discuss the dramaturgy of the play

On a practical front . . .

- Let's ban all writers who don't write with the audience and event in mind
- Let's ban all writers who bore audiences to death
- Let's ban all writers who don't shock us *and* make us laugh
- In fact, let's force all playwrights to write at least one play that is as shocking, provocative, disgusting, outrageous, funny, and as perverse as possible . . .

Or, at the very least, let's not forget these options are available to us.

2.10 WRITE A POSTDRAMATIC PLAY

I wanted my show *Reasons to be Cheerful* to be more than a play with songs, I wanted it to be an *event*. I didn't want the audience to sit down and watch something, I wanted them to be a part of something; to be on the inside with the actors, not on the outside looking in; to feel part of the occasion and not like an onlooker. It was important to me that there was as little artifice as possible. This was achieved in our production by having what is known as a *soft start* – this meant having the actors chatting to the audience as they took their seats, rather than the archetypical 'lights down, lights up, curtain rises, play begins' opening. We kept this connection up throughout the play and it proved to be a wonderful way to keep the audience inside the show. It was almost postdramatic in concept, apart from the fact we were asking the audience to suspend disbelief by buying into the idea that they were in a pub with us circa 1981. If we had wanted to create a postdramatic play, we wouldn't have used such a framework – there would have been no pretence. But there were many postdramatic elements within this production that cemented my belief that playwrights should engage much more with postdramatic theatre techniques.

First things first: **What is postdramatic theatre?**

Postdramatic theatre is a term established by the German theatre theorist and professor, Hans-Theis Lehmann, that pulls together the experimental techniques of avant-garde theatre-makers from the 1970s onwards and prioritizes the audience and the heterogenous elements of the performance event over the written text.

Postdramatic theatre was and is a reaction to the primacy of text in theatre-making. In postdramatic theatre, the relationship between the performance and the audience is paramount. As Lehmann asserts in the prologue to his seminal book *Postdramatic Theatre*, 'Theatre means the collectively spent and used up lifetime in the collectively breathed air of that space in which the performing *and* the spectating take place.'[1]

Theatre is a sensory, spatial, temporal exchange between audience and performers, we inhabit the same space, we use up a small quota of our lifetime together. It is not 'us' the audience and 'them' the actors, it is 'all of us', together, in this space, now. All of which is more important to the postdramatic theatre-maker than the text of the performance.

In postdramatic theatre, every aspect of theatre-making has equal importance: words, bodies, props, lights, sound, audience, space, time, everything. Most theatre of this type is auteur-led, or put together collaboratively, devised, improvised. A writer may be involved in this process; indeed, it could be argued that everyone involved in the process is the writer, but the word on the page isn't the driver, it is just one component in the act of making a piece of theatre.

But here's the thing, although text isn't usually at the heart of postdramatic theatre, I think there is a great deal we, as playwrights, can learn from postdramatic performance. In fact, the term postdramatic is sometimes applied to the more innovative playwrights among us; to playwrights like Jon Fosse, Sarah Kane and Martin Crimp, who dare to play with the very idea of text, who eschew cause and effect dramatic conflict, who challenge form and who write with ambition, adventure, curiosity, non-linearity and intellectual flair. These writers are inimitable, but I have always been curious as to how they came to write their plays in the way they do. This led me to conjecture that they may have been influenced by the work of avant-garde, postdramatic theatre-makers, and this, in turn, led me to ask myself what the rest of us might learn from postdramatic theatre.

For the playwright, writing a postdramatic play means thinking beyond plot, character and language. To write postdramatically, the playwright must take into consideration the entire potential of the event. They must embrace the liveness of the event, the temporal, spatial, transient nature of production, the relationship between audience and performers, and the possibility of confronting and shaking audiences out of pre-conditioned passivity to live performance towards a more visceral shared experience. The postdramatic playwright needs to think about the unique opportunities that live performance offers, and to exploit them, mercilessly.

1. The words

Ask yourself what you can do to disturb conventional text. Perhaps stagger your words across the page like an army of ants, use numerals instead of words, use graphics instead of words, use bodies instead of words, use sound effects instead of words.

Ask yourself how you want actors to relate to your text. As characters? As actors?

Ask yourself how you want your audience to relate to your text. As spectators? As participants?

Ask yourself how you can break the actors' relationship to dialogue. Perhaps by using choric incantation instead of conversation.

Think poetically. Not only about poetic text, but about the poetry of sound, light, movement, media, music and spectacle.

Think flexibly. Create a text which is flexible and transferable. Dare to move text from your play's beginning to its end or to have text spoken backwards! Experiment with the attribution of lines; take a scene between two characters and give the lines to ten actors or one actor or even to members of the audience.

Let your words offer options for a performance rather than dictate terms. Create shapes, colours, textures of language that invite the audience to investigate meaning on an individual level, where the opinion of one audience member may be entirely at odds with the person sitting, or standing, or lying next to them. A totally different understanding, or no understanding at all.

Let different styles of writing bang up against each other – mix prose, poetry, journalism, stream of consciousness, political rhetoric, verbatim – anything you like. Let them walk shoulder to shoulder through your text, liberated from the novels and anthologies and newspapers and journals and parliamentary reports and recipes where you would normally find them.

Think of your text as an event rather than a play. The moment a spectator enters the performance space, the event has begun. As a playwright this opens a new channel of investigation – what does an audience member experience when they walk through the entrance to the event? Do they see rows of exhausted red velour seats? Do they see the bare blue breeze block walls of an industrial unit? What does this say to them? What do you want it to say?

Perhaps think of writing not as the authorship of a text but as the composition of a situation. You could write a history, a family tree, a sequence of doctor's reports, newspaper articles, online dating profiles, tweets. You could write a world rather than a narrative. You could write the backstory of a building, of the cultural landscape of a location not as preparation for the text but **as the text**. Maybe create a world that is more like a video game, in which the player-spectator can interact with any other character or non-player character and follow any quest they wish, a kind of 'choose your own adventure' experience outside of the digital realm that might lead to further postdramatic audience emancipation.

2. The performer

The performer viewed through a postdramatic prism can offer up a host of new refractions for the playwright. Consider the physical presence of the performer – their body, their body in time, their body in this space. What does their body represent? How might they use their body? How might we, the playwright, instruct them to use it?

Consider the question of mimesis – to what extent is the actor's performance mimetic? We need to decide if the performer is representing, presenting or simply being. Is your actor asking the audience to believe they are someone else; are they acknowledging that they are presenting someone else; or are they simply standing before us as the performer.

Character does not have to be at the centre of your play. Think performer rather than character. Think performance rather than play. Consider every element of performance as a performer. The lighting as actor, the sound as actor, the space as actor, time as actor, a prop as actor, audience as actor.

Ask yourself who attributes meaning to a performer – author, actor or audience? All? Or none?

3. The audience

The audience is not a passive receiver. The audience is part of the performance. The audience is a tool for the playwright.

The majority of audiences expect a story with a beginning, a middle and an end. What happens when these expectations are subverted? Potential boredom. Potential irritation. Potential walkouts. The challenge for us as playwrights is to find ways to encourage audiences to engage with a non-linear, more disruptive form. To do this we need to write plays that explode their imagination, plays that take them to new and unexpected places, plays that excite and enthral. Easy to say, very hard to do. But we cannot advance our artform by sitting around and playing the game as it has been played over and over again for two and a half thousand years. With innovation comes true progress in art. Human beings are inquisitive, and the more creative we are at asking questions, the more likely it is that our audience will want to join us in our search for the answers.

Think about how a performance can question, even upend the perception of the audience. Think about how you can turn the world of the audience on its head, like Tim Crouch does in his play *The Author* in which the audience *is* the setting of the play.

Perhaps you can involve your audience as co-creators of the event? Create templates, options, fragments – elements that only come together with the input of the spectators. Ask yourself what might happen if you turned everything on its head. What might happen when light becomes sound, sound becomes light – when yellow is loud, when a crashing wave is blue. What might happen when the actor becomes the spectator, the spectator becomes the actor – when the actor watches the audience. If you can imagine it, there will be a way to do it.

Every performance of every play is different. A live event can never be precisely replicated. Why not harness that and take it further. Perhaps ask yourself what elements of ceremony, event, gathering, you can make anew every time.

Predictability. Don't we all like to play 'Guess the Plot'? She's going to kill him. He's going to marry her. They will all end up dead. The joy of a postdramatic text is that such a game becomes redundant. The play doesn't follow an established narrative arc, it can veer off anywhere. It isn't comprehensible. However, because we are human, we will try to impose sense on the performance, but the joyful thing is that an audience of 200 can have 200 different interpretations. It is in the meeting of the imagination of the production and the imagination of the individual spectator that the play will find its sense (or non-sense). You can author this. Embrace the deprivation of dramatic 'meaning' that postdramatic theatre offers and replace it with intellectual and creative engagement from the viewer. Perhaps try to encourage your audience to 'feel' a performance rather than interpret it. I know that sometimes when I am watching a performance that makes little or no narrative sense, I simply let it wash over me and enjoy the experience of receiving the performance. It can be liberating.

4. Time

We live in the present moment. Life is a succession of lived present moments. Theatre exists in the shared present moment. The moment a performer screams, the moment a trap door opens, the moment a spectator laughs. Many philosophies exhort us to live in the present moment. Theatre *is* the present moment. It is the present moment shared. In postdramatic theatre we don't need to deny this fact. Of course, one could argue that all theatre happens in the here and now, the difference with postdramatic theatre is that it isn't pretending that the here and now is happening there and then (on stage). So, let's address this in our texts, let's acknowledge that the play is performed in the present. Let's allow our collaborators to know we expect them to embrace the present moment of the present performance.

Never forget the versatility of time on stage. We can make time stand still, we can make it jump, bend, speed up, slow down, repeat, go backwards. Time is one of the most extraordinary tools that *every* playwright has at their disposal – and it is always *now.*

5. Space

I'm not talking about the stage set, I'm referring to the performance space, the physical space, the performers relationship to that space and the audience relationship to that space. These are things that, in my experience, a playwright rarely considers in depth.

We need to ask ourselves if the space is part of the performance or coincidental to the performance. We need to understand and utilize the space. Tim Crouch informs us that no matter where his play *The Author* is performed, it is always Upstairs at the Royal Court – it is a play about writing a play that is produced Upstairs at the Royal Court, so it makes sense.[2] But what do the postdramatic playwrights usually say about space? Very little or nothing at all. And for good reason, they don't want to dictate the terms of the space when they can't know where their play is being performed or what their future collaborators might want to do with it. However, I don't think we can simply dismiss the idea of the performance space – especially if it is an essential part of the performative experience, as it is in *Immersive Theatre.*

Immersive Theatre literally immerses the audience inside the performance. As designated by American theatrologist, Marvin Carlson, this can work in a number of ways: a promenade performance, in which the audience are guided from place to place, perhaps in a park or in a building, with scenes acted out in a set sequence in one space after another; a performance space similar to that of a promenade production, usually in a non-theatre building, through which spectators are allowed to roam freely, with action taking place simultaneously in some of these spaces so that the audience can choose their own journey; a single performance space which contains several specifically designated performance areas within it, and places the audience inside the action by making them part of the community of the play and by giving them the freedom to come and go as they please.[3]

Immersive Theatre is sometimes viewed as the enemy of the postdramatic because of a commitment to representational performance.[4] Basically this means that the audience pretend they are actually at the event they are watching, if the play is *Julius Caesar*, we must be in Rome. It is an accusation you could lay squarely at the feet of my show, *Reasons to be Cheerful*, but I'll leave the arguments about this to the purists, I just want us to write great plays. For us, the important thing is that it If you are going to write an *Immersive* play you are going to have to think hard not only about the location but the audience and their relationship to that location, and if and how they belong there.

6. Symbol

Symbol is, and always has been, a strong element in all theatre. Put a vase on stage – it will say something; take a cigarette from another character's coat pocket – it will say something; climb to the top of a mountain – it will say something. We even created a form of drama called *Symbolism.*[5] The question for the postdramatic writer is, how can I exploit sign and symbol in new and invigorating ways? We need to make the ordinary extraordinary because it is. Elevate the props. Spin the action around the prop rather than the human. Use Brecht's hammer to reshape things. Use Heidegger's hammer and when the head flies off re-examine the hammer as a more abstract object.[6] Or use a mirror and ask what it shows us. Does it reflect who we are? Does it reflect what we are? Is it just glass and silver nitrate? If we smash it with a hammer, is it broken, or does it continue to reflect in different ways?

A postdramatic playwright can also engage with the minutiae of gesture and the potential symbolic meaning of physicality and movement. Should you be so inclined you could even codify your own treatise on the meaning of certain movements. The tiniest movement can mean so many things.

7. Logic

Does each text suggest its own logic? Are there rules that need to be obeyed? How do we shake off the Aristotelian logic of beginning, middle and end? Perhaps have some fun by setting up narrative expectations and then defying them. Defy the unities.[7] Defy logic. Dreams, desires, nightmares, work, love, sleep, play – none of them need be tied to any dramatic logic. Set yourself free. Build your own entropic paradise. Leave your logic to the ironing and the dusting, let your unconscious tell the stories.

Perhaps try to disrupt the traditional idea of form in order to shake the audience from their comfortable preconceptions, to challenge the dramatic unities, to surprise, to dispute conventions, and to open the door on a new experience.

Is this reality on stage or is it fiction? Or is it both? Or neither? Up to you.

8. Revolution

Let's challenge ourselves to remake the theatrical universe for performer and audience alike.

Think of theatrical conventions, then see how you can explode them. Don't destroy every dramatic tool for the sake of it, such revolutionary zeal is not necessary, instead see what you can do to remake them. But don't strive for perfection. Drama, like life, can never be perfect. It is messy, so don't be afraid of the mess.

Magic. Theatre can make the mundane magic. It can turn convention to chaos, politics to posturing. Magic doesn't have to mean pulling a rabbit out of a hat. Everything and anything can be made magical by a theatre that knows no bounds.

Chaos. Life as chaos. Drama as chaos. Let's create the chaos of life on our stages. The late, great dramaturg, Marianne van Kerkhoven, thought we should investigate the idea of chaos.[8] And I agree. But what does this look like? Perhaps we might create *chaos structure*: structure that is unknown, structure that could be anything that happens. *Chaos text*: words that can be misused, misunderstood, misplaced. *Chaos character*: characters that don't exist or split into multiple conflicting existences. *Chaos image*: images that aren't what they appear to be, a mirage, a chimera. *Chaos sensation*: sensations that aren't what they seem, hot as cold, dry as wet, optical illusions, hallucinations. Chaos is an open book. Tear out the pages.

9. The new

How can we create something new? By writing the present event, by re-hearing and re-inventing the structures of language; by re-seeing the context of the body, the soundscape of old words and neologisms, and the visual representation of ideas; by generating image through the sense of smell, fear through the sense of touch, catharsis through silence, and metaphysics through spectacle; by creating a text in which no one thing is subservient to another, with everything pulling, distorting, speaking in theatrical tongues, taking us to extraordinary places. And, I would say, by remembering diversity, remembering inclusion, and by thinking about *access*. Anyone who wants to go to a performance should have *access* to every moment of that performance, irrespective of whether they are D/deaf, blind, disabled or non-disabled. *Access* should be at the beating heart of our theatrical evolution.

2.11 WRITE ACCESSIBLY

I have been incredibly fortunate to work as a playwright and dramaturg with the disabled-led theatre company Graeae in the UK. Working with this company and its Artistic Director, Jenny Sealey, has been one of the greatest theatrical adventures of my life, and for a very simple reason, working with this company requires the playwright to think with *total* theatricality.

The difference between writing for Graeae and writing for other theatre companies is very straightforward, it is called *access*. In writing *Reasons to be Cheerful* and my adaptation of Ted Hughes' children's book, *The Iron Man*,[1] I had to write in a way that I had never written before. I had to write with an access aesthetic at the heart of the work. Access is inclusion. It means that *everyone* can access every moment of the play being performed for them. In other words, disabled, blind, and D/deaf audience members are not excluded like they often can be. In a Graeae production they can access every grunt, sideways glance and custard pie, along with everybody else in the audience. This is important, not only because it means the play you write is accessible to everyone, but also because it opens up an aesthetic treasure chest of theatricality.

Access usually works like this: during the run of a play there will be one performance for visually impaired audience members with in-ear audio description, and one performance for D/deaf audience members with either sign language interpretation and/or captions. It is not enough, and it is a missed opportunity. Access should not be an afterthought, it should be seen as what, at its best, it can be – inclusion *and* enhanced theatricality.

Writing with access as part of the brief isn't restrictive, it is liberating. One of the first effects an accessible play has in performance is that it blasts the fourth wall sky-high. Typically, this happens because the playwright is challenged to come up with creative solutions for reaching

D/deaf and visually impaired audience members which necessitates reaching out through the fourth wall.

A visually impaired audience member will usually only have access to one audio described performance during the run of a play. If they miss the audio described performance and still want to go to the play, their only option will be to attend one of the other performances and try to guess what is happening on the stage. If they do manage to make the designated audio described performance, they will be given some headphones when they arrive to put on at the start of the play. The action on stage is described to them by a specialist audio describer sitting somewhere in the theatre, usually watching the play on a TV monitor. In the early days of audio description, the account of what was happening on stage could be very literal – *red light, green light, walks to the front of the stage* – however, in recent years the description has become much more engaged and creative and there are some excellent audio describers doing a terrific job. But far too often the audio describer is still only employed for one performance. Some theatres have tried to remedy this by using pre-recorded audio description, this is progress in terms of access, but it isn't perfect. Theatre is a live event and performances can and do change during a run, which means that pre-recorded audio will either become redundant or misleading, and surely it also flies against the basic pre-requisite of an artform that is a living, breathing, present experience.

The challenge for the playwright is to write a play without the need for disembodied audio description, and doing this requires the playwright to transgress the unwritten law: *show don't tell.* How can a visually impaired audience member know precisely what is happening on stage if you don't tell them? It demands that the information is somehow delivered by a character or assimilated into the dialogue, which forces the writer to think tangentially. Instead of writing dialogue in the way that they usually do, the writer needs to think about finding creative solutions to imparting visual information. Anyone who has written audio drama will already be ahead of the game in this.

Often, it isn't possible to include all the necessary audio description in the dialogue and a compromise will be needed in the use of an audio describer. But this doesn't have to mean someone tucked away in an alcove by the props table whispering into a microphone, you don't have to hide your audio describer. In *Reasons to be Cheerful*, we put the audio describer on stage in the middle of the action. The conceit was that he was on the phone in a pub, telling a mate, *Blind Derek*, about a play that was being performed in the public bar. Of course, he wasn't speaking to Derek, he had a direct line to every visually impaired member of the audience through their headphones. Visually impaired members of an audience can sometimes feel excluded when they hear people laughing at a visual gag they can't see, in this production it was the other way around, the other members of the audience were jealous of them because of their direct line to the stage and the joking commentary from the on-stage character (created and played by the brilliant Pickles Norman).

D/deaf audiences usually have to rely on a sign language interpreter apologetically tucked away on a corner of the stage for the one access performance they are offered during the run of a play. This is frustrating because of the way it forces D/deaf audience members to have to keep switching from the action in front of them on the stage and the interpreter downstage left under the exit sign, a bit like watching a game of tennis. A partial solution for this is to have D/deaf characters in the play who sign – you can have these characters converse with other characters using sign language and perhaps let them use direct address sign language to interpret the other characters' speech for the audience when not in a scene. Alternatively, you can introduce actors playing smaller roles who sign, both in and out of the action. Or you can double the characters. I have seen and worked on productions with D/deaf and disabled practitioners in which D/deaf actors have been doubled with hearing actors playing the same part. This doubling has a stunning theatrical impact. In a production of Bryony Lavery's *Frozen* by a brilliant company called Fingersmiths, each of the three parts was doubled.[2] It was like watching two plays for the price of one, with the two actors reflecting alternative personalities, strange cohesions and creating an extraordinary sub-textual dynamic. Again, think *creatively*! And please, never stick your interpreter/actors on the corner of the stage like an apology – put them in the middle of the action and see what that does to the play! Don't pretend they aren't there, use them. Break the fourth wall with them.

Another solution is to use captions. If you are going to use captions, please use your imagination, don't just leave it to someone else to type the text into a word processor and have it projected above or below the stage. Ask yourself how you can use captions creatively. For instance, you might have captions projected onto your characters' bodies, or suggest that the set embodies captions, or even embrace captions as a way to communicate the play's creative vision. In a play about a tech guru, captions could be embedded in code on screens that frame the set. In a play about a television newsreader, captions could run beneath the stage like the headlines on a 24/7 news channel. Be resourceful and use that artistic brain of yours.

In *Reasons to be Cheerful* we were faced with the added challenge of how to interpret song lyrics for D/deaf audience members. We solved this problem two ways – we used captions as part of a video film made by one of the characters, and we embedded sign language in the performance of the songs so that the lyric was signed as well as sung. The wonderful thing about doing this was that the signing became part of the choreography, so that singing and dancing and signing became one. I would encourage everyone writing plays with songs or musicals to embed sign language in the choreography. It works brilliantly.

If you put access at the centre of your play you will be challenging yourself to think more creatively. You will be reaching out to your audience. You won't be pretending they aren't there. You won't be able to hide behind the fourth wall. And that's a wonderful learning curve for a writer. Try it. Take one of your scripts and re-work it for *total* access, you will be surprised at how quickly it is reborn as a more vividly theatrical play.

Access is not an add-on.

PART THREE

3.1 THE WAY TO WRITE

The first play I wrote – after failed attempts to channel my inner-Ionesco at university and a few years of prancing around in PVC trousers, dark glasses and a silly hat playing pop music – was called *Blackshirt*.[1] It was about a working-class East London man who got sucked into the world of Oswald Moseley's British Union of Fascists (BUF) in the 1930s. I read some books about Moseley and the BUF, made some notes, and then sat down and wrote the play. When I'd finished, I sent it to four theatres, crossed my fingers and waited. One theatre never replied, two sent encouraging rejections with offers of setting up a reading, and the fourth, Theatre Royal Stratford East, invited me to join their writers' group. I got lucky.

I had studied drama at university, I had acted in plays, but I had never been taught how to write plays, I just liked doing it, so I did it. Basically, my writing process was instinctive trial and error based on whatever it was I had soaked up through osmosis. In terms of craft, I didn't really know what I was doing. My next play was called *A Night in Tunisia*, it was a play about a jazz saxophonist set in the 1960s. Again, I didn't think about how I was going to craft the play, I just sat down and wrote it. Fortunately, Jeff Teare, the Associate Director at Stratford East who had invited me to join the writers' group, liked it enough to want to direct it. And so, my 'first' play was produced.[2] On the back of this production, I managed to secure a position as writer-in-residence at Essex University for a year. Great. Except that as part of this residency I had to teach playwriting at Colchester Arts Centre. Suddenly, I was going to have to teach people how to write plays, without ever having sat down and worked out how to do it myself.

I realized that teaching my approach to playwriting – sit down and see what happens – would take about two minutes and the workshop participants would not be very happy. So, I broke the craft of playwriting down into basic areas of dialogue and structure and character, read as much as I could, and taught by keeping one week ahead of my students. It wasn't ideal, but I learned a lot, probably more than my students did.

By teaching playwriting, I realized that I already knew the basics. In other words, I had read, studied and performed in enough plays to have a basic grasp of the fundamentals of playwriting. The question now was: to what extent did I need to use the knowledge gleaned from teaching the craft in my own writing? It is a question that we all need to grapple with. Instinct, or Craft. Or both. If you are a new writer, I would suggest you embrace the happy rule-breaking accident of your first play, just write it and see what happens. Then, when you decide to make a career in this joyous and infuriating business, learn your craft.

There usually comes a point when you will have to make a decision about how you are going to write your next play. There is a spectrum of approaches – at one end of which is the *start-writing-and-see-what-happens* method, and at the other end is the *plan-it-in-minute-detail-and-then-write-it* method. The question for you is, where do you position yourself?

In Harold Pinter's Nobel Prize for Literature acceptance speech, he explains that most of his plays are 'engendered by a line, a word or an image' and that, 'In each case I had no further information.'[3] To find out who the characters were and what was going to happen in most of his plays, Pinter simply sat down and wrote. These plays were an act of improvisation based on a moment of inspiration.

The writer, Philip Ridley, would seem to be cut from the same creative cloth. He doesn't plan anything. He said, 'I deliberately get as lost as possible.'[4] That's incredible, isn't it? That's inspirational, isn't it? Except that when most of us sit down and try to write a play like Pinter or Ridley, it is usually a disaster, consisting of dead ends, diversions and total breakdowns. Sadly, most of us aren't Pinter or Ridley.

Writing like Pinter or Ridley is fun, but it can result in a horrible sprawling mess of a play. And it can be doubly disastrous if you buy into the *legend-of-the-untouchable-first-draft* myth. For reasons best known to the muses, some writers seem to think that a first draft is a magical, sacrosanct thing that must never be re-written. I don't know how much re-writing Pinter did or Ridley does, but for most of us I believe it is self-defeating to think that our first draft is untouchable. We must re-write.

And if you are willing to re-write, the act of improvisation on the page can be a wonderful method of writing your way into your story, a way of finding the heart of your play.

At the other end of the process paradigm, you will find the writers who plan everything in granular detail before even typing a single word of dialogue.

In Lajos Egri's book *The Art of Dramatic Writing*, a book that was hugely influential on the golden age of mid-twentieth century American playwrights, he writes that no playwright should start to write their play without first having a clear-cut premise.[5] To do so would be a waste of valuable time. According to Egri, a moment of inspiration must be moulded into a coherent shape before starting to write your script. The message is clear: PLAN BEFORE YOU WRITE.

I once heard playwright David Edgar in a debate with Alan Plater strongly advocate the necessity of planning your play before writing it; he seemed astonished that anyone could contemplate doing it any other way. If you plan your play, you won't get lost. If you know where it starts, you can start; if you know how it ends, you can drive all the way there without having to circumnavigate the creative planet unnecessarily.

Evidently, the writing process is often framed as a choice of opposites. The first time I came across this idea of a dialectically opposed processes was in a book called *The Sound of One Hand Clapping* by Sheila Yeger. Sheila writes about the difference between an ORGANIC writer, someone who makes it up as they go along; and a SCHEMATIC writer, someone who plans the play before they start writing.[6] Since reading that book, I have read many other articles and books with chapters on process that basically say the same thing but use a slightly different vocabulary. A list (not exhaustive, by any means) is as follows:

Making it up as you go along:	Planning what will happen before you write:
INSTINCT	CRAFT
ORGANIC	SCHEMATIC
IMPROVISED	PLANNED
FLUID	CONCRETE
INSPIRATION	PERSPIRATION
RIGHT (artistic) BRAIN	LEFT (organized) BRAIN
ARTIST	ARTISAN

ROMANTICISM	ENLIGHTENMENT
INDUCTIVE	DEDUCTIVE
EXPERIMENT	REASON
DIONYSIAN	APOLLONIAN

So, what works best? The answer is, whatever suits you, whatever gets the results you want. But before deciding whether you are a *fluid* or a *concrete* playwright, it might be worth reminding yourself that these options are at opposite ends of the spectrum. Most playwrights are likely to use both approaches when writing a play, navigating a dialectical process:

THESIS: Make it up as you go along
ANTITHESIS: Plan everything
SYNTHESIS: Do a bit of both

If the wild *artist* writes the first draft, they are likely to need the reliable *artisan* to help them knock the second draft into shape. If the *Apollonian* playwright carefully crafts the first draft, they are likely to need the inebriated *Dionysian* dramatic poet to give the second draft more vibrancy. Mix it up. Find out what works for you. Swing between the two.

Alice Birch has gone on record as saying that it took her three days to write *Revolt. She Said. Revolt Again.* She had been storing up ideas for some time, but she wrote it in a blistering seventy-two hours. Most of the playwrights I know visibly sag when they learn this. How could she write a play that is so utterly fantastic in such a short time? Firstly, because she knew what she wanted to say. Secondly, because she knew how she wanted to say it. Talking about writers who plan everything before they write Alice Birch said, 'I am definitely not one of those writers,' but she wasn't writing into a void, 'I had the form in my head.'[7] She knew what she wanted to say, backed up by the knowledge of the form it would take, backed up by the intellect, backed up by the drive, backed up by the talent, backed up by the craft.

Don't make the mistake of thinking that you have to be able to write a play in three days. Don't make the mistake of thinking that you have to plan everything meticulously before you start tapping out a rhythm on your keyboard. Try a bit of both. And always consider that different plays may require different approaches, a commissioned community play about a local sixteenth-century witch trial is going to need research and planning; a play about the feeling of loss may require you to dig deep into your emotions and start by writing from the inside out.

To study or not to study, that is the question . . .

Does the obsessive study of plays make you a better writer? Does seeing as many plays as possible make you a better writer? Answer: yes. Caveat: but only for some people. One of the reasons I work as a dramaturg as well as a playwright is that I love the challenge of trying to understand what makes a play work, but not every playwright does.

Can you tell the difference between Aeschylus, Sophocles and Euripides? Can you tell the difference between Shakespeare, Jonson and Fletcher? Can you tell the difference between Prebble, Hickson and Birch? Yes? No? Does it matter? Will knowing the difference make you a better writer? For some, maybe. For others, no, it won't.

The truth is that reading every play produced at the Royal Court over the last sixty-six years doesn't guarantee you that the next play you write will be produced at the Royal Court. You will certainly have a much better sense of the history of the company, but the last thing the Court want is a pastiche Royal Court play, unless you're Tim Crouch of course in which case you write a play about writing a Royal Court play. The Court, according to successive generations of their literary department, are always looking for the next thing, the play that leads the way for the next generation, the play that gives us the shock of the new, not the old thing, or even the now thing. The next thing. Where do these plays come from? You are unlikely to find the answer by studying the plays of Edward Bond or Sarah Kane, but it might stimulate you to develop your own theatrical pyrotechnics.

The fact is that some writers never read other writers' plays, they never go to the theatre, yet they are brilliant playwrights. Perhaps they are brilliant precisely because they are only interested in what is in their own heads and don't care about what is in another writer's head. They just do their thing and to hell with all those dramaturgs and critics who think they know everything. If knowing everything was the most important thing about being a playwright, wouldn't they be the great playwrights themselves? In the end, I think the choice comes down to the individual, if studying the work of others feeds your beast, then feed it; if studying the work of others is anathema to you and you only want to write what you want to write and you don't care what anyone else is writing, so be it. However, I'm not convinced a writer can sustain a long career on maverick talent alone. They might write an extraordinary play one day and then spend the rest of their writing life trying and failing to replicate it, because they don't know how they did it. On the other hand, plays also need maverick talent to help them stand out from the crowd, those idiosyncratic moments that make them different. The trick is to understand this and make the most of it. If you know what you are doing and are able to give yourself permission to be playful and idiosyncratic now and then, great. If your writing is entirely wild and nonconformist but no one ever wants to produce your plays, perhaps the time has come to learn a bit more about how other writers do it.

In the UK we are obsessed with the idea of the *gift*. The *gift* is the idea that one day a hopeful wannabe playwright sat down and with no previous knowledge or experience, wrote a play and it turned out to be a work of genius. It doesn't happen. When Shelagh Delaney was working as an usher in a theatre in Manchester as a nineteen-year-old in 1958 she allegedly stood at the back of the auditorium one day watching a play and thought to herself, I could write a better play than that. So, she went home and wrote a play about a seventeen-year-old girl who becomes pregnant by her black, sailor boyfriend and then goes to live with her homosexual friend who becomes a surrogate father to her child. Shelagh called the play, *A Taste of Honey*. She sent it to Joan Littlewood at the Theatre Royal Stratford East. Joan loved it, put it on straight away, and Shelagh became an overnight sensation. It's a great story, except that what people tend to overlook is the fact that Shelagh had already been working on the story as a novel and had been watching plays every day of the week for something like three years. She knew her story, she had a basic idea of how plays worked, she had a fantastic, raw talent, but one piece of the jigsaw was missing, a practical understanding of what is needed to make a play really work. Shelagh found that in Joan Littlewood. Joan Littlewood helped Shelagh to shape her play. The fact is: if you haven't got a Joan Littlewood, it helps to know a bit about what you are doing.

Do you have an idea?

Do you get your ideas from the news? From something you see? From something you imagine? From something someone says? From something you feel? From a blinding flash of inspiration?

I remember reading an interview with Stephen Sondheim in which he told his interviewer that he often took a nap when he was working – not because he was lazy, but because many of his best ideas came from the liminal space between his conscious and unconscious waking mind.[8] For a playwright, this means taking a nap and making a note of the ideas you have when you are in the process of waking up. It's hard work being a playwright, isn't it!

If you prefer the conscious manifestation of ideas, it may be that your inspirations are linked to your *vision* (if you have one) or it may be that they are totally random and unconnected. Whatever the case, your process is likely to begin with an idea or a story. The challenge is to develop it.

Perhaps it's an idea for a specific theatre company? Perhaps it's a commission? Perhaps it's a play you are writing with no performance space in mind? Whatever the case, these factors are likely to inform your writing process.

Developing an idea will involve asking a lot of questions. Does the content dictate a certain form, or do I feed the content into a preconceived form? Does my idea come complete with genre? Do I need to visualize the space as I write? Can I see the play from the audience perspective? Are my characters talking to me or am I putting words in their mouths? Is my idea intrinsically theatrical or would it work better as an audio drama or a film? How many actors do I need? How many actors can the company afford to employ?

There are a lot of practical/pragmatic considerations before you even start to make notes. Unless you are the kind of writer who doesn't give a damn about such boring questions.

And what do you do if you have run out of ideas? My solution for this problem is to suggest that you write down one idea every day for thirty days without censoring that idea. Some will be awful, but it doesn't matter because at the end of the month you will have thirty ideas, and maybe one of them will be quite good.

Procrastination

A lot of writers, myself included, find it incredibly hard to get started. Even when we do, eventually, get started, there are all those emails and messages we need to check. Then there is that research question that sends us spiralling though websites that eventually leads to a quick check on our social media. Then there are the snacks and cups of coffee that are essential to our writing process. And just look at all those pencils that need sharpening!

We all know how to procrastinate. The only way to defeat it, is to start doing the actual work. Crossing the threshold into the work is the hardest thing. Trick yourself. Tell yourself you are just going to do five minutes work and then stop. Chances are you'll keep going a lot longer. We all have to learn how to crack our own whip and get on with it. Just start.

Precipitateness versus perfectionism

You've just finished the first draft of your new play. JOY! Now what? There are two extremes: *Precipitateness* and *Perfectionism*.

The Precipitators: It's done! Send it out!

The Perfectionists: I'm not going to send it out until it's perfect.

Rushing to send your play out before it is ready is a very bad idea. You only get one first chance to impress, don't waste it by being impetuous. Once your play has been read and rejected, it is extremely hard to get a company to read it again.

However, waiting until your play is perfect before sending it out is also a very bad idea. If you try to write the perfect play, the chances are you will never finish it. Take the advice of one of the finest playwright's agents that ever lived, Margaret Ramsay, who is reputed to have told her clients that they should never try to write the greatest play every written, just to try to write good plays – that way, one of them might turn out to be great.

Re-writing

When you have finished your initial, let's call it *rough draft*, you should put it away for at least a couple of weeks. Then, read it. Make notes. Then, re-write it. You should also consider showing it to someone you trust and asking them for feedback BUT this must be someone who knows what they are doing, you should never ask anyone for feedback who doesn't know how to read and analyse a play, this isn't a favour you should ask of a friend who 'knows what they like', handing your play to a mate who doesn't know the difference between Aeschylus and Ayckbourn will be at best counterproductive and at worst disastrous.

If it helps, you can use this list of questions as a starting point for thinking about your re-write:

(Some) basic questions for the second draft

The BIG one:

- Is my play intrinsically theatrical?

Structural nuts and bolts:

- Is this the most appropriate overall structure?
- Is every scene essential?
- Is every scene structured appropriately?
- Is this the most appropriate form?

Character

- Does each of my characters serve the purpose for which I created them?
- Are all of my characters necessary?

Language

- Is my use of dramatic language appropriate?
- Is my use of dramatic language distinctive?
- Does everything I've written demand to be in the play? (If not: can I cut it?)

Overall

- Is it self-indulgent?
- Is it what I expected? (If not: Is this a good thing?)
- Is it too ambitious?
- Is it not ambitious enough?
- Is it overwritten?
- Is it underwritten?
- Have I underestimated the intelligence of the audience?
- Have I overestimated the intelligence of the audience?
- Have I used any crude devices?
- Are there any (enough) surprises for the audience?
- Is my research complete?
- Does my play challenge conventions? (Do I want it to?)
- Am I true to the world of my play? (Does it have an internal logic?)

Character-driven Naturalistic Causal Drama (Aristotelian Cause & Effect)

- Do cause and effect / intention and obstacle / conflict drive the story?
- Is there a clearly identified protagonist?
- Is there a clearly identified antagonist?
- Does my protagonist have three clearly drawn levels of conflict?
  - Inner conflict
  - Intra conflict
  - Extra conflict
- Have I pushed my protagonist to the furthest limit within the parameters of my story?
- Does each character have a clearly defined voice?
- Are my characters consistent?
- Does the climax of my play work?

- Have I used subtext?
- Do I need a(nother) twist?

Bigger picture

- Will the idea behind this play make it stand out for a Literary Manager?
- Will the writing [my use of language] stand out for a Literary Manager?
- Will the first five pages of this play grab the reader's attention?
- Does my play demand to be produced *now*?

Once you have re-written the play you will now have your official *first draft*. If this is a commissioned play and you are confident in your relationship with the producing theatre you can submit your play and continue to develop the play with them.

If you intend to submit your play unsolicited to a producing theatre or competition, I suggest that you give it one last read and tinker before submitting it.

An experienced reader will make up their mind about whether the play they are reading is good or not in the first few pages. I have run several playwriting competitions, often there isn't enough money to pay for all the scripts to be read in their entirety. This leads to a sifting process, a process by which the reader will decide on the strength of a few pages whether a script is worth reading in full or not. Always try to ensure that the first few pages of your play are a strong representation of the potential of your play as a whole.

Re-writing after rejection

It is sometimes the case that if your play is rejected you will receive some written feedback. You should take the time to consider this feedback carefully and decide if you agree with the comments. You may need to wait a week or two before seriously thinking about the feedback, so that you can get over your initial fury or sense of being gravely misunderstood. Ultimately, you will need to decide if implementing re-writes dictated by the comments, or some of them, will improve your play. If you think they will, you should do a re-write. BUT don't send it back to the theatre that rejected the play saying that you've done what they told you to do and now they should produce the play. You have been rejected by that theatre, move on, send it somewhere else. The same is true even if they asked to see your next play, send them your next play, not a re-write of the old one.

NB. Don't spend hours analysing rejection letters, it isn't worth the effort. The euphemism 'not right for us' can mean a multitude of things – none of them worth agonizing about. I know. I have written hundreds of them. Move on.

Re-writing after feedback

If you get sent notes and an invitation to re-submit, you need to think very seriously about your re-write. If you get invited in for a chat about your play: Eureka! Now you will need to learn how to deal with notes from directors and/or dramaturgs. The key to this process is simple: listen, be polite, and always ask for clarity if there are things you don't understand. Some of the notes you receive will be genuinely illuminating. Some of the notes will be useful. Some of the notes will be bad. Your job is to identify the notes that are useful to you and disregard the ones that are not.

Never try to implement a note if you don't agree with it, and never try to do everything they suggest. If you try to implement every note you are given, your play is likely to become a swollen mess of a thing. A short wistful chamber piece can swell to become a boated monster of a play, be selective. Every play you write will be different. Every play you write will require you to adjust the parameters of your approach to it. An epic with a cast of thirty will need a very different approach to an intimate two-hander. The type of notes you receive will be different. Your application of the notes will be different. One play might require a lot of intervention to make it work, another might require very little. You need to develop the confidence to know which is which. You need to know what you want your play to be. Don't let others bend it out of shape. You need to serve the play you have written. The best directors and dramaturgs will help you to do this.

Subsequent re-writes

Chances are you will be asked to do more than one re-write. Dig deep every time to understand the reasons why your director/dramaturg still aren't convinced. Try things. I have often found that, following a conversation about something in a script that isn't working, the director might make a suggestion for a fix. Sometimes it is a great idea, sometimes it isn't. Your job is to decide which. In my experience the best solutions come from the writer after they have gone away, thought long and hard, and come up with something entirely new that hasn't even been discussed. Something I often refer to as the *third way* – something different to the original idea, not the suggested fix, but something new.

The tipping point

Beware: there will come a time when any further re-writes could kill your play. You need to try to identify when you hit this moment. It might come after the third full draft, it might come after twenty drafts, but every play will reach a tipping point. A point at which it stops getting better. A point at which it starts to get worse with every subsequent re-write. I once wrote twenty-seven drafts of a pantomime, yes, twenty-seven! Draft seven was good. Draft twenty-seven was terrible. I learned the hard way. I should have said, *no more!* Don't kill your play with re-writes. You need to be able to say, *enough is enough.*

Production

If the theatre decides to produce your play, a whole new set of rules kick in, more re-writes inside and outside the rehearsal and preview process (more on this in the next chapter *Theatre Is Collaboration*).

Or final rejection

If, after all that work, you and your play get the boot, suck it up and send your play somewhere else. In other words, get your play produced by a rival new writing company to prove what a terrible mistake the company that rejected your play has made. It happens! However, if your commissioned play is rejected and you submit it to another theatre, be prepared to start the development process all over again. Different people will have different opinions and give different notes.

Finally . . .

If you are feeling a little jaded about the idea of beginning a new play, perhaps try something different to see what it does to your writing. Experiment with process. If you are a *schematic* playwright, try an *organic* approach, or vice versa. If you usually write in the mornings, try writing later in the day. If you take a year to write a play, challenge yourself to write a play in three days. If you usually write a play in three days, make yourself take longer. If you use playwriting software, try writing a play without it. If you use a specific font and pagination, do it differently. Change it up. See what happens when you try a different process. Do what you need to do to keep the process fresh and alive.

3.2 THEATRE IS COLLABORATION

I once did a diabolical thing.

During rehearsals for my second play at Stratford East, *Worlds Apart*, the director, Jeff Teare, asked if he could cut a line in one of the scenes. I wasn't convinced. He had asked to cut what I was certain was the funniest line in the entire play. It was a line that had me in fits of giggles when I wrote it at 2.00 am one morning. It was my favourite line in the entire play. I asked Jeff why he wanted to cut it, and he said, bluntly, it wasn't funny. The actor who had to deliver the line agreed. The actor who the line was delivered to agreed. I didn't want to cause a fuss, it was only my second play, after all, so I reluctantly caved in. I remained convinced, however, that the line was an absolute killer, and that Jeff had made a terrible mistake. I had heard that horrible writers' maxim that we need to learn to *kill our babies*, but this felt like a *baby* too far. Every time we rehearsed that scene, the gap where that funny line should have been, pierced my writerly soul like a knife. But it was no good, it was gone. Forever. Or was it? I can't now remember why, but Jeff couldn't make it to the second preview, so I did what all misunderstood writers would do in my situation: I asked the actors to put the line back in. They were reluctant, but I convinced them. I told them if the line worked – which it obviously would – I would tell Jeff about it in the morning, take the consequent bollocking, and get the line reinstated. If it didn't work, we would say no more about it. They agreed. The play began, the moment came, the funniest line I had ever written was uttered . . . and was greeted with total and utter silence. There wasn't a solitary chortle. Tumbleweed rolled through the theatre. In that moment, I heard the devil take a rasping in-breath and a deep chasm opened up at the back of the stalls, and I fell in – metaphorically. I was horrified, humiliated and humbled. In the bar, after the preview, the actor looked at me and shrugged. I shrugged back. We didn't need words. I was an idiot. Someone told Jeff the following day, he wasn't bothered at all, he just looked at me and said, 'Told you.'[1]

I had learned the lesson that we all need to learn, sometimes, other people know better than we do: THEATRE IS COLLABORATION.

These days, I often suggest to writers that when it comes to cutting their play in rehearsals, they identify their favourite line in the play and prepare to cut it, that way, none of the other cuts will hurt anywhere near as much.

Theatre is collaboration. If you don't like the idea, then go and write a novel. For a play to live, it requires other people. If you are fortunate and you write a hugely successful play, you are unlikely to be present at every production around the world. However, you are likely to be there at the first production, and you will need to learn to collaborate.

Perhaps the first thing you will discover is that not everyone thinks the playwright is the most important person in the production equation. A playwright is certainly to be found higher up the food chain in theatre than in TV or film, but it is rare today for a director and actors to pay total, worshipful reverence to the writer, and defer to every dot, dash and syntactical quirk of the text without question. You are just a cog in the production machine – an important, initiating cog, yes, but just a cog.

'But if it wasn't for me there would be no play!' I hear some of you cry. True. But if it wasn't for the producer, the director, the actors, the stage management team, the crew, and everyone else working in the theatre, there would be no production. And a play without a production is just another file on your laptop.

To investigate the chain of collaboration for a new writer, I'm going to outline a hypothetical process from submission of an unsolicited new play to its eventual production by a building-based, new writing theatre company. I should perhaps point out that in the real world, it is very rare for an unsolicited play from an unknown writer to be produced. What will typically happen is that your play, if it is any good, will get some interest from the theatre, and that will result in some kind of relationship that will eventually result in a play you write being produced. But once in a blue moon it does happen that an unsolicited play is produced. We can all dream.

The dramaturg / literary manager

So, you've written and submitted the first draft of your new play. You have received an email from the dramaturg, aka Literary Manager, aka Literary Associate, aka Associate Director (Literary), etc., asking you to come in for a chat. You interrogate the email for any subtextual clues as to what they really think, there are none, but you will probably find some anyway.

I have worked on both sides of the dramaturgical fence, as both a dramaturg and a playwright, so I have a good understanding of this process. I'll be honest with you, it's a lot easier being the dramaturg than it is being the writer. The dramaturg asks questions, and the playwright needs to answer them. Then, they need to re-write. Given that the focus of this manifesto is you, the playwright, I will write this process from the playwright's perspective.

Playwrights, the dramaturg is not your nemesis; they do not want to dehumanize or humiliate you. Rather, they want your play to be brilliant, and to be the very best play you can write. Why? Because it makes them look good. The dramaturg – if they are any good – is your friend and companion on this adventure. Don't be suspicious of their motives, they want your play to work. And you need them to be your advocate, so behave yourself. Get your dramaturg onside, and build a solid relationship; unless, of course, they have completely misinterpreted your play, in which case you might want to cut your losses. However, the dramaturgs I have worked with have always been very smart, very well-read, creative, inspirational individuals who care passionately about their work, and yours! You would have to be very unlucky indeed to meet a bad one. I honestly believe this to be true.

The best dramaturgs will ask you questions. They will not provide answers. That's your job. Be prepared to have an open conversation. Don't be unnecessarily protective or defensive. When I first started writing plays and was asked a question about a character or an idea, if I didn't know the answer, I would make one up, on the spot. I would have been better off admitting that I didn't know. A collaboration with a dramaturg will only work if you can both be honest. After all, it isn't a test of intellect or a battle of smartarses, it's a conversation, an investigation, a quest. Listen to what your dramaturg has to say and ask for clarity if they say something you don't understand. Ask them questions. Try to build trust, because if there is no trust between you it will be the play that suffers. If your dramaturg tells you something you disagree with, have a robust discussion about it, don't tell them they are an idiot. And when you get home to do your re-write, go through your notes, action the ones that are useful, discard the ones that aren't, and provide the answers that make sense to you. The best solutions are always the ones that the writer comes up with themselves.

As well as being a specialist in play development, a dramaturg can seem akin to a therapist or a diplomat. For you, the playwright, their most important role to play is as the advocate for your play. Get them onside and invested. The deeper you can go, the more you can engage with your dramaturg, the better your chances of the dramaturg singing the praises of your play to the Artistic Director. Aim for an alliance rather than an adversarial relationship. If you can imbue them with just a tiny sense of ownership, they will fight like hell for you in the meetings you don't get to go to – the meetings where they decide which plays they are going to produce.

The director

In our scenario, you will probably redraft your play once or twice more before the director gets involved. However, it might be the case that the company you are writing for does not employ a dramaturg and the director will have been working exclusively with you on the development of your play from the start. Whether you have been working with a dramaturg and the director now joins, or you have been working solely with the director throughout, there is one thing you need to remember: your relationship with your director is the most important relationship you will ever have in the theatre. If you can find a director who likes your work, who admires your writing, who wants to direct your plays, *Hallelujah!* If that director is an associate at a new writing theatre, *Hallelujah!* If that director is the Artistic Director of a new writing theatre, *Hallelujah!* The reason *why* this is so important should be self-evident: it's all about getting your play on. A director with no affiliations will be a friend to bang on doors with, but an associate can go straight to the theatre where they are an associate and say, 'I've got a great new play from [*insert your name here*].' An Artistic Director doesn't even have to talk to anyone, they are the feudal rulers of their own private fiefdoms, and if they like your play, they can do it! While the Executive Director may have something to say about this, it is rare that an Artistic Director passionate about a play will be told by their Executive Director that they can't do it (other than for financial reasons, of course).

It might happen that you meet, and work with, a great director straight away. For example: your dramaturg likes your play; they recommend it to their Artistic Director, who just happens to be the best director of new writing in the country; you meet the Artistic Director; you get on marvellously, and you live happily ever after.

Or, it might be that you need to identify the right director for you and then try to get your work to them. How do you do that? Go to the theatre, watch as many new plays as you can afford to watch, and make a note of the directors whose work you genuinely admire. If they are an associate or an Artistic Director, send your plays directly to them at the theatres where they work. If they are freelance, you may need to go via their agent or corner them in the bar after a preview of their new production (if you've got the nerve for that kind of thing). Whatever the case, it is important to work out who you think will respond to your writing and get the best out of it.

Remember: writers need directors, but directors don't always need writers – there is a great big graveyard full of dead playwrights they can work with who won't give them any trouble!

You also need to bear in mind that even if you do manage to hook up with someone fantastic you are both going to have to be unfaithful from time to time. And you, or they, might even find someone better to work with …

Back to our scenario: the Artistic Director is only likely to get involved in the development process if they have a serious interest in your play, either for themselves as a director, for an associate, or freelance director they want to work at their theatre. In our scenario, you hit the jackpot, the Artistic Director wants to direct your play, but it's not a done deal, production isn't guaranteed, they've got notes for you.

You may have been introduced to the Artistic Director at a performance or event at the theatre, but the first time you are likely to meet them properly will be in a meeting to discuss your play, probably with the dramaturg. You can safely assume that the Artistic Director and dramaturg will have already met to discuss your play before they meet with you. This is basic common sense, no Artistic Director or dramaturg wants to turn up at a script meeting and give contradictory notes. They will have a plan for how to approach the conversation, meanwhile you're just praying the Artistic Director likes you and wants to do your play.

Now the small-talk, buddying-up process begins all over again with the Artistic Director. Remember: the Artistic Director likes your play, they wouldn't be here if they didn't like it, they want to like you, they want to direct your play, and have the world tell them they are a genius for 'discovering' you. New writing theatres can be extremely proprietorial, they love to have their name associated with the next big thing, and there is a chance, however slim, that it might be you! So, you are valuable to them. But they are even more important to you, they are your gateway to a career. I usually advise writers to behave themselves and act like the nicest person on earth in meetings during their early career, even when meeting people they don't like. Why? Because you need to get your play on! Get your play on, and if it's a success, you can be a total arsehole afterwards. But be warned, a playwright is only ever as good as their last play, so don't antagonize too many people. Don't burn all your bridges. What matters most is that there is trust. You need to have established trust with your dramaturg, and you now need to establish trust with your director.

For a time, you are likely to be in a triangular relationship of playwright–dramaturg–director. If it is the dramaturg's job to help you make the play as good as it can be, it is the director's job to help you make the play as good as it can be AND to direct it. This brings an added set of considerations. Your director will have one eye on the art and one eye on the pragmatic considerations of the production. They might flag up practical problems: quick changes, entrances and exits, the number of actors they can afford to pay. You can't ignore these things. You need to collaborate to find solutions.

You may find that the Artistic Director will take the lead in discussions about your next draft, supported by the dramaturg. Your dramaturg, if they are good, will feel like an ally in the room, but hopefully you won't need to think like that because the notes you receive will be so good that you are desperate to do another draft. One thing to remember is that you still need to be making decisions that you are happy with. Take risks. If the Artistic Director and dramaturg don't like what you have done, they can always ask you to change it again.

Moving towards production, dramaturgically you will move ever closer to the director. The dramaturg will still be there, but it is likely to be the director giving you the most notes. You may be fortunate in finding a director who considers it their job to revere your text, but chances are, it won't be quite that simple. Directors have been elbowing playwrights off their pedestal for a long time now. Your director is likely to have a vision.

The question for you is: do you buy into it? If you don't, there's a chance your journey will be rocky, and your play may even end up not getting produced. I'm not advocating caving in, I'm suggesting that if you need to have a tough conversation have it as early in the process as possible, don't let the feeling that they've got something wrong drag on. A good relationship should mean a robust conversation is not the end of the world, you may win some arguments, and lose others. Only you will know where to draw the line.

So, you've done your re-write(s), and now comes the great news that the theatre is going to produce your play! Job done? No. No way. There is still a very long way to go. There are likely to be further re-writes before rehearsals, some easy fixes, some irritating problems, some things that you don't think need fixing. But you still haven't got dates. Stay calm. Do the work. Keep smiling. A month passes, then another, then another. The theatre announces their Spring Season, and your play isn't in it. You ask nervously if they still intend to do your play. And they give you dates. It's next year. But you've got dates.

One of the best pieces of advice I ever received came from the brilliant Scottish playwright Patrick Prior. When I told Patrick I finally had a date for the production of my first play at the Theatre Royal Stratford East, he said, 'Make sure you've got the next one ready . . .' So, don't just sit there waiting for the dates to come around, get on with that new play. The time will pass, it has a habit of doing that.

At some point before rehearsals begin you will deliver your 'Rehearsal Draft'. Now comes a deluge of further collaborators, and most, if not all of these collaborative relationships will be facilitated through the medium of your director.

The designer

Your designer is likely to be a long-term collaborator of the director, they will probably have built up a trust over several productions, and you are now entering their story.

As with all collaborations you will need to be open, to listen, and to think like a shrink, in other words, analyse them, try to work out what makes them tick, try to get an idea of how their relationship with the director works, and consider the best way to offer your feedback. If you like the design for your play, great, if you don't, you will need to have a discussion about your reservations, perhaps privately with the dramaturg or director in the first instance. Remember, a designer is an artist, they too will have a vision: your words, their images.

Your director and designer may have cooked up a design idea for your play without your input. You'll be invited to a meeting one day, the director will introduce you to the designer who will plonk a model box down in front of you, and you will be astonished to discover that your opening stage directions detailing every realistic inch of the Italian restaurant in which the action of your play takes place has been interpreted as a lunar landscape inside a giant Perspex cube. This, for me, is one of the great joys of collaboration: the surprise of others' interpretations of your work. Once again, if you like the designer's idea, great, but if you don't, you will need to negotiate your way into a constructive conversation. You might even be shown two or three alternative deigns. Whatever the case, you must not panic – these are early days! Instead, try to understand the choices your collaborators have made and to interrogate them carefully and intelligently. You never know, it might well be a great idea to set your play in a Perspex cube on the moon! It might unlock the meaning and theatricality in ways you could never have envisaged. I have seen productions of well-known naturalistic plays in Europe given a fantastically new theatrical lease of life by abstract design concepts.

If you have a strong visual imagination, you will probably know precisely what you want to see on stage, if you don't, you perhaps need to think about it. What are the designs that stick in your mind? Do you like detailed realistic sets, or do you prefer a bare stage? Thornton Wilder, who was a big fan of Elizabethan and Spanish Golden Age drama, had this to say about stage sets, 'In its healthiest ages the theatre has always exhibited the least scenery.'[2] Wilder preferred the use of imagination to realistic sets, and he made his opinions manifest in his plays. The opening stage direction in *Our Town*, reads:

No curtain.
No scenery.[3]

No messing about.

Duncan Macmillan would appear to be of a similar persuasion. In the writer's note at the start of his play *Lungs*, he informs his collaborators that, 'This play is written to be performed on a bare stage.'[4] You can't get much clearer than that.

Cards on the table, I love this. Set descriptions like these make me almost faint with joy, BUT I also love an abstract, metaphorical and thematic design. For instance: a naturalistic family feud set in an abattoir; a play about loss set in a wilderness; a play about a group of friends on a drunken night out in the city during which the set starts to tilt as the characters get more inebriated.[5]

You don't even need to stipulate a bare stage, if you don't want to, you can just jump straight into dialogue. However, most writers will probably include a set description of some kind. But don't forget that the stage magnifies actions AND design/props. Everything on stage takes on a meaning; so, if there's a fishing rod leaning against a wall, it needs to be there because it has something to *say* to the audience. We look for these things. At least, we should.

Not many playwrights think too deeply about costume, but what a character wears reveals something about who they are. An item of clothing can be a statement of how a character wants the world to perceive them. Does it matter to you? It will matter to the designer. It will help everyone if you have an opinion – especially if you voice it early on so that everyone knows what you think, then they can react to your ideas, rather than you having to react to theirs.

If you absolutely have to have a hyper-realistic set and authentic costumes, so be it. But please never forget the power of the imagination to create and say things even more potent that the real represented thing.

Let's not forget technology. Your designer might want an animatronic Minotaur. They might want a stage filled with video screens. I love poor theatre, but sometimes designers can come up with amazing ideas to serve your play with technology, and you need to be receptive. We need to be careful not to kill our imaginations with tech, but sometimes it will be what the play needs, and, if that's the case, use it.

First productions of new plays are usually faithful to the playwright's original vision of the set, but not all. And you will need to get used to the idea that you may travel to Rotterdam one day to see a new production of an old play that doesn't look anything like the play you originally wrote.

Stage designers are artists. One of the greatest joys of making theatre is to work with other great artists to bring our plays to life, possibly in ways we could never have imagined. Respect your designer. Listen to what they have to say. They will have very good reasons for doing what they have done. A great designer has the ability to take your play to a higher level.

So, you now have another artist in the game. As a team you will continue to grow in number. While you might not meet every artist that will work on your play early on in the process, by this point, you may also encounter the lighting designer and the sound designer. Again, these roles are liable to be filled by long-term associates and friends of your director, they will be collaborators your director trusts to deliver. You are not likely to get too deeply involved with lighting and sound, but you are likely to be asked your opinion on aspects of the work related to sound and light so you need to build a collaborative relationship with these artists too. These people are experts in their fields, they read magazines about noise and light bulbs for fun! They love it! They are as passionate and possessive and precious about their work as you are. Respect them.

Casting

Next collaborator: casting agent. Likely to be another of your director's friends. You will probably be asked about ideas for casting. You may have some good ideas (some writers may know who they want); you may not have any ideas (it is surprising the number of playwrights who don't know the names of many actors). It's not your job to be a casting expert, but you will soon learn that a play is only ever as good as its cast – so it is *very* important to take casting *very* seriously.

I love actors, how they cope with the audition process is beyond me. As playwrights, we have to learn to deal with rejection on a regular basis because every play we write, and submit, is open to rejection. But for actors, rejection is on a whole other level. If you are a good actor, you should get a lot of auditions. If you achieve the success of getting a lot of auditions, you will also be guaranteed a lot of rejection. And you have to keep smiling the whole time. Actors, you have my admiration.

As the writer, you should be invited to attend auditions. If you are: go. Perhaps you don't think this is something you need to do. Think again. You will learn a lot, especially when you hear different combinations of actors reading the same scene from your play over and over again. The audition process itself is arduous. You might know the moment an actor walks into the room that they are wrong for the part, but you will still need to go through the casting motions: a bit of a chat, a bit of a read, a bit more of a chat, a quick dance through their CV, and goodbye. It is hard to judge potential at an audition, an actor may give a poor audition, but grow into a part beautifully; they may give a quite good audition but never move beyond that performance. It is very hard to tell, which is why you need a good director and a good casting agent to steer the process. Listen to them, chances are, they will know better than you which actors are right for your play. Collaborate.

When you go to see plays in the future, make a note of the actors you thought were good. Keep a list. Use it to remind yourself the next time you're casting one of your own plays. One more time in case you missed it: your play will only ever be as good as the actors in it.

Executive producer

At some point during this process, you are likely to be introduced to the company's Executive Producer, or perhaps Chief Executive, or Executive Director (basically the same thing). This person is likely to be the joint CEO of the company, alongside the Artistic Director. Reductively speaking, this means that the Artistic Director does the art, and the Executive Producer does the business. In reality it's more complicated than that: the Artistic Director needs to know their way around the business, and the Executive Producer needs to understand the art. Whatever the case, the Executive Producer is a Very Important Person. They had to agree to finance your play. If your play loses the theatre a small fortune, they are the ones who will need to take a long hard look at the budgets, appease the board of directors, and try to make something miraculous happen. In my experience, the people in this role have – without exception – been amazing, committed, intelligent people. They make our world function. They deserve our total respect.

NB: In some companies the Artistic Director holds both jobs.

The rehearsal room

Your play has been cast and is in rehearsal. You are going to go to rehearsals by the way, this is – most definitely – not the time to step back. Don't make the mistake I made with my first semi-professional production when I thought there was no need for me to go to rehearsals, and I would just leave the director and actors to get on with it. Seeing the first performance of that play was like watching my entire aesthetic life disintegrate in slow motion. GO TO REHEARSALS. Not all of them, but go to the first week, some of the second, and then drop in as and when required for runs. In the UK, we have it enshrined in our writers' contracts that the playwright can not only attend rehearsals, but that they should be paid an attendance fee for doing so. Thank you, Writers' Guild of Great Britain!

Now the real collaborative work begins: working with the director and the actors on the text in the room. It may be that you have seen productions previously directed by your director, but you may not know their rehearsal process. Do yourself a favour, seek out those who have rehearsed with this director before so that you don't turn up on day one without a clue as to what awaits.

You might be working with a director who jumps straight in every day with a series of energetic and cognitively demanding warm-up games that actors seem to think are great fun, but which often terrify the living daylights out of most playwrights. Are you going to join in? Or are you going to go to make an excuse and get the hell out of the rehearsal room as soon as possible? I often find that I need to check if the photocopier is working at this moment in the process.

Perhaps the first morning of rehearsals will begin with a read-through. I always find the first read-through at least a little bit excruciating. All those words, all those inflections, all those reactions that you have rehearsed intimately in your own head over the last year, ridden roughshod over by your cast. But don't panic! It's the first read-through, they don't know the play yet. Any and all stumbles, slips and spoonerisms can be sorted out later.

It might be that you are working with a director who has a very specific process. Some directors spend the first week of rehearsals sitting around a desk breaking the play down into units and actions. This can be a long and arduous process involving giving every line a transitive verb. The chances are that not even when you were writing the play did you interrogate the play in this amount of detail. It can be daunting but rewarding. A quick word of advice: don't use adverbs like *anxiously*, *urgently*, *softly*, to instruct your actors how to say a line. Actors are smart, they are perfectly capable of working out their own adverbs.

It is always a good idea to chat with your director or dramaturg before rehearsals to ask how best to offer feedback. In the rehearsal room, the director is the boss, and no director will want you butting in every five minutes with suggestions. So, ask how best to communicate your thoughts; it may be that the director is open to interventions, or they might be the kind of director who will regularly turn to you for an opinion, or they might want to talk when there is an appropriate break. Whatever the case, try to work out the best course of action before rehearsals begin. Set up a protocol.

Now is when the director and the actors will start to question certain lines. Prepare to hear, 'Can we use this word instead of that word?', 'I don't think my character would say this!', and 'Can we cut this line?' This is the time when you really need to collaborate. You will agree with some things, be ambivalent about others, and every now and then disagree with what is being suggested. You need to balance your reactions. I can promise you that you will know when to say 'No!' It will hurt too much.

Most actors will show you respect, some actors will just get on with their job, a small number of actors may think they know better than you. It can get a bit overwhelming. Hopefully, your director will be able keep control of the room and make everyone happy. One of the director's hardest jobs, in my opinion, is keeping the room happy – which is not easy with all those ideas and insecurities flying around.

There is usually one other person of major importance in the rehearsal room: the Stage Manager. Stage managers are fabulous human beings. They make the whole play function. They rarely get involved with the creative decisions, they usually sit there mapping the decisions in pencil in the prompt book, then rubbing them out and re-doing them again, reminding the actors where to go and what to say, telling the director when it's time for a break, and doing a multitude of other mysterious things. They are one of the most important, underappreciated people in the whole process. A good stage manager is like gold. Befriend your Stage Manager. Without them, the production of your play is likely to be a disaster.

Someone from wardrobe might also appear with a tape measure during rehearsals. The job the wardrobe department do is vital to a production, the things they can do with Velcro, or a needle and thread, are to be marvelled at.

There are several other people you may well meet during rehearsals. If there are fights or other physical confrontations in your play, you will need a Fight Director. Fight directors are great, they know how to pretend to really hurt people! If there is a physical or dance sequence in your play, you will need a Movement Director. A Movement Director can bring a new energy and dimension to your play, they are like magicians.

Throughout this process, you will be doing re-writes – some small, some not so small. You will learn that actors used to working with new plays will take your re-writes in their stride, you will also learn that actors not used to working on new plays will not be so enthusiastic about changes. Be supportive, you are all in this together! At some point, probably towards the end of the third week of rehearsals, the director will get the actors to do a run of the play. As a moment, this can be thrilling, but it can also spawn more re-writes – especially if something isn't quite working.

Into the theatre

When you move into the theatre, you will meet the Production Manager, crew, and the rest of the backstage team for the get-in and technical rehearsal. This is a whole new universe. These are the people responsible for making the play and the set and the lights and the sound function. Utterly brilliant people! For a short time, I worked backstage at the Adelphi Theatre in London's West End. The crew were amazing, and I will always have total respect for anyone working backstage. Without these people, there is no show. They are on your team. Some of them will be wonderful, some of them will be grumpy as hell, it doesn't matter, they are also your collaborators.

You will probably continue to fiddle with your script through previews up until Press Night. You may even do some major re-writes during this time. It never ceases to amaze me that, no matter how much work we do on a play in the rehearsal room, it is only when we see it before an audience that we truly know what works and what doesn't. A word of warning: be strategic about *when* you talk to your director during this period, and don't forget that they not only have to direct your play, but they also have to direct the tech rehearsal, run the theatre, placate their board of directors, and continue to fend off the hordes of other playwrights who all think they should be directing their new play instead of yours. People can get a little bit irritable during this period, it's not surprising. On the positive side, you will probably be so sick with nerves you won't notice

By this point, the marketing team may have set up some interviews for you with the press. Some writers like nothing more than to discuss their work with the press, others hate it. Talk to the marketing department, let them know what you are comfortable with, hopefully they will be able to balance it with their needs. Along with the marketing team, by now you will probably have become familiar with all kinds of other theatre staff, such as the Front of House team, box office, ushers, bar staff. Usually, all of these people will be working in this theatre for a reason: because they love theatre. Many of these people will become writers, actors, directors and executive directors themselves. They are smart people, and they might just turn out to be the stars of the future. Platitude: be nice to people on your way up, because you never know who you might meet on your way down.

Press Night will come and go, and now you're into the run (I talk more about Press Nights in the chapter *Look After Your Mental Health . . .*). You will go to see the play every now and then, you might even give the director a couple of notes if something isn't working, or if the actors have decided to paraphrase a line here and there.

And then, it's over. Your director and all your collaborators will now be working with someone else on another play. You'll be alone, once more, in your garret writing your next great play.

Collaborators

I think the most important thing I have learned as a collaborator in the production process is that when the process is well managed, the play is enhanced with the addition of every new brain. We think differently. And that is a glorious thing. When each collaborator's contribution improves the artistic whole, you are really onto something. It's like financial compounding. When your director or actors come up with an idea that benefits the play, that would never have occurred to you sitting at home writing your play, you really start to appreciate the potential of collaboration.

Fact: your play will only ever exist through collaboration.

Fact: sometimes your collaborators will thrill you with their interpretation of your text.

Fact: sometimes your collaborators will kill you with their interpretation of your text

Conclusion: live dangerously.

How to collaborate when you are not there

I've got some good news for you, the play you just had produced was a massive hit and there are going to be multiple productions all over the globe. Congratulations! The only slight downside to this is that there is no way you can be there for every rehearsal process, so you need to ask yourself what you can do to make sure your intentions are clear for the various teams of creatives interpreting your play. The answer: you don't need to do anything, because your intentions should already be embedded in your text. Your text is your instruction to the director and actors, and it is the closest you will get to collaboration when you can't be in the room. You need to make sure that the words on the page speak for you.

There are four basic ways of doing this:

1 A Writer's Note
2 Dramatic Punctuation
3 Dialogue
4 Stage Directions

1. Writer's Note

You can put anything you like in your writer's note at the start of your play, but don't get too carried away. In this case, less is probably more.

After all, no one wants to read an essay about your demands for how your play has to be produced before they get to the actual text. At best, a writer's note is a collaborative statement. You may choose to say nothing at all, which is absolutely fine, but you should remember that by saying nothing, you give your collaborators permission to do anything.

In the writer's note at the start of his play *Attempts on her Life* Martin Crimp states that he wants the company of actors (there are no named parts) to, 'reflect the composition of the world beyond the theatre'. He also requests his collaborators to approach the words and design in a way which, 'best exposes its irony'.[6] Creatives with no sense of irony need not apply.

In her writer's note at the beginning of *Dance Nation*, a play about a group of adolescent dancers, Clare Barron informs us that, 'Cuteness is death. Pagan feral-ness and ferocity are key'.[7]

And at the end of Alice Birch's writer's note in *Revolt. She Said. Revolt Again.* she writes, in bold, '**Most importantly, this play should not be well behaved.**'[8]

Tell your collaborators what you want from your play. If it needs to be feral, tell them. If it needs to misbehave, tell them. And, if you really want them to guess, then by all means tell them nothing.

2. Dramatic Punctuation

I'm going to keep repeating this until it is second nature: all those dots, dashes and slashes are there to ensure that the actors know the rhythm of your language. They are your instruction to the actor. When you aren't in the rehearsal room, this becomes your method of collaboration with the actors. It is your musical score.

Because there is no standardized way for how playwrights can use punctuation, it is always best to include your way of doing things at the start of your play so that your director and actors know what you mean by the use of certain punctuation marks.

3. Dialogue

The way your dialogue sits on the page is incredibly important and informative to your collaborators. Most of your text will probably be left aligned, but if you centre some text and/or right align text, you are sending a message to your collaborators that this text needs to be interpreted differently. Similarly, text that is *italicized*, in CAPS, in **bold,** in different font, or in smaller or larger font, will inform your collaborators that these words are to be interpreted differently to the standard text.

Is the letter at the start of each line in lower case? Are there no full stops at the end of some lines? Are there gaps on the page? You can use all of these devices, and more, as a way of whispering in the ear of your future collaborators.

4. Stage Directions

There is a fashion today for fewer stage directions which, I think, is another encouraging sign when it comes to collaboration. As a fashion choice, it shows that we don't feel the need to tell our collaborators everything, and that we are leaving room for interpretation. However, stage directions are still very important, at their best they can be the gateway for your collaborators to the aesthetic of your play.

Most great directors and designers will love a challenging stage direction. As playwrights, I think we need to rise to the challenge set down by Shakespeare in *The Winter's Tale*: 'Exit, pursued by a bear.'[9]

Clare Barron offers some great challenges in *Dance Nation;* one of the characters grows fangs and 'chews off a chunk of her own arm.'[10] Soon after this, another character 'grows taller' and turns into a red-eyed pagan god with a shadow twelve feet long.[11] How are your collaborators going to do that? Not your problem. It's an invitation to be creative.

Jasmine Lee-Jones also loves to set her collaborators a challenge. In her play *Seven Methods of Killing Kylie Jenner*, she includes Tweets, Memes, gifs and emojis, and invites her collaborators to interpret them in whatever way they will. What a fantastic way to invite a collaborative adventure. She also likes to play with text in her stage directions, using a jumble of overlapping, refracted text to literally show us in typeface that 'The Twittersphere completely explodes',[12] and at one point she warps a character name in the text to suggest that we are entering a warped Twittersphere world.[13] Another simple device she uses is the repetition of the letter 'i' to suggest that one of her characters is silent for a long time by writing, 'CLEO is silent. For tiiiiiiiiiiiiiiime.'[14] So much more fun than just writing 'CLEO is silent for a long time'. And towards the end of her play, she also challenges her collaborators to solve the problem of what to do when one of her characters 'expands and swells in space.'[15]

In *An Octoroon*, Branden Jacobs-Jenkins has an ongoing conversation with his reader (and therefore any potential collaborators) in his stage directions. He doesn't have a problem with telling it like it is – at the end of the Prologue, he writes a note informing the reader that there's something he needs to say right now so he can get it over with: 'I don't know what a real slave sounded like. And neither do you.'[16] Refreshingly honest, and something that will hopefully stop his collaborators from agonizing too much about this during rehearsals. We then move into the first scene of the play, borrowed and bent from the original 1859 play it is based on, with stage directions describing the plantation, the winding Mississippi, and the planter's dwelling, which Jacobs-Jenkins undercuts beautifully by adding the words, 'Or not.' at the end.[17] Later in this play he writes, 'I worry about the whole thing becoming too Brechtian?'[18] Ponder that, creative team! Later still, he suggests that when a character throws money in the air it can either literally or figuratively rain, and then adds for good measure, 'The theatre is a space of infinite possibilities.'[19] Spoken like a true man of the theatre. He ends his play with the suggestion that there is singing.[20] If only more plays gave us that option!

At the end of Act Two in *Revolt. She Said. Revolt Again.* we get the stage direction, 'They chop their tongues out.'[21] How might a director and actors interpret this? Literally? Symbolically? Who knows, the fact is, it's a wonderful invitation to investigate. But Alice Birch doesn't stop there, a little later we get the stage direction, 'She chops her head off.'[22] Excellent.

To suggest a moment of huge magnitude, in *The Inheritance*, Matthew Lopez uses the simple but effective stage direction, 'The Grand Canyon.'[23] That is how **BIG** this moment should be!

In Ella Hickson's, *The Writer*, the stage directions sometimes inform us that we glimpse the director watching the play from the wings as the world of the production bleeds into the performance of the play. The lines between the world of the play, the production, and the audience blur.[24] Scenes and characters evaporate. Illusions are shattered and removed. Both the source of the illusion and the tricks of the trade are revealed. This is what the writer of *The Writer* wants.

In *People, Places & Things*, Duncan Macmillan uses his stage directions to invite his collaborators to see the world through the sense-experience of his protagonist, Emma: lights glow brighter, lights flicker, lights flash, music slows down, time speeds up and slows down, time jumps, walls lose definition, walls move away and dissolve, people move in slow motion, an

EXIT light glows and grows, a thousand TV channels play at the same time, a voice sounds like it is underwater, Emma multiplies into a chorus of Emmas. Duncan Macmillan allows us to experience the world through the senses of an addict in rehab.

There are two types of stage direction in Tarell Alvin McCraney's play *The Brothers Size*, stage directions in parentheses, which are to be played by the actors, and stage directions that are both spoken and played by the actors. The play begins with a half-spoken, half-sung invocation before stepping into the wonderful world of articulated stage directions, dialogue and action. It is a mesmerizing opening and the effect of the performed and spoken stage directions in theatrical terms is both magical and magnificent: magical because it beautifully reveals the actors' movements and intentions; magnificent because it makes poetic the usually hidden stage directions, and makes the play accessible to a visually impaired audience by describing what is happening on stage not as additional audio description, but as beautiful, poetic and dramatic writing.

There are very few stage directions in Martin Crimp's *Attempts on Her Life*. There are no stage directions in Sarah Kane's *4.48 Psychosis*. Sarah Kane and Martin Crimp were way ahead of their time. They have been a huge inspiration to the best playwrights of recent years. Credit due.

If you are brave enough to write a play with no writer's note or stage directions, I want to remind you that this too is a form of collaboration, you are giving permission for your collaborators to roam freely through your text. You are asking them to work hard, creatively and imaginatively to bring the world of your play to life. It gives your collaborators room to express themselves and enough rope to hang themselves with. It will be a challenge, but what a wonderful challenge for brilliant collaborative minds.

Perhaps the last word on all this should go to the great Peter Brook, who said:

Some writers attempt to nail down their meaning and intentions in stage directions and explanations, yet we cannot help being struck by the fact that the best dramatists explain themselves least.[25]

Devising

Sometimes a director and group of actors who want to devise a new play might invite a writer into the devising process. This can be fantastically rewarding work that brings forth extraordinary drama. However, it is essential – if you ever get involved in a process like this – to establish from the very start your role and rights in the finished play. If you don't have this conversation at the start of the process, even if you are working with your very best friends, the chances are that you will get into some horrible tangles later on, and, if you write something that becomes very successful, you could end up involved in some nasty litigation.

It's great to set up a project with friends in which you will be the writer, but if you are going to remain friends you need to set the rules at the start and try as hard as you can to stick to them, which won't always be easy because the process and contributions of individuals can change.

It's not easy to know where to draw the line. For example, a director suggests a scene and then films the actors improvising that scene. The writer goes home that night, watches the video, and then writes a scene based on the improv. Next day the scene is handed out to the actors, it isn't the same as the scene they improvised the day before, but there are still fragments of their original improvised dialogue in there, and don't forget it was the director who suggested the idea in the first place. So, who owns the material? Who gets the writing credit? In an example like this, I would suggest that it should be a shared credit between the playwright and the devising company. However, things might change throughout the play's development and change necessitates new conversations. It could turn into an ongoing wrangle. If you want to stay good friends with the people you are working with, tell them up front what you anticipate. If you expect to be credited as sole author and to retain all rights in the written text, get everyone to sign a short, legally binding statement declaring this before you start work on the play together. It might feel a bit awkward, but it's better than a big fall out at the end. Think of it as a creative prenup. At least that way everyone starts on the same page.

Co-writing

Collaborators come in many shapes and sizes, but one potential collaborator I haven't mentioned yet is the co-writer. It is quite rare for a new play to be co-authored, and for good reason: we write plays to get our individual vision out there. It does, however, happen, and there are plenty of other instances in which you are likely to be working alongside another writer – in TV or film, for example. But let's concentrate on the sometimes wonderful, sometimes torturous experience of co-writing a stage play.

Before you begin your (hopefully) wonderful collaboration, I have a suggestion: discuss how you are going to do it *before* you do it.

- Are you going to sit in the same room and write together at the same time?

- Does one of you type while the other one paces?

- Do you take it in turns at the keyboard?

- Are you going to write alone and then exchange pages?

- Are you going to write the same scene or play leapfrog?

- Are you going to write separately-together on a shared online document?

- Do you have complete carte blanche to re-write your collaborators text?

- Do they have your permission to re-write your text?

Life is too short to spend all day arguing about syntax and verbal contractions, so try to plan your process ahead of time. You need to work out between you how to get the best out of each other. Talk about it before you start to write the play, discuss your strong points, your weak points. The most important thing is that you find ways to complement each other, and that the collaboration creates a spark that leads not only to a great play, but one that benefits from the 'two brains are better than one' theory. Perhaps you have complimentary skills, perhaps you both like the same things, perhaps you have diametrically opposed processes, whatever the case, you need to work out what's best. And you will have to learn to compromise, whether you like it or not.

If you decide to have a go at writing the book for a musical or the libretto for an opera, you will find yourself meeting some new and very important collaborators.

Musical theatre

Musicals require a book, a score and lyrics. As the playwright in the equation, your primary job will be to write the book, but there are a number of permutations in terms of the nature of the collaboration.

Collaborative permutations can involve:

1 Three people: Book Writer, plus a Composer, plus a Lyricist

2 Two people: Book Writer, plus a Composer-Lyricist

3 Two people: Book Writer-Lyricist, plus Composer

4 Two people: Book Writer-Lyricist, Plus Composer-Lyricist

5 One person: Book Writer-Lyrist-Composer

The fifth permutation isn't of concern, as I'm not convinced that working alone counts as collaboration. If you intend to do everything yourself, I wish you luck.

Permutation 1 – Book Writer, plus a Composer, plus a Lyricist

I've got some bad news for you: the composer is likely to be considered more important than you. Sorry. The lyricist too. Sorry. In the hierarchy of musical theatre writing collaboration, the book writer comes last. But that doesn't mean you do the least work.

Experienced composers and lyricists are likely to know just as much about story, structure and character as you, but less experienced ones won't. Therefore, it can sometimes fall to you to take the lead in pulling these strands together. And you need to bear in mind that composers will be using music to do a multitude of things beyond telling the story, as will lyricists with their words.

The first question (again) is: How is this going to work? The chances are that the composer and lyricist are already a team, and that they are used to working with each other. The question for you is, how do you fit into the creative relationship. You can make life a lot easier for yourself by having this discussion up front.

If you are beginning the whole process from scratch, you will need to spend several sessions together simply planning your story, and working out what the style as well as the musical language of the show will be. This can take a long time. At some point you are all likely to go off and start playing with ideas. Then you'll bring them back to the room, and the discussion will begin all over again.

At best, this will be a truly collaborative exchange of ideas, and to achieve that you need to listen, understand the job music and lyrics can do, and weigh that against the personalities of the people you are working with. Do they work quickly? Slowly? Are they getting in touch with you all the time? Never? How can you improve the process?

Working with a lyricist is not the same as working with another playwright. They have a different skillset, and you need to respect that. You also need to be aware that if you write a beautiful, elegant speech, a lyricist might use it as a springboard for a lyric. Before you even begin a collaboration with a lyricist, you need to establish a working protocol by asking questions such as: are they likely to take your prose and turn it into a lyric? Are they happy for you to make suggestions for re-writes to their lyrics? Whatever the case, you need to be careful not to step on their toes.

The writing and workshop process can take years, about five years on average, so you better make sure you get along, or at least be prepared to pretend to get along. And the matrix of collaborations is substantially increased in the production of a musical, not just the composer and lyricist, but everyone mentioned in the first part of this chapter from the director to the stage manager and actors to everyone beyond and in-between, as well as the musical director, musicians, dancers, singers, and another hugely important collaborator in musical theatre, the choreographer.

Dance is phenomenally important in musical theatre. Music, lyrics and dance have huge narrative and emotional applications, so learn to think flexibly and porously when your team insists on cutting that great scene you wrote in favour of a dance that says what you were trying to say in half the time with no words. Let your choreographer speak with the bodies of the performers, it can be absolutely magical.

As ever, be open and collaborative with all these people. And don't forget that many of the greatest directors in American musical theatre were once choreographers, dance is probably going to be way more important to them than that flash of brilliant dialogue you just penned.

You need to be prepared to make some tough decisions. You need to write the best things you have ever written, and then get ready to cut them in the name of serving the show. It's the same for all of us, even Lin-Manuel Miranda; 'Lin and his collaborators needed the creativity to generate thousands of ideas and the pragmatism to test them all . . . Again and again they sacrificed little pleasures (a beautiful melody, a big laugh) in pursuit of an overarching goal.'[26]

Another thing to bear in mind during the preview process is that if you want to change some dialogue it is likely to have more ramifications than in a play. For example, if you want to extend some dialogue spoken during the middle of a song, the composer and/or the musical director will need to know exactly how much time the new dialogue will take up so that they can extend the number of bars, and adjust the score accordingly. You might not be working directly with the musical director, but you need to bear in mind that you probably just gave them a big headache. Changes to the book in musical theatre has consequences.

Permutation 2 – Book Writer, plus a Composer-Lyricist

In this permutation you are basically working with a songwriter. All the factors outlined in the first permutation still exist, except that the human component and all its attendant complications has been cut by one-third. You are still likely to get your dialogue 're-imagined' in a lyric every now and then, and you are still likely to experience that slightly sinking feeling that you aren't getting enough credit for all the hard work you've put in. If you want to write for musical theatre, get used to it.

Permutation 3 – Book Writer-Lyricist, plus Composer

So, you've done a couple of musicals and you want to have a go at writing lyrics. You might hand a sheaf of lyrics to the composer only for them to be returned because they didn't inspire your collaborator. Perhaps your composer will hand you some music and ask you to find lyrics to fit the melody. You may sit down and write a number together. Whatever you do, the composer is still more important. (See chapter 2.6 *Get Musical* for more about how to write lyrics.)

Permutation 4 – Book Writer-Lyricist, plus Composer-Lyricist

This is my favourite permutation because this is the creative paradigm that meets in the middle. There is a good balance to the creative input. You will still need to agree on how to write the lyrics, in other words, do you write separate songs, can you re-write your collaborator's lyrics, can your collaborator change your lyrics to fit the melody they have just written? Up to you. The composer is still more important though . . .

Opera

If you think I am overstating the importance of the composer in musical theatre, I would like to up the hyperbolic stakes and suggest that in opera, the composer is GOD.

As essential as the librettist is in the creation of an opera, the likelihood is that their status will never equal that of the composer. Composers love good librettists, without them their operas wouldn't exist, but we don't even know the names of some librettists from the seventeenth century, they were never recorded! At least these days librettist's get their names recorded, even if it is in little letters at the bottom of the page towered over by the composer's credit. I exaggerate, but it is galling.

You may be asked to write the libretto before the composer has selected a single note. Perhaps you will be given some music before you have written a single word. Perhaps you will be locked in a room together and not let out until you've written something. Possibly the most important consideration is the question of what you are going to write. If you have been asked to come up with an original idea, your process is likely to be a lot longer and have more false starts than if you have been asked to adapt something. In any case, the same rules apply: listen, be respectful, discuss how you are going to work together, make a plan. It may be the case that more face-to-face collaboration is necessary in writing an opera – conversations about scansion, recitative, arias, and dialogue (if there is any) – but the only essential is that you find the best way of working together. And after you have worked out how to work together and you have done the work, what next? Here comes that army of other collaborators again . . .

Composers are passionate about their work. You should be passionate about your work. And if furious rows are your style, just make sure they are the kind of furious rows that lead to phenomenal art and not irreparable damage.

Conclusion

Remember, almost everyone in the creative process will probably believe their job is the most important one. And, in a way, they are all right. Because we need each other; it is the sum of the parts that will make a great production. It is possible for a great director or actor to make a poor play seem a lot better than it actually is. It is possible for a bad director or actor to make a great play seem dreadful. Identify the best – according to you and no one else – and aim to work with them. If you can't find the magic in a collaboration, try something different, but don't forget that collaboration is the beating heart of theatre-making.

3.3 TAKE THE BUSINESS OF BEING A PLAYWRIGHT SERIOUSLY

I have an annoying little epigram that I like to trot out to groups of new playwrights I work with: *Take your playwriting seriously; take the business of being a playwright seriously.*

Writing plays and earning a living is hard. Really hard. Even successful writers – the writers whose plays are regularly produced – can struggle to make a living, and will have to balance their playwriting with other work; for instance, writing for other media, or teaching, or doing another job entirely. Even deciding what other work to do is difficult. Do you aim for a job in theatre? Perhaps in the literary department or in marketing or front of house? Or do you keep your theatrical powder dry by doing something entirely unrelated to theatre? An office job, temping, retail? Only you can answer this question. I know a playwright whose day job is being a lawyer; how they balance the demands of both is beyond me, but they do. I know a playwright who works in a theatre's marketing department; how they balance selling the work of other writers when they are burning to write their own plays is beyond me, but they do. The sad truth is that if you don't come from a family with the wealth to support you, your life will probably get a bit messy, I know mine did.

I spent my twenties playing the guitar in various bands, but when I got kicked out of the last band I was in at the ripe old age of thirty-one, I decided to do what any sensible person would do, and leave that precarious profession to get a proper job being a playwright. At least that's the way I usually tell it; the truth, as ever, is a bit more complex. I had already made the decision to commit myself to playwriting about a year earlier. I had sent a play to Stratford East and been invited to join their writers' group, and I knew I had found my aesthetic and spiritual home. My masterplan was to ease my way into my new career by making one more album and doing one more tour while I continued to write. Everything was going well: I had recently married, I was earning a living from the band, and writing in my spare time. But then I got the boot from the band, and suddenly found myself thrown into my brave new world prematurely. I decided against trying to get session work, or joining another band, so that I could focus on my playwriting. But there was a problem, I was now broke. So, I got a casual job working backstage in the West End so that I could continue to write. I won an award for an audio drama, but my wife was pregnant with our first child, and money was still tight, so when a friend said he could get me a 'proper' job I decided to take him up on the offer. Now I was working for a rapacious car parking company during the day and trying to write at night. But attempting to get into writing a play after a day of administering vicious Fixed Penalty Notices was not easy. Then, just over a year after joining the writers' group at Stratford East, I was awarded a writer's attachment bursary and told that my first play was going to be produced. So, I did what all sensible playwrights would do, I quit my job to write full time. My first play went on, and six months later, I was broke again. I trawled through every attachment scheme and bursary offer in the UK, and got a position as writer-in-residence at Essex University. Respite . . . for twelve months. My second play was produced. I managed to patch an income together from commissions, bits of TV and radio for a couple of years. My third play was produced. But I now had a young family, and I needed a more secure income. I had to think very hard about what I could and/or should do. I had tried balancing a brain-numbing job with writing and it hadn't worked, so when I saw a job advertisement for the post of Literary Manager at Soho Theatre Company, I applied, and was fortunate enough to get it. Ever since then, I have juggled writing and dramaturgy. And it works, sort of, when you factor in the teaching I do, and the bits and pieces of work I still do as a guitarist to earn a bit extra. Like I said, it's messy.

It doesn't matter what you do or how you do it, the important thing is that you make a commitment to writing. It is fine to work in a pub, or restaurant, or diner while you write your masterpiece. That's what Jonathan Larson, the writer of *Rent* did.[1] It's fine to be an usher and scribble ideas at the back of the stalls for the play you are going to write when you get back home. That's what Shelagh Delaney, the writer of *A Taste of Honey* did.[2] It's fine to be a woman in her forties, with four exhausting kids, and decide to have a go at writing plays. And succeed! That's what Pam Gems, the writer of *Piaf* did.[3] She began writing seriously in her forties and went on to write a string of brilliant plays. Find your balance. It won't be easy, but it is possible. The most important thing is to start, and then, endure. As the great James Baldwin said,

Talent is insignificant. I know a lot of talented ruins. Beyond talent lie all the usual words: discipline, love, luck, but most of all, endurance.[4]

James Baldwin, a truly great writer, had to endure years of rejection, slights and stupidity before his writing finally received the recognition it deserved. If you are going to be a playwright, you too will need to endure. If you are already a playwright, you will need to continue to endure. It is not an easy profession. You will not survive on talent alone. There is no point writing a wonderful new play, sending it to half a dozen new writing theatres, and then sitting on your couch with your feet up waiting for someone to call and tell you that you are a genius. You need to engage with the business of being a playwright. Everyone, EVERYONE, to a greater or – if you are lucky – lesser extent must play the game. In the face of rejection, of people saying stupid things about your play, people writing stupid things about your play, people telling you how to write your play, and people telling you not to give up the day job, you will need to endure. You will need to keep going.

Don't believe in the *Myth of Lazy Genius*. It doesn't matter how smart you are, if you don't do the work, you don't get the accolades. Believe this: *the harder you work, the more talented you get*. Don't sit around waiting for a lucky break. Believe this: *the harder you work, the luckier you get*. Believe this: *the harder you work, the more you engage with the business, the better your chances of achieving something*. You need to work hard at doing the writing. You need to work hard at taking responsibility for the writing.

So, don't wait to be discovered, be proactive. Build your knowledge of the industry, know where to look for opportunities, know where to send your next play. You need to identify theatre companies producing new writing, select the companies whose work resonates with you, and then do some research. Find out how these companies work, how many new plays they produce each year, and whether they work with co-producers. Make a list of the playwrights whose work they produce, the artistic director, associate directors, freelance directors that work there,[5] and other companies involved with the various productions. Work out what opportunities these companies offer for a writer like you. Find out if they accept year-round submissions or have a submissions window. Find out what initiatives they are running. Do they have a competition? Do they have a writers' group? You need to work out how you can get involved.

Or come at it from a different angle, identify the playwrights and directors whose work resonates with you and research these individuals. For playwrights, find out who directed their last three plays, who produced their last three plays, and where their last three plays were produced. For directors, find out what the last three plays they directed were, who produced them, and where they were produced.

By doing this, you will begin to build a web of connections that can inform your decisions about where to submit your new play. Knowing where to send your play will save you a lot of time in wasted approaches to companies and individuals who aren't likely to be interested in the plays you write. Now you need to get your play to the people and places that offer you the best opportunities, so you need to know when the script submission windows are, and you need to know when the competition deadlines are. ENTER COMPETITIONS! Why wait for someone else to win them! Think regionally. Most companies love discovering a local writer, it doesn't matter if it's where you live now, or where you grew up, press those local buttons. And attend writers' workshops, or join writers' groups. Joining writers' groups is one of the best ways of making connections in the industry. Tips and suggestions from other writers create a nexus that can lead to opportunities, and provide an invaluable support network. If you are new to playwriting, and nervous about joining a writers' group, I promise you that other playwrights aren't as scary as they might at first appear. You will make good friends and further your career at the same time, and where else can you talk passionately about the obscure fringe play that changed your life without your interlocuter making a quick excuse to leave the building. Having said that, a quick word of warning, don't become a workshop junkie and make the mistake of thinking that attending a workshop, and learning the same things again and again, is progress.

You will also need to network. Most of the playwrights I know hate networking, but I'm afraid that in the early days you will have to do it, and you will need to maintain your network. That tired old aphorism, it's *not what you know, it's who you know*, is, sadly, still very, very relevant.

Submitting your script

You may well have heard that if you are a new writer you need to make sure that the first few pages of your script really grab the reader's attention. This is true.

There used to be a time when new writing theatre companies read all submissions, all year round. Today, I'm afraid, this rarely happens. More often than not, there will be a submissions window and a sifting process similar to the one previously mentioned that is used in competitions to decide which plays will be read and which will not. A literary assistant will perhaps read the first few pages, have a quick look in the middle, and then peer at the last page. Does it look like it's worth reading? Yes, or no? It depends on those few pages. Does the writer know what they are doing? Is there something interesting about the play? Read or reject? Brutal. But true. There will be exceptions to this process – companies who assiduously read everything – and to those companies and individuals, I say, thank you! But the lesson is a simple one: you need to do what you can to convince the reader they HAVE to read your play. Five pages of stage directions detailing the objects d'art in a country house is unlikely to do you any favours, even if the play itself is sublime.

When submitting your script to a new writing company, you should accompany it with a short note. Tell the company who you are, why you have submitted this play to them, and the subject of your play. And please do keep it short, no literary manager is likely to have the time or desire to read an essay on how interesting your play is.

Usually, you will wait for approximately three months before you hear anything. If you don't hear anything after that time you should think about sending a polite enquiry as to when you might hear back. If you are still waiting after four months, hassle strategically, but don't be a pain in the arse. A polite reminder will probably trigger the guilt of the literary team. Remember, they are dealing with hundreds of people in the same situation as you, and you should be prepared to cut them a little slack

If you receive a rejection email, don't analyse it. I have written hundreds of rejections, don't try to find the subtext. If the company encourage you to send your next play, this is a very good thing, no literary manager wants to make extra work for themself reading plays from a writer they aren't interested in.

If you are invited in for a chat, you have hit the new writer jackpot. When you meet the literary team, or one of the directors, you don't need to pretend to be Sarah Kane, Annie Baker, Tony Kushner or Mark Ravenhill. Just be yourself.

Bigger picture

You need to understand the different types of contracts. In the UK, this means:

- ITC – Independent Theatre Council (small–medium scale).
- TMA – Theatre Managers Association (medium–large scale).
- TNC – contracts relating to the National Theatre, the Royal Shakespeare Company, the Royal Court Theatre.
- Commercial – beautiful, brilliant producers, and perhaps every now and then one or two total bastards.

Contracts from the first three organizations on this list are regulated and shouldn't cause you too much grief. A commercial contract will require an agent or advice from a lawyer or writers' industry body. If in doubt, consult the Writers' Guild of Great Britain (WGGB) or whatever body represents writers in your country. If there isn't one, form one.

You will also need to understand what the contract is for. If your unsolicited new play is going to be produced, the theatre company will need to acquire the rights to produce it. This is referred to as the *acquisition of rights*. If a company asks you to pitch ideas for a new play for them, and they decide to pay you to write a play based on one of your ideas, this is referred to as a *commission*. If a company want to produce one of your old plays, this will be referred to as a *license*.

You will need to look out for the important clauses. Who owns the rights to produce your play and for how long? Are their rights exclusive? How much are you getting paid, how are the payments divided, and when are they due? How much of what you are being paid is an advance against royalties? What are the royalty splits? Are you getting paid to attend rehearsals? (As mentioned previously, in the UK the playwright should have the legal right to attend rehearsals.)

Broaden your horizons

Because writing for the stage is such a precarious profession you will need to broaden your dramatic horizons. Think about:

- Audio/Radio
- TV
- Film
- Gaming
- Residencies: Hospitals / Prisons / Businesses / Universities.

It is a sad fact of life as a playwright that to live on the income from playwriting alone is almost impossible. If you spend twelve months writing a play, and then have the joy of seeing it produced in a studio theatre, you will earn something like eight thousand pounds. You will not be rich; you need multiple large-scale productions in multiple cities for that to happen. If you have a new play produced, and it does okay, it will usually open the door to working in other media: audio, TV, gaming, even film. As a playwright, your skills are transferrable to all of these media, BUT they are not the same. You will need to learn how to write for these different disciplines. Writing audio drama is not the same as writing a play, and is seismically different to TV and film. You need to learn the difference between writing for all five senses in theatre as opposed to writing with your ears in audio drama, and writing with your eyes for film. This may all seem quite reductive, but there are a two essential things to bear in mind. Firstly, to survive financially as a dramatist you will most likely need to write for other media. Secondly, you will need to invest time and effort into learning how to write for other media.

Other sources of income

In the UK you can apply for grants and bursaries from various trusts and foundations. There are also grants available from the Arts Council as well as the Peggy Ramsey Foundation, and fellowships and residencies from several theatre companies, schools and colleges. The types of grants and bursaries vary enormously, and change regularly. The best places to look for guidance in the UK are the WGGB; the Arts Council and/or your

Regional Arts Board; online groups like the London Playwrights' Workshop/Blog. Don't be lazy, do some research.

Agents

At some point you will need to get an agent. It's rare, but not entirely unknown, for a playwright to get an agent before they are produced, but it's much more likely that you will only get traction with an agent when you have had a play on somewhere. I don't think there's much point in agonizing over getting an agent until you need one. It is rare, in my experience, that an agent will make your career for you, but they are indispensable when it comes to negotiating contracts. It is worth following a similar process to the one outlined above for directors when contemplating which agent or agency to approach. Identify the agents and/or agencies that represent the playwrights you most admire, then, when you get a play on, approach the ones you feel might have an affinity with your writing. Bear in mind that agents sometimes specialize in theatre, TV or film, but can also cover all areas. Ask yourself what you want from an agent: for example, do you want a theatre specialist with connections in TV or a film agent who sometimes works with playwrights? Many agents – if not most – have too many clients, so it is often worthwhile to begin by contacting an agent's assistant(s). Agents' assistants will one day be agents in their own right, and will already be developing their own lists.

Balancing the practicalities of playwriting with paying your bills is not easy. It can be brutal. You need to learn to deal not only with the vicissitudes and uncertainties of writing, but also the impact of becoming a playwright on how to support yourself. You need to take your playwriting seriously and take the business of being a playwright seriously. You need to work out how it is going to work for you, and you need to learn to take care of yourself while doing it. All of which can take a toll on a playwright's mental health . . .

3.4 LOOK AFTER YOUR MENTAL HEALTH

I can't read reviews of my plays. I try, sometimes, but reading a review feels like having hot wax dripped onto my eyeballs. I think my problem dates back to my first full professional production at the Theatre Royal Stratford East. The first review I read was okay, not sensational, but okay. The second review I read was nasty. The play was about a bebop jazz saxophonist, and there was a strapline at the bottom of the poster for my play taken from a 1940s jazz advertisement that read, 'If you can't be good, bebop!' The critic obviously didn't like the play, but not content with just saying that, they decided to do what critics sometimes do which is to come up with an amusing little kick in the teeth to finish the review off. The critic in question mentioned the strapline on the poster before signing off with the witty epithet, 'If you can't be good, don't bother!' It should have been funny. Not to me. I could have died. This was my first play. It meant the world to me. But here I was, being told I shouldn't have bothered. It was humiliating. My mum and dad would read this, my friends would read this, people I knew, as well as complete strangers, would read this, and smirk at the critic's acerbic put-down. I wanted to run away and hide. But I didn't. I sat at home and felt shame instead. I didn't read any more reviews. I couldn't. Perhaps it was a good thing? Perhaps it taught me to toughen up. If you are going to stick your head above the parapet, snipers are going to take shots, right? In the age of social media, most of us have had to get used to that. The fact is, even in the face of this humiliation, I was never going to give up. I couldn't. It was going to take more than a throwaway remark to stop me writing. So, I kept going.

My next play at Stratford East, about a year later, was a big success. I won a prestigious best play award, and the play was critic's choice in several magazines and newspapers, but I didn't read the reviews. I didn't want to feel like that ever again.

Years ago, before the news became digital, I read an article in *The Guardian* newspaper about artists' mental health. The article discussed recent research that suggested the group of artists with the highest rate of mental health issues was playwrights. I was not surprised. Our is a profession strewn with potential mental health hazards like rejection, humiliation and vulnerability. The thing that struck me then, as it continues to strike me today, is that no one ever really talks about these things. It can be a joy to write a play, it can be a joy to see it produced, and it can be the most wonderful job in the world. But there is a dark side. For me, the time has come to drag the demons and black dogs out into the daylight, so that we can begin to name them, and start to think of strategies that might help us to deal with them.

If you are the kind of playwright who has total confidence in their ability, who knows they are a genius, who never ceases to remind people of that fact, and who has skin as thick as rhinoceros hide, you probably don't need this chapter. If, on the other hand, you sometimes (or often) have doubts about whether you can or should be writing plays, then please read on.

Having said that, writers of genius (if you are still reading this) please take note: over the years I have met playwrights who considered themselves to be of God-like playwriting stature – one or two of them (annoyingly) actually were – but most of them weren't, they just had an extraordinarily inflated opinion of their own talent. On the other hand, I have worked with many playwrights (predominantly women) who think they aren't very good, who are, in fact, absolutely brilliant, and, usually, far superior to the writers who consider themselves gods. I suppose what I'm trying to say is that your opinion of how good you are is not a very good guide to how good you are in practice.

In my experience, most playwrights suffer from at least some doubts about their ability. Doubts that begin from the moment we sit down to write our first play. Parents, partners and friends will respect the time we spend earning a living – whether by teaching, working in hospitality, or stacking shelves in a supermarket – but for some reason they seem to find it harder to respect the time we give to writing. In the early days, no one is paying us to write, so we need to motivate ourselves, and to have people around us question the fact we want to spend our time writing, makes it even harder. But if we don't do the work, we will never become the writers we want to be. It is time justifiably well-spent, and just because other people can't see it, and doubt us, it doesn't mean we shouldn't do it. It can be unsettling, but we need to overcome the doubt of others as well as the doubts we carry about ourselves. However, even if we can overcome these doubts, get our plays written, submit them to potential producers, and get them produced, our journey into the mental health maelstrom of playwriting has only just begun.

Usually, a playwright is left to deal with the slings and arrows of outrageous fortune on their own, but this needs to change. We need to open up a conversation about our mental health. We need to be open about the anxieties, worries and misgivings that most of us, most of the time, tend to keep hidden. We need to acknowledge that it is time to take our mental health seriously.

You might be a young playwright, filled with the ambition to write great plays, terrified by all those writers, and directors, and actors who seem to know precisely who they are and what they are doing. Don't worry about it, they are just as confused as you are.

You might be an older playwright, worried that you have left it too late and will never get your work produced. Don't worry about it, some writers write great plays in their twenties while some write them in their eighties. The most important thing is that you write your plays.

You might be a playwright with a long-term health condition, struggling to get your play written. Don't worry, just find solace in doing what you can, when you can.

You might be a playwright struggling to balance the demands of writing and looking after kids. Don worry, they will grow up, you'll get some time back, just keep the writing ticking.

You might be a playwright in a demanding full-time job, too tired to write at night. Don't worry, do what you can, when you can, and book yourself a holiday when you can pull it all together.

You might be a playwright who needs to take time out to focus on their mental or physical health. Don't worry about it, do it. You need your health to write, it is part of your creative paradigm, prioritize it when you need to prioritize it, and, when you feel you can, find purpose in your writing.

You might be a playwright whose writing is inextricably linked to their health condition. Don't worry about it, just take care of yourself, on a personal level, and as a writer. Do the work on yourself that you need to do, take the time you need to take to feel well. Your writing is a part of who you are.

You might be a disabled playwright concerned that you won't find the support you need to do your writing. Don't worry, the support is there for you in many theatre organizations as well as disabled-led companies, seek them out.

You might be a neurodiverse playwright worried that you won't find a place for your work. Don't worry, you will. The world is changing. We can make it change.

Whether you belong to one of these catregories or a combination of them, let's try to be honest for once. None of us are immune to all of the challenges that creative work presents. So, let's start to name it, and let's start to deal with it. Together.

Imposter syndrome

You want to be a playwright. You go to the Royal Court. There are all these clever, trendy people talking about plays. They look cool. They look confident. You think, what on earth am I doing here? I don't belong here! I don't belong with these people! I've never even heard the names of most of the writers they're talking about. It's mystifying. It's terrifying. It's another world. Welcome! You have just been hit by the dreaded Imposter Syndrome.

Fear not, you are not alone. We all began as outsiders. We all had to walk into that theatre, writers' group, or workshop for the first time. The feeling of being an imposter isn't unique to you. I've never liked the self-help mantra, *fake it till you make it*, but I do think it's worth remembering that it's important to connect with our peers in whatever way we can, even if it feels frightening. The life of a playwright is a bit odd in the way we yo-yo from total isolation to collegiate playmaking, but we need to get used to it. We are all imposters in the beginning.

Don't believe the myth that playwrights are born not made. Many of the greatest playwrights had to work like hell to get to where they are. Don't believe the great first play myth; you know, the idea that a young writer sat down one day to write their play and it was a work of genius. Even the 'greats' like Arthur Miller and Tennessee Williams had written many plays before they eventually got produced. Theatres like to present the myth of the great first play. It doesn't usually happen like that. You are not inadequate if you write a lot of plays before your first play gets produced. You are not in competition with other writers, you just need to keep writing. Don't judge yourself by the success of others, AND accept that sometimes you will write badly, just as Williams and Miller did.

You don't need anyone's permission to be a playwright, you just need to do the work.

Confidence

Some playwrights find it hard to even call themselves a playwright. This, I think, is a matter of confidence. I once met a playwright who had had one reading of their first play above a pub in north London to an audience of about a dozen (including their mum and dad) who talked with total confidence about being a playwright as if they were Tony Kushner. I know other playwrights who still don't think they are worthy of the name 'playwright' after years of writing. As far as I'm concerned, if you've written a play, and you want to continue writing plays, you are a playwright. You don't need to wait for someone to give you permission to be a playwright. It doesn't matter who you are. It doesn't matter about your circumstances. It doesn't matter if you haven't read every play written by Shakespeare. You don't have to be better than Shakespeare. You just need to write your plays.

Confidence doesn't come easily to every playwright, but every playwright will need to try to develop confidence. In the first instance, the confidence to write and finish a play. A lot of people want to write plays, a lot of people start to write a play, a lot of people never finish the play they started. Why? A lack of confidence tinged with the fear that they aren't good enough. You will also need the confidence to ask someone to read your play, and have the confidence not to fall to pieces if they tell you there are things they don't like. You will need the confidence to submit a play to a theatre, producer or competition; the confidence to deal with rejection; the confidence to deal with the opinions of dramaturgs, directors, actors, stage managers, marketing departments, front of house, bar staff, relatives, friends and strangers; the confidence to get through the rehearsal process, sit through previews, and endure Press Night (for some, the cruellest playwriting torture ever invented); the confidence to deal with reviews; and, finally, the confidence to do it all over again.

If you are not a naturally confident person, it is extremely hard to miraculously conjure up self-assurance from the void. Some advice from the Stoics: control what you can control and don't worry about what lies outside your control.[1] You can control whether you write a play or not. So do it. You can control whether you show it to someone and submit it to a competition or producing theatre. So do it. You can't control the reaction to your play by the people reading it. So don't obsess about it. You can control how you respond to feedback from dramaturgs, directors and actors. So, think clearly and engage in collaboration. You can control your input into the rehearsal process. So, make sure there is a protocol in place that means you can have your say. You can control your reaction to previews. So, get your notes to the director. You cannot control how the play goes on Press Night. So, try not to worry about it. You cannot control the reaction of individual audience members. So don't worry about it. You cannot control the reaction of critics. So, try not to worry about it. If you don't want to read your reviews, don't read them. If you've got a thicker skin, read them, and learn from them. Remember to ask yourself: is this something that is, or is not, in my control? If it is, do something about it, if it isn't, don't worry about it.

Pressure

Playwrights are great at heaping pressure on themselves: pressure to write, to write better, to write more, to write the greatest play ever written. Try to take the self-induced pressure off. After all, there are plenty of people waiting to pile the pressure on without you doing it to yourself.

Paranoia

The fear that you are being excluded for reasons that you have probably made up. The gatekeepers won't let you in! They won't read my play! They won't return my emails! They won't come to my readings! The truth: the gatekeepers are just trying to do their job to the best of their abilities. Sometimes you'll encounter inefficiency, but it's highly unlikely that you've been singled out for the cold shoulder.

I'm too old! I'm too young! Not every playwright is discovered at the same age. Some get lucky early, then learn. Others learn, then start writing later. Some have kids, then start *much* later. There is no rule that says that if you're not produced by the Royal Court before you are twenty-five that you are doomed to failure. I recall having to tell a 31-year-old playwright that the company I was working for were not going to produce his play, he crumpled and exclaimed, 'Shelley was dead by the age I am now!' I tried to explain to him that it probably wasn't a good idea to measure his career by the yardstick of Percy Bysshe Shelley, but he was inconsolable. The fact is that age is there as yet another stick to beat ourselves with. And almost all of us do. But we don't have to.

Anxiety and exposure

With every play you write, you are asking to be judged. If you want to be a playwright, there is nowhere to hide. At every stage of the process, once you have written your play, you are asking others, often strangers, to judge you. When you submit your new play to a theatre or playwriting competition, you are asking the readers to judge you. When you are fortunate enough to have your play optioned for production, you are asking the director, designer, actors, and everyone else involved to judge you. Then, when your play is produced, you are asking audiences, critics, family and friends to judge you. It's not like writing a novel where you can publish and then hide. You are visible at every stage. I sometimes think of this as the *Circle of Anxiety*, or, in more prosaic moments, the *Circle of Shit*. This is how the *anxiety* and *shit* go around: the anxiety that the play you are writing is shit; the anxiety that the people who are reading your play think it's shit; the anxiety that the people who are working on your play think it's shit; the anxiety that the audience, critics, family and friends who have come to see your play think it's shit; the anxiety that the new play you are working on is shit.

Round and around we go. If we are going to continue to write plays, we either just have to sit there and take it, or try to find strategies to deal with it.

The fact is that awaiting the opinion of others, awaiting acceptance, is always going to be anxiety inducing. And playwriting contains a double anxiety: the anxiety of showing your work to others, and the anxiety of others interpreting your work, then showing it to other others. You can't control it, but you shouldn't let it control you.

A true story: I remember when I was a teenage guitar player in a band at school visiting the house of a local, long-haired hippy guru with my friends to discuss the idea of him becoming our manager. He was all beads, incense and faux Indian art. I knew from the moment I sat down in front of him that he was a charlatan, but I was intrigued. The first thing he did was to stare intently at each of us, in turn, and tell us what we needed to do to find our true selves. When he got to me, he pulled back a little, widened his eyes, flicked his long, lank, dark hair, back behind his shoulders and announced that to fulfil my potential, and shake loose the chains of my conformity, I would first need to take off all my clothes and run naked through the streets of my hometown.

You may be disappointed to learn that I didn't take him up on his suggestion, but during the years that followed, I have regularly taken off all my clothes and stood naked before the world. Not literally. But by writing plays. As strange as it may sound, that is what it sometimes feels like to me when my plays are produced; like I am standing there, naked, asking to be judged. We need to learn to be able to deal with the anxiety of exposure; exposure not only of the quality of our writing, but also the content of our plays. We need to be brave and say the things we need to say, but sometimes we might feel we have exposed too much, and find that exposure overwhelming. It's important to say what we need to say, but we also need to keep an eye on our mental health, and to make sure that we have the support in place to help us through the process. We need to weigh up the fact that people will say things to us, newspapers and online platforms will write things about us, social media will assess us. Can we deal with this exposure? Perhaps the best thing to do is to have this conversation with a close friend or your collaborators as early in the process as possible. Writing a play is a brilliant thing, but you need to balance it with your mental health. You need to think hard before you take all your clothes off and run naked down the street.

Vulnerability as courage

If we do go ahead with our play, we need to understand that we will be making ourselves both visible and vulnerable. Every time you finish a play and send it out, you are making yourself vulnerable. This is especially true if you have exposed that 0.19 per cent of you that is uniquely you, if you have said things that others haven't dared to say, or if you have taken the risk of creating a character, or relating an event, that could be interpreted – rightly or wrongly – as autobiographical. But, as the American professor and researcher Brené Brown points out, vulnerability is not weakness, it is courage.[2] Being vulnerable means having the courage it takes to write your play, the courage it takes to get your play out there, and the courage it takes to deal with the snipers and detractors when there is nothing you can do to stop them. Have courage.

Rejection

Life as a playwright will always involve the possibility, or should that be the certainty, of rejection. It doesn't matter how good you are. Or how famous you are. It is a shadow that falls over us for our entire career. The first play I ever saw was *Death of a Salesman* by Arthur Miller.[3] I loved it. At university, I played Reverend Hale in a touring production of *The Crucible*.[4] I loved it. When I decided to take myself seriously as a playwright, I sat down to read Arthur Miller's autobiography, *Timebends*. I loved it. Arthur Miller is one of the main reasons I do what I do. I adore the man and his writing. However, when I was working as a dramaturg at the RSC, I received a new play by Arthur Miller from his agent, it was called *Resurrection Blues*.[5] The play had premiered in the USA and his agent was now looking for a London production. It still feels like heresy to say it, but I didn't think it was very good. So, I rejected it. I was that evil dramaturg reading your plays. But bear this in mind, it broke my heart to have to reject any play. I knew how hard it would have been to write it. The people reading and judging your plays don't reject them to humiliate you, they do it because it is their job. If you're on the receiving end, you need to move on. If one theatre rejects your play, send it to another one. You never know where, in the words of my friend and fellow playwright, Patrick Prior, you might land a lucky punch.

When collaboration goes wrong

Stay calm. Talk to someone. Get advice. Step away from the situation and think about it. Analyse what happened. Ask yourself if it can be fixed or if you are working with an idiot.

Let's say you're a young woman and you are working with an established male director with something like ten years' more experience than you. You have a disagreement about how a scene should work. He won't listen. He thinks he knows best. He's awfully nice about it, but he wants to do it his way. He tries the scene. You hate it. And it goes without saying that you need to be able to tell him what you think. Of course it does. If he remains intransigent, my advice is to let out your fury, upset and bewilderment with someone you can trust and whose advice you value – be it another writer, another theatre company, or a mentor. Don't stay quiet and let it fester, if you let it fester too long it can become fatal. If, after revisiting the conversation with your director, he still refuses to listen, you may need to find a way to communicate your problem to the producer, or Artistic Director (if you are working with a freelance or associate director), or Executive Director. Ideally, your agent (if you have one) or the Writers' Guild of Great Britain (WGGB) (if you are a member) will lead the charge on this. If you don't have an agent or aren't a member of the Guild, I would suggest setting up a meeting with the relevant people and taking one of your trusted friends/colleagues along in an attempt to find a solution. Hopefully, you will never find yourself in a situation like this, but if you do, you should try to find a way to resolve the problem as soon as possible. Most importantly, don't work with arseholes. Do your research. Find out everything you can about a director before you agree to work with them. A good director will do everything they can to find out about the personalities of the actors they are casting, you should do the same for the director. If you are fortunate enough to have a dramaturg, you can also use them as your sounding board and go-between.

The vast majority of directors are magnificent human beings, but if you are working with a director who won't listen, you need to find a way to get what you want to say across. You are a playwright. You are smart. One of your main jobs when writing a play is to problem-solve: how can I get this character to do this? What would this character do in this situation? And so on, ad infinitum. In a way, playwriting *is* problem solving. So, use your problem-solving skills to get your message across.

Moral dilemma: if you were offered a production of your new play at a prestigious new writing theatre on the condition that you changed the ending of your play to fit the director's vision, would you do it? If the answer is 'yes' – fine, get on with it, and don't beat yourself up about it. If the answer is 'no' – walk away, and don't beat yourself up about it. Be intelligent. Fight your battles strategically; win some, lose some, but win the war.

Sometimes a sneaky actor might talk to you behind the director's back to try to get you to add or change lines. Listen to them. If you agree, talk to the director about it. If you disagree, say no.

Critics and reviews

I have a problem with press nights. I hate them. Only once have I attended one of my own press nights and not wished I wasn't there. They are, for me, torture. I remember once seeing David Hare outside the West End theatre where his play *Amy's View* was having its Press Night in 1998. He looked wan and tortured. I remember thinking to myself, at the time, that if one of Britain's most established and successful playwrights can look so nervous on Press Night, what hope was there for mere mortals like me! Having said that, there are some playwrights who tell me they love press nights. If you're one of those, I envy you.

You know my feelings about reviews, I don't read them. But they are an essential part of the theatrical economy/ecology. A fellow playwright at Stratford East told me something I'll never forget that I think probably rings true for a lot of the less confident playwrights amongst us: in essence, 'you don't believe the good reviews and the bad ones just confirm your worst suspicions'. Your job is to learn to deal with them. Read them or don't read them, but don't let them dictate to you. You can't control what a critic writes, so try not to worry about it. It will only feed the self-loathing. The critics I have befriended over the years are intelligent, insightful people who love the theatre. They don't set out to make our lives a misery. They want the next play they see to be the best play they have ever seen. But when it isn't, it's their job to tell us why. We need critics, critics need us.

One thing I'm grateful I didn't have to contend with at the start of my career is the star rating system. That loathsome instant indicator of judgement. You might not read the reviews, but those star ratings are going to find their way into your orbit one way or another. One star: I might as well die now. Two stars: I'll never be able to leave my house ever again. Three stars: the kiss of death (the play is not bad enough to condemn, but not good enough to praise, which to any potential audience member translates as 'Don't bother!'). Four stars: thank God for that! Five Stars, I am God! ... But they will probably hate my next one.

The shame you feel when your play gets bad reviews is deep. But you need to park it and move on. The fact is that there will always be someone who thinks your plays stink, regardless of how successful you are. Your job is simply to get on with the job.

Humiliation

You need to deal with humiliation; whether it is the micro-humiliations felt in the rehearsal room, or the macro-humiliations of a poor national review. This is how we grow, how we learn, and how we find out if we really want to do this. If we can't take it, we stop. If we can learn to live with it, we evolve.

The humiliations might not even be your fault. An actor might dry, the set might fall over, an audience member might start shouting for no particular reason – none of it your fault – but the play is wrecked, and you are humiliated. Again, it's out of your control. Shit happens. In ten years' it will be easy to make a joke about it, so why not start now.

You need to be able to allow yourself to be thoroughly humiliated. You need to be able to face up to the prospect of public embarrassment. In fact, you need to learn to live with the constant possibility of humiliation. Be willing to make yourself look like a fool. And, when someone jokes about something in your play, tell them it's nothing compared to what happened in another of your plays one time . . .

Jealousy

No one wants your play. You are longlisted for yet another competition, but you never win. Every day you read about other playwrights, the great plays they have written, and what have you done? NOTHING! Naturally, you start to get very, very jealous.

You see other writers getting produced. You see other writers, your age or younger, doing really well. You go to see their new play. You think it's terrible. You don't understand why people think they are so great. You don't understand why your plays don't get produced instead. There's a simple way to avoid this jealousy: don't judge yourself by the success of others. Ignore them. Write a play. Write another play. Keep writing plays. You have control over this. Leave other writers to their successes and failures, and control what you can, control the work you do. Don't let jealousy turn into resentment, because your resentment might turn onto bitterness, and that bitterness could stop you writing altogether.

Whether we like to admit it or not, the wonderful world of playwriting is a competitive environment. Some playwrights will get breaks before others. Some playwrights will be praised more than others. It doesn't matter. What matters is that we do the work. Make people jealous of your work ethic, that's not a bad place to start.

Jealousy, doubt, hurt, these are tricky feelings that we all have to deal with. Perhaps you just need to find a friend, or therapist, you can talk to about it. Don't make hate or self-loathing your default position. I have read some sublime plays that have never been produced. The playwrights were unlucky. Their plays didn't land on the right desk, or in the right inbox, at the right time. The only thing you can do is to try to make your own luck. Keep writing. Keep submitting. Endure. But don't waste your time getting jealous, those writers you're jealous of have their own jealousies to deal with.

Giving up

When it gets bad – when the pressure, exposure, anxiety, vulnerability, rejection and humiliation get too much – you might start to think about giving up. Don't. At least, don't make an absolute once and forever decision. Give yourself some time off. Then come back and reconsider.

In the thirty or so years that I have been writing I have only seriously considered giving up once. A show I had written didn't go well; it was not entirely my own fault, but I wrote it, so I cannot absolve myself of all responsibility. I felt defeated. I felt humiliated. I felt ill. I started to think very seriously about giving up. Because I have a bit of an obsession with football, I wrote a list of all my plays, scored them like a football match – a successful play might be a 3–1 win, an unsuccessful play might be a 2–0 defeat – and entered my results into a league table. I worked out that at the end of the season, I would have been relegated. I really was that fed up. I decided to give myself a few more weeks to think about it before making a decision. I set a date. As the date approached, I was reading a book called *The Conquest of Happiness* by Bertrand Russell and, purely by chance, I came across a passage in the book about a test a playwright can take in order to know whether to give up or not, 'The test is this: do you produce because you feel an urgent compulsion to express certain ideas or feelings, or are you actuated by the desire for applause?'[6] I knew I liked applause. I knew I liked laughter. But I also knew I had things to say; things that I believed were important, and it was more important to me to get the things I wanted to say over to an audience in a theatre than to receive an ovation. I decided to keep writing.

How does a playwright endure other people's opinions? Know you are doing it for the right reason. Your right reason may be different to my right reason, but I tend to agree with Russell that if you are doing it because applause and adulation are more important than the work, you might find a more suitable career working on a reality TV show. If you really want to do this, and you know that you are doing it for reasons that make sense to you, above and beyond stardom, do it. And don't be so damn hard on yourself. If you so much as succeed in getting one play produced, that is one hell of an achievement.

Some advice . . .

Write. Get the work done. Control what you can. Don't obsess about what you can't control. Don't put unnecessary pressure on yourself. Remember that everyone was an imposter once. Theatre companies don't hate you. Find strategies to help deal with the exposure. Find a mentor, someone you can turn to when things get confusing, nasty or desperate. Don't forget that you are not alone: join a writers' group, or set one up, because it really helps to be surrounded by like-minds and spirits; join the WGGB, or whatever writers' organization that you think is right for you, organizations like the WGGB fight for your rights, they deserve your support. We all get jealous, but try not to let it take over. Rather than obsess about the success of [*insert writer's name here*] challenge yourself to work harder today than you did yesterday. Vulnerability is courage. Rejection is part of the job. Collaboration is unavoidable, so make the most of it. Some people will like your plays, some won't. You can't please everyone, so don't try. Critics will write what critics will write. Read it and deal with it. Or don't read it. Don't let star ratings dominate your life because one person's star rating is not an indication of universal praise or opprobrium. Humiliation is a part of the learning curve. Check in with Bertrand Russell before you give up. Talk to other writers about mental health, we need to admit to each other that this is a challenging occupation.

Finally . . .

If you are struggling, find a listening ear, seek support, get therapy, and don't suffer in silence. Perhaps take some time out, give yourself a month off, or two months, or six, or a year. Taking time out doesn't mean you have given up, it doesn't mean you're a bad writer, it just means you're taking a bit of a break. You don't need to be on the brink of a breakdown to write a great play. You don't need to *suffer for your art*, you need to look after yourself. Don't feed the *Myth of the Tortured Artist*, it is dangerous and unnecessary. Seek out help. Seek out yourself. Then write all those extraordinary plays that reside in that brilliant mind of yours!

3.5 YOU ARE THE FUTURE OF PLAYWRITING

If you are going to be the future of playwriting, and you *are* going to be the future of playwriting, it is essential for you to engage with what is happening *now*. Because it is only by understanding what is happening *now* that you can begin to think about what you are going to do next. And your next play is the future of playwriting.

You need to ask yourself what some of the best contemporary playwrights are doing and what you can learn from them. Not what they are writing about, but how they are writing about it; about their techniques; about whether you might want to build on some of their techniques, or whether, having identified what they are doing, you want to run in the opposite direction. It's all about *now*. Except that *now* is likely to be *then* by the time you read this, so you may have to sit down and do some work on your own *now*. You should also bear in mind that my assessment of what the playwriting animal is doing today is going to be somewhat slippery, given that it is subjective, and that the moment I try to pin it down, it will have moved again. Playwriting is an elusive beast at the best of times, but it is worth the effort because we can learn a phenomenal amount from the best of our peers.

You might discover your writing is very fashionable, in which case, perhaps ask yourself what you can do to give it a bit of extra edge. You might discover your writing is very unfashionable, in which case, you might decide to just keep doing what you are doing until the wheel of fashion rotates back around to the way you write, and your style of writing becomes all the rage again. You might be inspired to play more with structure, with language, form, character, audience perception or audience engagement. Most importantly, by connecting with what is currently happening, there is a better than average chance that you will grow as a playwright.

I think something has shifted in playwriting in the last decade, and the thing that seems to have shifted the most is the number of brilliant, theatrically driven plays written by a new wave of predominantly female playwrights. There are some men writing extraordinary plays, but it is mostly the work of the women that has excited me and suggests that new theatrical writing has a very bright future. Of course, it may well be the case that there have always been a lot of brilliant, theatrical plays by women, and the problem has been that these plays just weren't getting produced. It is sadly still the case that fewer women playwrights are produced than men, commenting on the 2020 Sphinx Theatre *Women in Theatre Report* in the Guardian, playwright April De Angelis said, 'I keep hearing how things have improved for women in theatre, and that it's not a problem but the reality is that only 35% of new playwrights are women.'[1] This is the kind of statistic that just doesn't make sense to me. I have run playwriting workshops for thirty years and, in my experience, the gender balance in those workshops is, on average, something like 80:20 in favour of women. How does that translate into an almost inverse proportion in terms of production? There is still a long way to go in terms of equality, but the women who are being produced today are writing some of the most incredible and intrinsically theatrical plays I have ever seen. These playwrights play more with form and idea, and don't seem to stick so rigidly to linear naturalistic narratives. There is so much we can learn from them.

If you like things the way they are, if you think all of the plays you go to see are brilliant, if you think all of the plays you read are written by geniuses and there is nothing more you or anyone else can do, then you are wrong. There is plenty you can do. You can do something new. You can do more. You can go further. You can be the playwright that shakes the world out of its aesthetic slumber.

I have a challenge for you: the next time you are writing a play for the stage I would like you to ask yourself this question: What is it about my play that is intrinsically theatrical? Or, to put it another way, what is it about my play that means it demands it be produced in a theatre space rather than in another medium? I want to challenge you to build upon some of the things that I have noticed some of the more interesting contemporary playwrights doing today, and to embrace the ideas that I have put forward in this book.

I challenge you

I challenge you to write plays that are intrinsically theatrical; to use music; to use movement and mime and dance; to use mask and puppets; to put ceremony into your plays; to use a chorus; to talk to the audience.

I challenge you to tear down the fourth wall and run rampant through the ruins.

I challenge you to find new ways to structure a play; to use other art forms to construct the framework; to shape the form to the inspiration; to let the form tell the story; to use alternative structures.

I challenge you to redefine characterization; to show the actor inside the character; to allow characters to comment on the action, to let them discuss the play they are in; to create a character based on the idea behind your play; to put yourself in your play.

I challenge you to be a dramatic poet; to use metaphor and symbol; to play with the way text looks on the page; to love words, love every single glorious one of them, love the meaning of them, love the sound of them, and never ever waste a single one; to invent your own grammar system and play with punctuation; to put some pictures in your play; to speak the stage directions; to use no stage directions; to use verse; to reflect the emotion in the play in the presentation of your text.

I challenge you to reinvent naturalism as a potent, new theatrical force.

I challenge you to use sign language, captions and audio description.

I challenge you to write large-scale plays.

I challenge you to write plays with BIG ideas.

I challenge you to take risks.

I challenge you to shock, to break things and to provoke.

I challenge you to write with every element of theatre-making given equal importance.

I challenge you to acknowledge and involve your audience.

I challenge you to utilize casting as a creative tool; perhaps by refusing to attribute parts or by casting against type; to use creative doubling.

I **challenge you** to play with metaphysics, with metamorphosis and with meta itself.

I **challenge you** to use a prologue, and an epilogue, and to tell your audience to clap.

And that is not all. As a human being who writes plays:

I **challenge you** to only write plays about what is important to you.

I **challenge you** to write like only you can write.

I **challenge you** to stand on the shoulders of giants so that through your eyes we can see further than we have ever seen before.

I **challenge you** to write with a different process every time you write a new play.

I **challenge you** to fully embrace collaboration.

I **challenge you** to take your writing seriously, and to take the business of your writing seriously.

I **challenge you** to look after yourself, to take care of your mental health and the mental health of other playwrights.

I **challenge you** to write plays because it is what you need to do. To write plays because it the most important thing for you to do. To take pride in the work you do. It's not easy being a playwright, the hours are long, getting a play produced is hard, the money is pathetic, the critics can be vile, and the public can be fickle. But at the end of the day, it's an incredible way to spend your life. And we still have so much to discover.

I **challenge <u>YOU</u> to be the future of playwriting.**

EPILOGUE

A Letter to the playwrights of the future

Dear Playwrights of the Future,

Please stand on our shoulders, as we did on those that came before us. Please learn from our innovations as well as our mistakes. Please always have an open mind, a willingness to listen and to investigate new ideas. Please stay inquisitive. Please let your plays be eclectic and never static. Please celebrate your fellow playwrights. We are all in this together. We need to appreciate and respect each other. Please surprise us with things we never thought of doing and make our ghosts jealous of your wonderful ideas. Please continue to question the very nature of playwriting and the dominant forms of theatrical presentation of your day. Push forward. Reframe playwriting for your own time. Please keep asking BIG questions. And please don't forget us. Please keep producing our plays. We wrote them so that we could talk to you when we are long gone.

Most importantly, please keep writing plays.

We wish you every success.

With love,

The Playwrights of Today

REASONS TO BE A PLAYWRIGHT

This final chapter is for the bad days. The days when you can't write, when you don't feel like writing, when you don't see the point in writing. On those days, perhaps come here, pick a number, and start reading.

1 A play can change people, minds and attitudes; it can enlighten, entertain and eviscerate.

2 A play can inform the debate; can initiate the debate; can close the debate.

3 A play can make, remake and record history.

4 A play can be a metaphor, a prism through which to view humanity, life and existence in a different way.

5 A play can remind us what it means to be human, to have empathy, to laugh, to cry; it can remind us what it is to be inhuman, to hate, to cause misery, to be cruel.

6 A play can ask questions – big questions, small questions, hard questions, very hard questions – and it can offer answers, or leave you to come to your own conclusions.

7 A play can be a starburst of imagination that brings joy, insight, recognition, understanding, fear.

8 A play can shape an idea, an opinion, a feeling, a country, a world.

9 A play can be a philosophical statement framed in darkness or light, as tragedy or comedy.

10 A play can enable us to see, hear, touch, taste, feel, think and reason.

11 A play is people; people like you and me; people from the past, present and future. Good people, bad people, complicated people

and people who are wonderful, evil, inspirational, vile, beautiful, downtrodden, happy and sad.

12 A play is the moods we have, the moods we might have, the moods we are.

13 A play is a living reflection of who we are, what we are, why we are; and, it can help us understand who we are, what we are, why we are.

14 A play can be like the blast of a trumpet, blaring out a truth; a shaft of light, illuminating an idea; a bell, that resounds deeply inside us.

15 A play is a conversation with other human beings. You can agree with a play. You can disagree with a play. A play can make you furious. A play can make you love the idea of love. A play can make you hate the idea of love.

16 A play can observe and comment. A play can observe and say nothing.

17 A play can reflect. It can reflect your life back at you. It can reflect the life of someone you know, love, despise or admire. It can reflect the lives of others. It can make you reflect.

18 A play can destroy. It can smash the world to pieces.

19 A play can educate, extend the moral imagination, offer insights into other lives, cultures, ways, choices, many of which we might never experience directly.

20 A play can be a window on another world, a world we never knew existed.

21 A play can be a meditation. Or it can provoke us to change the world.

22 A play can make us gasp in horror or scream with delight.

23 A play can help us to empathize, with an idea, with a character, with ourselves, with a stranger.

24 A play gives each of us the power to live another life, the life of the characters on stage.

25 A play can help us to forget our worries when we need to by taking us to another world.

26 A play can speak to different people in as many ways as there are individual audience members.

27 A play is a unique and communal human experience at the same time.

28 A play is an essential, living, human ritual.

29 A play can make us regret; make us applaud with joy.

30 A play can bring human beings together. It can push us apart.

31 A play can comment on the world we live in, or it can ignore the world we live in and make a new one.

32 A play can help us to see ourselves more clearly.

33 A play can articulate things we feel but have never managed to clearly express for ourselves.

34 A play is the essence of humanity.

35 A play can be an argument between conflicting points of view, a dialectical confrontation that can lead to a new truth.

36 A play can mean one thing to one person and another thing to someone else. A play can be a metaphor, a chameleon.

37 A play can celebrate our diversity; confront our bigotry; undermine the status quo and our stability.

38 A play is an ultimate expression of human existence.

39 A play can be a revolutionary act.

40 A play can make us feel more deeply, strive more intently, and experience happiness and sadness more profoundly.

41 A play can be a lesson in living. And dying.

42 A play can bring meaning and purpose to humanity; a communication of our common story that brings us together as humans.

43 A play is important because human stories are important.

44 A play is important because the world we live in is important.

45 A play is a vision of how one person (the playwright) sees the world, shared with everyone. It is unique and universal at the same time.

46 A play can take people in a different direction (or further in the same direction) aesthetically, intellectually, emotionally, spiritually.

47 A play is a testimony of the human condition. It encompasses our struggles, our successes, our tantrums, our celebrations; it can touch every aspect of what it means to be human.

48 A play is a statement. A way to understand ourselves.

49 A play enables you to tell people exactly what you think for two and a half hours without being interrupted!

50 A play is who you are.

51 A play is your obsessions and preoccupations, shared with the world. Offered as a salve or a provocation to others.

52 A play is what you want to say.

53 A play is your imagination, your memory, a distorted experience, an incident reinvented, peopled with inventions, real people and composite characters from the life you have lived.

54 A play is your unique fingerprint, your unique contribution to this mad, mad world that we all live in.

55 A play is how you articulate your ideas, thoughts, opinions.

56 A play is a sharing. Sharing your life. Your past. Your present. Your beliefs. Your passions. Your private thoughts. Your public thoughts. A play is sharing your story. Your experiences. Your obsessions. Your vision. Your dreams. It is your life's experience shared.

57 A play can be what scares you.

58 A play is your gift, offering meaning, ideas, participation.

59 A play that you write can make people feel less alone.

60 A play that you write can be a rational recourse in an irrational universe.

61 You can explore tiny, microscopic worlds, or a universe, or infinity.

62 You can investigate myths – and, you can create your own myths.

63 You can write BIG ideas or miniscule moments.

64 You can write on a huge scale or for just one person.

65 You can write a play that is the length of one breath or a play that lasts days or years.

66 You can live content in the knowledge you have given something of yourself to the future.

67 You can write a play as an antidote to the absurdity of life.

68 You can write a play confirming the absurdity of life.

69 You can write a play that causes an outpouring of emotion.

70 You can write a play that brings happiness.

71 You can write a play that causes a riot.

72 A play is the individual expression of the human experience – we are the only animal that does this.

73 Seeing ourselves reflected in a play makes us feel the shared human experience.

74 A play is the ultimate expression of our conscious and unconscious existence.

75 A play can be aesthetically as well as politically rebellious.

76 A play can be an act of solidarity.

77 A play is an act of freedom.

78 A play is an act of dignity.

79 A play is an act of joy.

80 A play is an act of peace.

81 A play is an act of kindness.

82 A play is an act of love.

83 A play is an act of fury.

84 A play is a human and humane act.

85 A play is the art form most like life. It's performed by real people in a real space in real time.

86 A play is a laboratory for life.

87 A play can be ridiculous. And so can life.

88 A play can be chaotic. And so can life.

89 Life can be sublime. And so can a play.

90 Life can be terrible. And so can a play.

91 A play can offer catharsis, the cleansing of fear and pity.

92 A play can sear a moment into our minds for the rest of our lives.

93 A play can be spectacular, or it can be a bare stage and our imagination.

94 A play can heal.

95 A play can wound.

96 A play can energize.

97 A play can educate and elevate our souls.

98 A play can help us live good lives, better lives, wiser lives.

99 A play can remind us that we are not alone.

100 A play can help us to re-see the things we thought familiar.

101 A play can teach us that the things we thought we knew – we don't.

102 A play can help us to feel involved – it can speak to us.

103 A play can reinforce beliefs, destroy beliefs.

104 A play can make us hopeful.

105 A play can rebalance us.

106 A play can enable us to think in new ways, see things in a new light, embrace new ideas.

107 A play can challenge us to look again at the world, to look again at ourselves.

108 A play can tell us what really matters, directly or indirectly.

109 A play can put us back in touch with ourselves.

110 A play is a corporeal, breathing imprint of our lives.

111 A play is a living thing.

112 A play is immortal.

113 A play is life.

114 A play is us, reflected back at us, and we are the only thing that we have got.

NOTES

Chapter 1.1

1 Friedrich Nietzsche, *The Birth of Tragedy,* Shaun Whiteside (trans.), Michael Tanner (ed.) (London: Penguin Classics, Penguin Books, 2003 – first published 1872) p. 13. Some people might claim that when Nietzsche talks about 'art', he is referring explicitly to music, however I would argue that the music that truly moved him was that of Wagner, to whom this remark was addressed, it was opera, it was music and spectacle, it was performance, it was drama, it was theatre. And we shouldn't forget that his love of art was initially spawned by his love of Greek literature, by Homer and the tragedians of ancient Greece.

2 Eric Bentley, *The Life of the Drama* (New York: Applause Books, 1991 – first published 1964) p. 147.

3 Elinor Fuchs, *EF's Visit to a Small Planet, some questions to ask a play,* The Routledge Companion to Dramaturgy, Magda Romanska (ed.) (Abingdon: Routledge, 2016) pp. 403–7 (p. 403).

4 Interview with Thornton Wilder, 1956, *Playwrights at Work,* George Plympton (ed.) (London: Harvill, 2000) p. 13.

5 Shakespeare, William. *Hamlet,* G. B. Harrison (ed.) (Harmondsworth: Penguin Books, 1978) 3.2.21–23 p. 86.

6 The quote often attributed to Brecht is, '*Art is not a mirror to hold up to society, but a hammer with which to shape it.*' However, there is no source for this quote which seems to have been appropriated and paraphrased from Leon Trotsky who wrote, '*Art, it is said, is not a mirror, but a hammer: it does not reflect, it shapes.*' *Literature and Revolution* (1923) Rose Strunsky (trans. 1925) uncopyrighted 1957 Russell & Russell, New York edition, Ch. 4: Futurism, p. 120. https://www.marxists.org/archive/trotsky/1924/lit_revo/ch04.htm

7 '*Ars Longa, vita brevis*' – Seneca quotes Hippocrates in the opening paragraph of his essay, *On the Shortness of Life,* 49 CE (London: Penguin Books, 2004) p. 1.

8 Sophocles entered *Oedipus Rex* as part of his trilogy in the City Dionysia in 427 BCE, but the first prize that year went to a playwright called Philocles. One of the most famous plays in the history of drama was entered into a competition and came second. Think about that next time you get shortlisted for a prize but don't win.

Chapter 1.2

1 *The Hostage* was first produced at the Damer Theatre, Dublin, in 1958 in an Irish language version entitled *An Giall*, before being translated by the author and developed by Joan Littlewood and Theatre Workshop and produced at Stratford East later the same year.

2 Stratford East, 1958.

3 Stratford East, 1963.

4 Paula Vogel quoted in *Fifty Playwrights on their Craft*, Caroline Jester (ed.) and Caridad Svich (London: Bloomsbury, 2018) pp. 54–5.

5 Lucy Prebble quoted in *Fifty Playwrights on their Craft*, Jester, Svich pp. 214–15.

6 Bentley, *The Life of the Drama*, pp. 143–6.

7 Bentley, *The Life of the Drama*, p. 146.

Chapter 1.3

1 Caryl Churchill, *A Number*, in *Plays: Four* (London: Nick Hern Books, 2009) p. 205. First produced at the Royal Court, London, 2002.

2 James Graham, *This House*, first produced at the National Theatre, London, 2012.

3 Peter Morgan, *The Audience*, first produced at the Gielgud Theatre, London, 2013.

Chapter 1.4

1 *A View from the Bridge* was first produced at the Coronet Theatre on Broadway in 1955.

2 *Guys & Dolls* by Frank Loesser, Jo Swerling and Abe Burrows was first produced in an out-of-town try-out at the Schubert Theatre, Philadelphia, before moving to Broadway in 1950.

3 *The Interval*, interview with Paula Vogel, 2017 https://www.theintervalny.com/interviews/2017/04/an-interview-with-paula-vogel/

4 Paula Vogel, *The Long Christmas Ride Home* (New York: Theatre Communications Group, 2004) p. 5. First produced at the Long Wharf Theatre, New Haven, in 2003.

5 *Indecent*, first produced by Yale Rep and La Jolla Playhouse in 2015.

6 *Our Town*, first produced at the McCarter Theatre, Princeton, 1938.

7 *The Interval*, interview with Paula Vogel.

8 Newton wasn't the first to make this assertion, the idea can be dated back to the twelfth century and possibly beyond to the blind Greek mythological giant, Orion, whose servant, Cedalion, sat on his shoulders to serve as his eyes.

9 T. S. Eliot, *The Sacred Wood: Essays on Poetry and Criticism* (London: Methuen, 1920) p. 59.

10 Harold Bloom, *Foreword: Who Else Is There, Living with Shakespeare*, Susannah Carson (ed.) (New York: Vintage Books, 2013) pp. vii–xiii (p. vii).

11 At the date of publication this play had yet to be produced.

12 *Hamilton: The Revolution*, Lin-Manuel Miranda and James McCarter (London: Little, Brown, 2016) p. 94. *Hamilton* was first produced at the Public Theatre, New York, in 2015.

13 Interview with Lynn Nottage in *The Guardian* (2016). https://www.theguardian.com/stage/2016/feb/17/lynn-nottage-sweat-donald-trump-bernie-sanders

14 Thornton Wilder, Preface to *Our Town and Other Plays* (London: Penguin Books, 1962) p. 14. Joyce's novel *Finnegan's Wake* was published in 1939; Wilder's play, *The Skin of Our Teeth* was first produced at the Shubert Theatre, New Haven, in 1942.

15 *Baltimore Waltz*, first produced by Circle Repertory Company, New York, 1992; *How I Learned to Drive*, first produced by Vineyard Theatre, New York, 1997; *Indecent*, 2015 (see note 5).

Chapter 2.1

1 August Comte (1798–1857) developed his Positivist Philosophy in a series of writings between 1830 and 1842 and in his book *A General View of Positivism* (1844) which advocated the empirical, scientific study of society and rejected intuitive knowledge and theism.

2 Charles Darwin (1809–82) was an English Naturalist who is credited for developing the theory of natural selection.

3 Emile Zola (1840–1902) was a French writer who is best known for his naturalistic novels and plays, including *Thérèse Raquin* which he wrote as a novel in 1868 and adapted for the stage in 1873.

4 Nick Payne, *Constellations*, first produced at the Royal Court, London, 2012.

5 David Mamet, *Oleanna*, first produced by Back Bay Theatre Company, Cambridge, Mass. 1992.

6 Alice Birch, *Anatomy of a Suicide*, first produced at the Royal Court, London, 2017.

Chapter 2.2

1 *Reasons to be Cheerful* was first produced on tour by Graeae Theatre Company in 2010.

2 *The Big Life* was first produced at the Theatre Royal Stratford East in 2004.

3 *Bad Blood Blues* was first produced at the Theatre Royal Stratford East in 2008.

4 Denis Diderot, *Discours sur la poésie dramatique* in *D. Diderot Ouvres Complètes III* (Paris: Larousse 1970) p. 453.

5 Shakespeare, *Romeo and Juliet*, Prologue 1–14 (Cambridge: Cambridge University Press) p. 3.

6 *An Octoroon* was first produced at Soho Rep, New York, 2014.

7 Branden Jacobs-Jenkins, *An Octoroon* (London: Nick Hern Books, 2018) p. 10.

8 Duncan Macmillan, *People, Places & Things*, first produced at the Dorfman, National Theatre, London, 2015.

9 Matthew Lopez, *The Inheritance*, first produced at the Young Vic, London, 2018.

10 Donja R. Love, *One in Two*, first produced at the Pershing Square Signature Center, 2019.

11 Lucy Prebble, *Enron*, first produced at the Festival Theatre, Chichester, 2009.

12 Alice Birch, *Revolt. She Said. Revolt Again.* First produced at the Royal Shakespeare Company, 2014.

13 Ben Jonson, *Bartholomew Fair* in *Ben Jonson Four Plays*, Robert N. Watson (ed.) (London: Bloomsbury Methuen Drama, 2014) pp. 519–25 (p. 524).

14 *A Very Expensive Poison* was first produced at the Old Vic, London, 2019.

15 Lucy Prebble, *A Very Expensive Poison* (London: Methuen, 2019) p. 144.

16 Prebble, *A Very Expensive Poison*, p. 117.

17 *Jesus Christ Superstar* was first produced at the Mark Hellinger Theatre, New York, in 1971.

18 *Amadeus* was first produced at the National Theatre, London, in 1979.

19 *Fun Home* was first produced at the Public Theatre, New York, in 2013.

20 Robert Bolt, *A Man for All Seasons*, first produced at the Globe Theatre, now the Gielgud Theatre, London, in 1960 (originally a radio play).

21 *Dancing at Lughnasa* was first produced at the Abbey Theatre, Dublin in 1990.

22 David Edgar's adaptation of *Nicholas Nickleby* was first produced at the Royal Shakespeare Company in 1980.

23 *Navy Pier* was first produced at Soho Theatre, London, in 2001.

24 Shakespeare, William, *Hamlet*, G. B. Harrison (ed.) (Harmondsworth: Penguin Books, 1978) 1.2.67. p. 33.

25 Shakespeare, *Julius Caesar*, D. R. Elloway (ed.) (London: Macmillan Shakespeare, 1974) 2.2.132–3. p. 101.

26 *Fleabag* began life as a one-woman play that was first produced at the Edinburgh Festival Fringe in 2013.

27 Shakespeare, *Hamlet*, G. B. Harrison (ed.) 3.1.56–58. p. 81.

28 Clare Barron, *Dance Nation* (London: Oberon Books, 2018) pp. 53–8. First produced at Playwrights Horizons, New York, in 2018.

29 Jasmine Lee-Jones, *Seven Methods of Killing Kylie Jenner* (London: Oberon Books, 2019) pp. 73–8. First produced at the Royal Court, London, 2019.

30 Brian Friel, *Faith Healer*, first produced at the Longacre Theatre, New York, 1979.

31 Duncan Macmillan and Jonny Donohoe, *Every Brilliant Thing*, first produced at the Edinburgh Festival, 2014.

32 Arinze Kene, *Misty*, first produced at the Bush Theatre, London, 2018.

33 Roy Williams and Clint Dyer, *Death of England*, first produced at the National Theatre, 2019.

34 Annie Baker, *John*, first produced at Signature Theatre, New York, 2015.

35 Richard Bean, *One Man, Two Guvnors*, first produced at the National Theatre, 2011.

36 Ella Hickson, *The Writer* (London: Nick Hern Books, 2018) pp. 33–5. First produced at the Almeida Theatre, London, 2018.

37 Paul Sirett, *Rat Pack Confidential* (London: Oberon Books, 2002) pp. 9–10. First produced at Nottingham Playhouse, 2002.

38 Tim Crouch, *An Oak Tree*, first produced at the Traverse Theatre, Edinburgh, 2005.

39 Tim Crouch, *The Author*, first produced at the Royal Court Upstairs, London, 2009.

40 Birch, *Revolt. She Said. Revolt Again.* (London: Oberon Modern Plays, 2014) p. 19.

41 Jacobs-Jenkins, *An Octoroon*, p. 72.

42 Jonson, *Volpone*, Robert N. Watson (ed.) Epilogue 1–6. p. 169.

43 Shakespeare, William, *A Midsummer Night's Dream*, Stanley Wells (ed.) (Harmondsworth: New Penguin Shakespeare, 1981) 5.1.427–8. p. 122.

44 Lee-Jones, *Seven Methods of Killing Kylie Jenner*, p. 85.

Chapter 2.3

1 Aristotle, *Poetics* 330 BCE, Aristotle, Horace, Longinus *Classical Literary Criticism* (Harmondsworth: Penguin Classics, 1982) T. S. Dorsch (trans.) p. 41.

2 Aristotle (Dorsch), p. 41.

3 Aristotle (Dorsch), p. 43.

4 Aristotle (Dorsch), p. 43.

5 Bharata Muni, *The Nāṭyaśāstra*, Adya Rangacharya (ed.) (New Delhi: Munshiram Manoharlal Publishers, 2007) p. 159.

6 John Carley writes: 'Master Zeami reputedly likened jo-ha-kyū to the course of a mountain river: *jo* is the tributary's gentle rill; ha the river in spate as it cuts back and forth between mountain peaks; and *kyu* the plunge of a mighty waterfall into a deep and silent pool.' John Carley, *Renku Reckoner* (Darlington Richards, 2015) pp. 90–1.

7 Lope de Vega, *The New Art of Writing Plays (1609)* Brewster, W. T. (trans.) (Charleston: Bibliobazaar, 2009) p. 34.

8 Steve Waters, *The Secret Life of Plays* (London: Nick Hern Books, 2010) p. 13.

9 Arthur Laurents, *Original Story By . . .* (New York: Applause, 2000) p. 350.

10 Sarah Kane *4.48 Psychosis* in *Sarah Kane Complete Plays* (London: Bloomsbury Methuen, 2019) p. 208. First produced at the Royal Court Upstairs, 2000.

11 Laura Wade, *The Watsons*, first produced at the Minerva Theatre, Chichester, 2018.

12 August Strindberg, *A Dream Play*, first produced at the Swedish Theatre, Stockholm, 1907.

13 Arthur Miller, *After the Fall*, first produced at the ANTA Washington Square Theatre, New York, 1964

14 Florian Zeller, *The Father (Le Père)*, first produced at the Théâtre Hébertot, Paris, 2012.

15 Albert Camus, *The Myth of Sisyphus* (London: Penguin Classics, 2013) p. 89.

16 Samuel Beckett, *Waiting for Godot (En attendant Godot)*, first produced at the Théâtre de Babylone, Paris, 1953.

17 Arthur Schnitzler, *La Ronde (Reigen)*, written in 1897 but not produced until 1920 in Berlin because of the play's dissection of sexual morality.

18 Enda Walsh, Glen Hansard, Markéta Irglová, *Once*, first produced at the American Repertory Theatre, Cambridge, 2011 (based on a 2007 film of the same name).

19 Dylan Thomas, *Under Milk Wood* had its first reading at The Poetry Center, New York, 1953, before being recorded for BBC Radio in 1954. The first stage production was at the Théâtre de la Cour Saint-Pierre, Geneva, 1954.

20 Moira Buffini, *Loveplay*, first produced by the Royal Shakespeare Company, 2001.

21 Thornton Wilder, *The Long Christmas Dinner*, first performed by Yale Dramatic Associate and Vassar Philaletheis Society, 1931.

22 Harold Pinter, *Betrayal*, first produced at the National Theatre, London, 1978.

23 Caryl Churchill, *Top Girls*, first produced at the Royal Court, London, 1982.

24 Caryl Churchill, *Blue Heart*, first produced at the Royal Court, London, 1997.

25 For an inspiring exploration of story, including meandering and branching structure, please see John Truby *The Anatomy of Story: 22 Steps to Becoming a Master Storyteller* (New York: Faber and Faber, 2007).

26 Nick Payne, *Constellations* (London: Faber and Faber) 2012, p. 2.

27 Simon Stephens, *Heisenberg*, first produced at Manhattan Theatre Club, New York, 2017.

28 Samuel Beckett, *Happy Days*, first produced at Cherry Lane Theatre, New York, 1961.

29 Paula Vogel, *Indecent*, (New York: Theatre Communications Group, 2017) p. vii.

30 Hickson, *The Writer*, p. 57.

31 Christopher Booker, *The Seven Basic Plots* (London: Bloomsbury Continuum, 2019).

32 Rory Johnson, *Letter in the Guardian*, September 1991. https://www.theguardian.com/notesandqueries/query/0,,-1553,00.html For a brilliant explication of these seven stories, with two further additions, please see Stephen Jeffreys *Playwriting* (London: Nick Hern Books, 2019) pp. 218–44.

33 Stan Heywood, *Letter in the Guardian*, September 1991. https://www.theguardian.com/notesandqueries/query/0,,-1553,00.html

Chapter 2.4

1 David Edgar, *How Plays Work* (London: Nick Hern Books, 2009) p. 48.

2 Harold Pinter, Introduction to *Four Plays* (London: Faber and Faber, 1986) p. ix.

3 Aristotle (Dorsch), p. 51.

4 Eddie Carbone is the protagonist is Arthur Miller's play *A View from the Bridge*.

5 Thornton Wilder, 'Some Thoughts on Playwriting' in *Collected Plays & Writings on Theater* (New York: The Library of Congress, 2007) pp. 694–703 (p. 700).

6 A somewhat more sanitized form of the *satyr play* can be found in the rustic romantic comedies of Elizabethan writers like John Lyly and Robert Greene – plays that, in turn, influenced the more bucolically infused plays of William Shakespeare.

7 *Blasted* was first produced at the Royal Court, London, in 1995.

8 *The Trackers of Oxyrhynchus* was first produced at the *Stadium of Delphi* in Greece in 1988 before a run at the National Theatre two years later.

9 debbie tucker green, *Random,* first produced at the Royal Court, 2008.

10 *Beauty and the Beast* by Laurence Boswell, first produced at the Young Vic, London, 1996.

11 *Caroline, or Change* by Tony Kushner and Jeanine Tesori, first produced Public Theater, New York, 2003.

12 Paula Vogel, *The Long Christmas Ride Home,* written underneath the title on the cover and title page.

13 Bunraku originated in mid-sixteenth-century Japan and uses large puppets manipulated by three puppeteers dressed in black. The character dialogue is spoken by a single performer/narrator who voices the different characters using a range of vocal techniques.

14 Paula Vogel, *The Long Christmas Ride Home,* p. 6.

15 Prebble, *A Very Expensive Poison*, p. 56

16 Barron, *Dance Nation,* p. 9.

17 Barron, *Dance Nation,* p.19.

18 Paula Vogel, *How I Learned to Drive* (New York: Theatre Communications Group, 2018) p. 7.

19 Gregory Burke, *Black Watch*, first produced by National Theatre of Scotland at the Edinburgh Festival, 2006.

20 Jacobs-Jenkins, *An Octoroon,* p. 9.

21 Oscar G. Brockett, Franklin J. Hildy, *History of the Theatre* (Harlow: Pearson, 2014) p. 111.

22 Duncan Macmillan, *People, Places & Things* (London: Oberon Books, 2015) p. 59.

23 Mark Joyal, *Authors of Classical Greece,* British Museum Website https://www.bl.uk/greek-manuscripts/articles/manuscripts-of-classical-greek-authors

24 Martin Crimp, *Attempts on Her Life* (London: Faber and Faber, 1997) pp. 65–73. First produced at the Royal Court, London, 1997.

25 Birch, *Revolt. She Said. Revolt Again.*, p. 51

26 Birch, *Revolt. She Said. Revolt Again.*, p. 60

27 Hickson, *The Writer,* pp. 11–30.

Chapter 2.5

1 Aristotle (Dorsch) p. 65.

2 Shakespeare, William, *Macbeth*, G. K. Hunter (ed.) (Harmondsworth: New Penguin Books, 1967) 5.5.19–28. p. 132.

3 Peter Hall, *Advice to the Players* (London: Oberon Books, 2003) p. 18.

4 Shakespeare, William, *Hamlet*, G. B. Harrison (ed.) (Harmondsworth: Penguin Books, 1978) 3.1.56–59. p. 81.

5 David Harrower, *Blackbird* (London: Faber and Faber, 2006) p. 1. *Blackbird* was first produced at the Edinburgh International Festival in 2005.

6 Peter Gill, *The York Realist* (London, Faber and Faber, 2001) p. 7. *The York Realist* was first produced at the Lowry, Manchester, 2001.

7 Also known as the 'Churchill-Slash' due to this being a technique first used by Caryl Churchill.

8 At the time of writing this book, the text of *Shed: Exploded View* was unpublished.

9 debbie tucker green interview in *The Independent* 27 April 2003 https://www.independent.co.uk/arts-entertainment/theatre-dance/features/debbie-tucker-green-if-you-hate-the-show-at-least-you-have-passion-117081.html

10 Barron, *Dance Nation*, p. 38

11 Barron, *Dance Nation*, p. 12.

12 Barron, *Dance Nation*, p. 16.

13 Birch, *Revolt. She Said. Revolt Again.*, p. 19.

14 Lucy Kirkwood, *Chimerica* (London: Nick Hern Books, 2013) p. 11. First produced at the Almeida Theatre, London, 2013.

15 Annie Baker, *The Antipodes* (London: Nick Hern Books, 2019) p. 9. First produced at Signature Theatre, New York, 2017.

16 Lucy Kirkwood, *Mosquitoes* (London: Nick Hern Books, 2017) p.10. First produced at the National Theatre, London, 2017.

17 Barron, *Dance Nation*, pp. 53–8.

18 Lee-Jones, *Seven Methods of Killing Kylie Jenner*, pp. 74–8.

19 Birch, *Revolt. She Said. Revolt Again.*, pp. 65–74.

20 Tarrel Alvin McCraney, *The Brothers Size*, first produced at the Young Vic, London, 2007.

21 Mike Bartlett, *King Charles III*, first produced at the Almeida Theatre, London, 2014.

22 Vogel, *How I Learned to Drive*, pp. 39–41.

23 Brian Friel, *Translations*, first produced at the Guildhall, Derry, Northern Ireland, 1980.

24 debbie tucker green, interview in *The Guardian*, 30 March 2005 https://www.theguardian.com/stage/2005/mar/30/theatre

Chapter 2.6

1 Leonard Bernstein, Stephen Sondheim, Arthur Laurents, *West Side Story*. After try-outs in Washington DC and Philadelphia, the musical opened at the Winter Gardens Theatre, New York, 1957.

2 Frank Loesser, Jo Swerling, Abe Burrows, *Guys & Dolls*. After a try-out at the Schubert Theatre in Philadelphia, the musical opened at the 46th Street Theatre, New York. (now the Richard Rogers Theatre) in 1950.

3 Rogers and Hammerstein, *Carousel*. The first Broadway production opened at the Majestic Theatre, New York, in 1945.

4 Brockett, Hildy, *History of the Theatre*, p. 131.

5 Prebble, *Enron*, p. 20.

6 Prebble, *Enron*, p. 33.

7 Vogel, *The Long Christmas Ride Home*, p. 5.

8 Jule Styne, Stephen Sondheim, Arthur Laurents, *Gypsy*. The original Broadway production opened at the Broadway Theatre, 1959.

9 Arthur Laurents, *Original Story By . . .* (New York: Applause, 2000) p. 15.

10 Laurents, *Original Story by . . .*, p. 348.

11 Laurents, *Original Story by . . .*, p. 348.

12 Miranda and McCarter, *Hamilton: The Revolution*, p. 174.

13 Stephen Sondheim, *Finishing the Hat* (London: Virgin Books, 2010) p. 23.

14 Philip Furia, *Ira Gershwin: The Art of the Lyricist* (Oxford: Oxford University Press, 1997) p. 62.

15 Furia, *Ira Gershwin*, p. 81.

16 Miranda and McCarter, *Hamilton*, p. 88.

17 Miranda and McCarter, *Hamilton*, p. 103.

18 Sondheim, *Finishing the Hat*, p. 33.

19 Cole Porter, Bella Spewack, Samuel Spewack, *Kiss Me Kate*. After a try-out at the Schubert Theatre, Philadelphia, the Broadway production opened at the New Century Theatre, New York, in 1948.

20 George Abbot, Richard Rogers, Lorenz Hart, *The Boys from Syracuse*. After try-outs in New Haven and Boston, the show opened on Broadway at the Alvin Theatre in 1938.

21 Castellucci, Cecil. Email to the author. 26 October 2021.

22 Giacomo Puccini, Luigi Illica, Giuseppe Giacosa, *La Bohème*, first produced at the Teatro Regio, Turin, in 1896.

23 Muir-Smith, Emma. Email to the author. 4 January 2022.

24 In recent years I have been fortunate to work with writer/director Peter Rowe and composer/musical director Ben Goddard at the New Wolsey Theatre in Ipswich on a number of new plays with songs.

25 Jonathan Larson, *Rent*. First workshop production at New York Theatre Workshop, 1993. First full production at the same venue, 1996.

26 In her top five tips, Emma Muir-Smith recommends that you watch and listen to Puccini's *La Bohème*, I would recommend that you watch and listen to Puccini's *La Bohème* AND Larson's *Rent* – produced exactly 100 years apart, these two pieces offer a wonderful short education in the scope of words and music in a theatrical context.

27 Styne, Sondheim, Laurents, *Gypsy*, Act 2 Scene 1 p. 2 https://kupdf.net/download/gypsy-script_58c83c1bdc0d60b51333902d_pdf

Chapter 2.7

1 John Rwothomack, *Far Gone* (London: Nick Hern Books, 2022) p. 12.

2 Rwothomack, John. Email to the author. 6 February 2022.

3 Prebble, *Enron*, p. 36

Chapter 2.8

1 Jez Butterworth, *Jerusalem*, first produced at the Royal Court, London, 2009. *Jerusalem* has sixteen characters, usually played by fourteen actors.

2 Vogel, *Indecent*, p. 6.

3 Robert Lepage, *The Far Side of the Moon*, first produced Théâtre du Trident, Quebec City, Canada, 2000.

4 Suzie Miller, *Prima Face*, first produced at Griffin Theatre, Sydney, Australia, 2019.

5 Suzan Lori-Parks, *Top Dog/Underdog*, first produced at the Public Theater, New York, 2001.

6 Michael Frayn, *Copenhagen*, first produced at the National Theatre, London, 1998.

7 Tony Kushner, *Angels in America*, first produced Eureka Theatre Company, San Francisco, 1991.

Chapter 2.9

1 Ian Dury is a superb lyricist, and his lyrics often feature superb wordplay, but at the more *earthy* end of his writing you can find songs like *Plaistow Patricia*, which begins with the immortal line: 'Arseholes, bastards, fucking cunts, and pricks!'

2 Edward Bond, *Saved*, first produced at the Royal Court, 1965.

3 Howard Brenton, *Romans in Britain*, first produced at the National Theatre, 1980

4 *'Five people faint due to violence in National Theatre's Cleansed'* article in *The Guardian* 24 February 2016. https://www.theguardian.com/stage/2016/feb/24/five-people-faint-40-leave-violence-cleansed-national-theatre-sarah-kane

5 For example, John Webster's play *The Duchess of Malfi*, first produced in 1614, and John Ford's *'Tis Pity She's a Whore*, first produced between 1626 and 1633.

6 Grand Guignol was a popular form of cabaret entertainment in nineteenth-century Paris, consisting of grotesque short plays featuring horror, violence and sadism.

7 Respectively, *Blasted* by Sarah Kane (Royal Court, 1995); *Lear* by Edward Bond (Royal Court, 1971); *Snatch* by Peter Rose (Soho Theatre at the Pleasance, 1998); *Jet of Blood* by Antoine Artaud (written 1924, first produced by the RSC in 1964).

8 Jeremy O. Harris, *Slave Play*, first produced at the New York Theatre Workshop, 2018.

9 Vogel, *How I Learned to Drive*, pp. 100–3.

10 Tim Etchells, *Step Off the Stage*, Sheffield and Gent, April 2007. https://timetchells.com/step-off-the-stage/

11 Prebble, *Enron*.

12 Paula Vogel quoted in an interview with Backstage.com, 2001. https://www.backstage.com/magazine/article/paula-vogel-pulitzer-winner-playwright-getting-way-42997/

13 Lisa Goldman, *The No Rules Handbook for Writers* (London: Oberon Books, 2012) p. 15.

Chapter 2.10

1 Hans-Thies Lehmann, *Postdramatic Theatre* (Abingdon: Routledge, 2006) Karen Jürs-Munby (trans.) p. 17.

2 Tim Crouch, *The Author*, (London: Oberon Books, 2009) p. 16.

3 Marvin Carlson, 'Postdramatic Theatre and Postdramatic Performance' (*Revista Brasileira de Estudos da Presença*, Volume 5, Issue 3, 2015) pp. 577–95 (p. 587) https://www.researchgate.net/publication/293328477_Postdramatic_Theatre_and_Postdramatic_Performance

4 Carlson, 'Postdramatic Theatre and Postdramatic Performance', p. 588.

5 Symbolism was a late-nineteenth-century movement in the arts using symbol and metaphor to represent what the artist wanted to say. Maurice Maeterlinck is perhaps the best-known symbolist playwright.

6 Jens Zimmermann, *Hermeneutics: A Very Short Introduction* (Oxford: Oxford University Press, 2015) Section on *Heidegger's hammer* p. 36.

7 The three unities usually attributed to Aristotle are unity of action, unity of time and unity of place. However, these unities were established during late eighteenth-century French neoclassicism; the only unity emphasized in the *Poetics* is the unity of action, there is one brief mention of the unity of time, and no mention of the unity of place.

8 Marianne van Kerkhoven, 'The Burden of the Times', an essay in *Tat-Zeitung*, (Frankfurt-am-Main: Journal of the Theater am Turn, 1991) as cited in Lehmann, *Postdramatic Theatre*, p. 83.

Chapter 2.11

1 *The Iron Man* was first produced by Graeae at the Greenwich & Docklands International Festival in 2011.

2 Bryony Lavery, *Frozen*, first produced at Birmingham Rep., 1998. Fingersmiths production, 2014.

Chapter 3.1

1 This play eventually metamorphosed into a play called *Skaville* about the National Front in Britain during the 1970s. It was first produced by Abacus Arts at the Bedlam Theatre, Edinburgh Festival, 1995.

2 *A Night in Tunisia*, Theatre Royal Stratford East, 1992.

3 Harold Pinter, Nobel Lecture, 2005. https://www.nobelprize.org/prizes/literature/2005/pinter/25621-harold-pinter-nobel-lecture-2005/

4 Philip Ridley quoted in *Fifty Playwrights on their Craft* Caroline Jester (ed.) and Caridad Svich (London: Bloomsbury, 2018) pp. 117–18.

5 Lajos Egri, *The Art of Dramatic Writing* (New York: Touchstone, 2004) p. 6. Originally published in 1942.

6 Sheila Yeger, *The Sound of One Hand Clapping* (Oxford: Amber Lane Press, 1990) pp. 91–2.

7 Alice Birch in an interview with Daisy Bowie-Sell for *Whatsonstage* in 2016. https://www.whatsonstage.com/edinburgh-theatre/news/alice-birch-interview-revolt-edinburgh_41421.html

8 Stephen Sondheim quoted in an article by Erica Hansen in *Deseret News*, 2011. https://www.deseret.com/2011/2/3/20171426/stephen-sondheim-brings-his-greatness-to-kingsbury-hall#features-logo

Chapter 3.2

1 The line in question came at a moment when an immigration officer suspected they might have unearthed a mole working inside immigration control at Heathrow, except she got a bit mixed up and said, 'We've got a mouse!' Hilarious isn't it! No. It's not. I know. All I can say is, watch out for those 2.00 am moments of inspiration when you think you've written a great line – and get ready to cut it.

2 Thornton Wilder, *A Preface for 'Our Town'* in Thornton Wilder, *Collected Plays & Writings on Theater* (New York: The Library of America, 2007) pp. 657–9 (p. 658).

3 Thornton Wilder, *Our Town and Other Plays* (London: Penguin Books, 1962) p. 21.

4 Duncan Macmillan, *Lungs* (London: Oberon Modern Plays, 2019) p. ix.

5 Courtesy of Adam Bock's play, *The Drunken City*, first produced by Kitchen Theatre Company, New York, 2005.

6 Crimp. *Attempts on Her Life*, writer's note before text begins on p. 1.

7 Barron, *Dance Nation*, writer's note, p. 9.

8 Birch, *Revolt. She Said. Revolt Again.*, writer's note, p. 19.

9 Shakespeare, William, *A Winter's Tale* (London: Macmillan, 1963) K. Deighton (ed.) 3.3.58, p. 45.

10 Barron, *Dance Nation*, p. 51.

11 Barron, *Dance Nation*, p. 56.

12 Lee-Jones, *Seven Methods*, p. 78.

13 Lee-Jones, *Seven Methods*, p. 74.

14 Lee-Jones, *Seven Methods*, p. 69.

15 Lee-Jones, *Seven Methods*, p. 74.

16 Jacobs-Jenkins, *An Octoroon*, p. 22.

17 Jacobs-Jenkins, *An Octoroon*, p. 22.

18 Jacobs-Jenkins, *An Octoroon*, p. 57.

19 Jacobs-Jenkins, *An Octoroon*, p. 62.

20 Jacobs-Jenkins, *An Octoroon*, p. 78.

21 Birch, *Revolt*, p. 59.

22 Birch, *Revolt*, p. 64.

23 Lopez, *The Inheritance*, p. 197.

24 Hickson, *The Writer*, pp. 37–56 (p. 48, 53, 56).

25 Peter Brook, *The Empty Space* (Harmondsworth: Penguin Books, 1968) p. 15.

26 Miranda and McCarter, *Hamilton: The Revolution*, p. 223.

Chapter 3.3

1 Jonathan Larson worked for nine and a half years at the Moondance Diner in New York while he wrote his musicals.

2 Shelagh Delaney worked as an usher at the Opera House, Manchester.

3 *Piaf* was first produced by the RSC at the Other Place, Stratford upon Avon, 1978. Other plays include, *Dusa, Fish, Stars and Vi*, (Edinburgh Festival, 1976), and *Stanley* (National Theatre, 1996).

4 James Baldwin, *The Writers' Chapbook* (New York: Modern Library, 1999) George Plimpton (ed.) p. 58.

5 Artistic directors run the companies and direct the plays they want to direct; associate directors are – like the name suggests – associated with the company and regularly direct plays there; freelance directors are directors who are invited on an ad hoc basis to direct plays for the company.

Chapter 3.4

1 'Happiness and freedom begin with a clear understanding of one principle: Some things are within our control, and some things are not. It is only after you have faced up to this fundamental rule and learned to distinguish between what you can and can't control that inner tranquillity and outer effectiveness become possible.' Epictetus, *The Art of Living* (San Francisco: HarperCollins, 1994) Sharon Lebell (ed.) p. 3.

2 Brené Brown, *Rising Strong* (London: Penguin Random House, 2015) p. 4.

3 *Death of a Salesman* was first produced at the Morosco Theatre, New York, 1949. I first saw it at the Oxford Playhouse in the late 1970s.

4 *The Crucible* was first produced at the Martin Beck Theatre, New York, 1953. I toured in a university production of this play in Denmark in the early 1980s.

5 *Resurrection Blues* was first produced at the Guthrie Theater, Minneapolis, in 2002. It was first produced in the UK at the Old Vic, London, 2006.

6 Bertrand Russell, *The Conquest of Happiness* (New York: Liveright, 2013) p. 112.

Chapter 3.5

1 April De Angelis, quoted in *The Guardian*, 13 December 2021. https://www.theguardian.com/stage/2021/jan/13/uk-report-reveals-disgraceful-gender-inequality-in-the-arts Full report available on the Sphinx Theatre website https://sphinxtheatre.co.uk/new-women-in-theatre-survey-report/

BIBLIOGRAPHY

Books and essays

Aristotle, Horace, Longinus (Raddice, B. ed., Dorsch T. S., trans.), *Classical Literary Criticism*, Harmondsworth: Penguin Books 1965.

Aristotle (Twining, T., trans.), *Aristotle's Poetics and Rhetoric,* London: J.M. Dent, 1953.

Ayckbourn, A., *The Crafty Art of Playmaking*, London: Faber and Faber, 2003.

Baldwin, J. (Plimpton, G., ed.), *The Writer's Chapbook*, New York: Modern Library, 1999.

Baker, G. P., *Dramatic Technique*, Boston & New York: Houghton Mifflin Company, Eibron Classics Replica, 2006.

Banham, M., *The Cambridge Guide to Theatre*, Cambridge: Cambridge University Press, 1995.

Bentley, E., *The Life of the Drama*, New York: Applause Theatre Books, 1964.

Bentley, E., *The Playwright as Thinker*, Minneapolis: University of Minnesota Press, edition 2010.

Berger, C., *Feminism in Postdramatic Theatre: An Oblique Approach*, Contemporary Theatre Review, 29:4, 2019.

Bharat Muni (Rangacharya, A., trans.), *The Nāṭyaśāstra*, New Delhi: Munshiram Manoharlal Publishers, 2007.

Bloom, H. (Carson, S., ed.), *Foreword: Who Else Is There, Living with Shakespeare*, New York: Vintage Books, 2013.

Booker, C., *The Seven Basic Plots*, London: Bloomsbury Continuum, 2019.

Brockett, O. G., Hildy, F. J., *History of the Theatre*, Harlow: Pearson Education Limited, 2014.

Brook, P., *The Empty Space*, Harmondsworth: Penguin Books, 1968.

Brown, B., *Rising Strong*, London: Penguin Random House, 2015.

Caird, J., *Theatre Craft*, London: Faber and Faber, 2010.

Carley, J., *Renku Reckoner*, Darlington Richards, 2015.

Carlson, M., 'Postdramatic Theatre and Postdramatic Performance', *Revista Brasileira de Estudos da Presença*, Volume 5, Issue 3, 2015.

Cole, T. (ed.), *Playwrights on Playwriting*, New York: Hill and Wang, 1982.

Diderot, D., *Discours sur la poésie dramatique* in *D. Diderot Ouvres Complètes III*, Paris: Larousse, 1970.

Edgar, D., *How Plays Work*, London: Nick Hern Books, 2010.

Edgar, D. (ed.), *State of Play*, London: Faber and Faber, 1999.

Egri, L., *The Art of Dramatic Writing*, New York: Touchstone, 1960.

Eliot, T. S., *The Sacred Wood: Essays on Poetry and Criticism*, London: Methuen, 1920.

Epictetus (Dobbin, R., ed. and trans.), *Discourses and Selected Writings*, London: Penguin Books, 2008.

Epictetus (Lebell, S., ed.), *The Art of Living*, San Francisco: HarperCollins, 1994.

Esslin, M., *The Theatre of the Absurd*, Harmondsworth: Penguin Books, 1980.

Etchells, T., *Certain Fragments: Texts and Writings on Performance*, London: Routledge, 2002.

Fountain, T., *So You Want to be a Playwright*, London: Nick Hern Books, 2007.

Fuchs, E., *The Death of Character: Perspectives on Theatre after Modernism*, Bloomington and Indianapolis: Indiana University Press, 1996.

Furia, P., *Ira Gershwin, The Art of the Lyricist*, Oxford New York: Oxford University Press, 1996.

Goldman, G., *The No Rules Handbook for Writers*, London: Oberon Books, 2012.

Gooch, S., *Writing a Play*, London: A&C Black, 1988.

Grace, F., Bayley C., *Play Writing*, London: Bloomsbury, 2016.

Greig, N., *Playwriting: A Practical Guide*, Abingdon: Routledge, 2005.

Hall, P., *Shakespeare's Advice to the Players*, London: Oberon Books, 2003.

Hartnoll, P. (ed.), *The Concise Oxford Companion to the Theatre*, Oxford: Oxford University Press, 1981.

Italie, J. C. van, *The Playwright's Workbook*, New York: Applause Books, 1997.

Jeffreys, S., *Playwriting*, London: Nick Hern Books, 2019.

Jester, C., Svich, C. (Jester, C., ed.), *Fifty Playwrights on their Craft*, London: Bloomsbury Methuen Drama, 2018.

Kerkhoven, M. van, 'The Burden of the Times', *Frankfurt am Main TAT-Zeitung*, Journal of Theatre am Turm, 1991.

Laurents, A., *Original Story By Arthur Laurents*, New York: Applause Theatre Books, 2000.

Lehmann, H-T., *Postdramatic Theatre*, Abingdon: Routledge, 2006.

Lehmann, H-T., Jürs-Munby, K., Barnett, D., 'Taking Stock and Looking Forward: Postdramatic Theatre Symposium', *Contemporary Theatre Review*, Volume 16, Issue 4, 2006.

Mamet, D., *Three Uses of the Knife*, London: Methuen, 2007.

Miller, A., *Timebends: A Life*, London: Methuen, 1987.

Miller, A. (Roudané, M., intro.), *The Collected Essays of Arthur Miller*, London: Bloomsbury Methuen Drama, 2015.

Miranda, L-M., McCarter, J., *Hamilton: The Revolution*, London: Little, Brown, 2016.

Nelson, R., Jones, D., *Making Plays*, London: Faber and Faber, 1995.

Nietzsche, F., *The Birth of Tragedy*, London: Penguin Books, 1991.

Pinter, H., *Four Plays*: Introduction, London: Faber and Faber, 1986.

Plato (Rowe, C., ed.), *The Republic*, London: Penguin Books, 2012.

Plimpton, G. (ed.), *The Paris Review Interviews: Playwrights at Work*, London: Harvill, 2000.

Prebble, L., *A Very Expensive Poison*, London: Methuen, 2019.

Roberts, M., 'Vanishing Acts: Sarah Kane's Texts for Performance and Post-dramatic Theatre', *Modern Drama*, Volume 58, Issue 1, 2015.

Romanska, M., *The Routledge Companion to Dramaturgy*, Abingdon: Routledge, 2016.

Russell, B., *The Conquest of Happiness*, New York: Liveright Publishing Corporation, reissue 2013.

Seneca, L. A. (Costa, C. D. N., trans.), *On the Shortness of Life*, London: 1997.

Sierz, A., *In-Yer-Face Theatre: British Drama Today*, London: Faber and Faber, 2001.

Sondheim, S., *Finishing the Hat*, London: Virgin Books, 2010.

Sondheim, S., *Look I Made a Hat*, New York: Virgin Books, 2011.

Sugiera, M., 'Beyond Drama: Writing for Postdramatic Theatre', *Theatre Research International*, Volume 29 Issue 1, 2004.

Sweet, J., *The Dramatist's Toolkit*, Portsmouth NH: Heinemann, 1993.

Szondi, P. (Hays, M., ed. and trans.), *Theory of the Modern Drama*, Minneapolis: University of Minnesota Press, 1987.

Tomlin, E., *Acts and Apparitions: Discourses on the Real in Performance Practice and Theory, 1990–2010*, Manchester: Manchester University Press, 2018.

Trotsky, L. (Strunsky, R., trans.), *Literature and Revolution*, New York: Russell & Russell, 1957.

Truby, J., *The Anatomy of Story: 22 Steps to Becoming a Master Storyteller*, New York: Faber and Faber, 2007.

Vega, L. de (Brewster, W. T., trans.), *The New Art of Writing Plays (1609)*, Charleston: Bibliobazaar, 2009.

Viertel, J., *The Secret Life of the American Musical*, New York: Sarah Crichton Books, 2017.

Vogel, P., *Baltimore Waltz and Other Plays*: Introduction, New York: Theatre Communications Group Inc., 2005.

Vogel, P., *The Long Christmas Ride Home*: Notes, New York: Theatre Communications Group Inc., 2004.

Vogel, P., *How I Learned to Drive*: Preface, New York: Theatre Communications Group Inc., 2018.

Vogler, C., *The Writer's Journey*, London: Pan Macmillan, 1999.

Waters, S., *The Secret Life of Plays*, London: Nick Hern Books, 2010.

Watson, Robert N. (ed.), *Ben Jonson Four Plays*, London: Bloomsbury Methuen Drama, 2014.

Wilder, T. (McClatchy, J. D., ed.), *Thornton Wilder Collected Plays & Writings on Theater*, New York: The Library of America, 2007.

Wilder, T., *Our Town and Other Plays*: Introduction, London: Penguin Books, 1962.

Williams, R., *Drama in Performance*, New York: Basic Books, 1968.

Yeger, S., *The Sound of One Hand Clapping*, Oxford: Amber Lane Press, 1990.

Yorke, J., *Into the Woods*, London: Penguin Books, 2014.

Zeami, M. (Rimer, J. T., Masakazu, Y., trans.), *On the Art of the No Drama: The Major Treatises of Zeami*, Princeton: Princeton University Press, 1984.

Zimmermann, J., *Hermeneutics: A Very Short Introduction*, Oxford: Oxford University Press, 2015.

Plays and musicals referenced

Abbot, George; Rogers, Richard; Hart, Lorenz – *The Boys from Syracuse*
Aeschylus – *Agamemnon*
Artaud, Antoine – *Jet of Blood*
Baker, Annie – *John; The Antipodes*
Barron, Clare – *Dance Nation*
Bartlett, Mike – *King Charles III*
Bean, Richard – *One Man, Two Guvnors*
Beckett, Samuel – *Waiting for Godot; Happy Days*
Behan, Brendan – *The Hostage*
Birch, Alice – *Anatomy of a Suicide; Revolt. She Said. Revolt Again.*
Bock, Adam – *The Drunken City*
Bond, Edward – *Saved; Lear*
Bolt, Robert – *A Man for All Seasons*
Boswell, Laurence – *Beauty and the Beast*
Brenton, Howard – *Romans in Britain*
Buffini, Moira – *Loveplay*
Burke, Gregory – *Black Watch*
Butterworth, Jez – *Jerusalem*
Churchill, Caryl – *A Number; Top Girls; Blue Heart*
Corwin, John – *Navy Pier*
Crimp, Martin – *Attempts on Her Life*
Crouch, Tim – *An Oak Tree; The Author*
Delaney, Shelagh – *A Taste of Honey*
Éclair-Powell – *Shed: Exploded View*
Edgar, David – *Nicholas Nickleby*
Euripides – *Medea; Cyclops*
Ford, John – *'Tis Pity She's a Whore*
Frayn, Michael – *Copenhagen*
Friel, Brian – *Dancing at Lughnasa; Faith Healer; Translations*
Gems, Pam – *Piaf; Stanley; Dusa, Fish, Stas and Vi*
Gill, Peter – *The York Realist*
Graham, James – *This House*
Hare, David – *Amy's View*
Harris, Jeremy O – *Slave Play*
Harrison, Tony – *The Trackers of Oxyrhynchus*
Harrower, David – *Blackbird*
Hickson, Ella – *The Writer*
Jacobs-Jenkins, Branden – *An Octoroon*
Johnson, Catherine; Andersson, Benny; Ulvaeus, Björn – *Mamma Mia*
Jonson, Ben – *Bartholomew Fair; Volpone*
Kane, Sarah – *4.48 Psychosis; Blasted; Cleansed*
Kene, Arinze – *Misty*
Kirkwood, Lucy – *Chimerica; Mosquitoes*

Kron, Lisa; Tesori, Jeanine – *Fun Home*
Kushner, Tony – *Angels in America*
Kushner, Tony; Tesori, Jeanine – *Caroline, or Change*
Larson, Jonathan – *Rent*
Laurents, Arthur; Styne, Jule; Sondheim, Stephen – *Gypsy*
Lavery, Bryony – *Frozen*
Lee-Jones, Jasmine – *Seven Methods of Killing Kylie Jenner*
Lepage, Robert – *The Far Side of the Moon*
Littlewood, Joan and Theatre Workshop – *Oh What a Lovely War*
Lloyd-Webber, Andrew; Rice, Tim – *Jesus Christ Superstar*
Loesser, Frank; Swerling, Jo; Burrows, Abe – *Guys & Dolls*
Lopez, Matthew – *The Inheritance*
Lori-Parks, Suzan – *Top Dog/Underdog*
Love, Donja R. – *One in Two*
Macmillan, Duncan – *People, Places and Things*; *Every Brilliant Thing* (with
    Jonny Donohoe); *Lungs*
Mamet, David – *Oleanna*
McCraney, Tarell Alvin – *The Brothers Size*
Miller, Arthur – *A View from the Bridge*; *After the Fall*; *Resurrection Blues*; *Death
    of a Salesman*; *The Crucible, After the Fall*
Miller, Suzie – *Prima Face*
Miranda, Lin-Manuel – *Hamilton*
Morgan, Peter – *The Audience*
Payne, Nick – *Constellations*
Pinter, Harold – *Betrayal*
Porter, Cole; Spewack, Bella; Spewack, Samuel – *Kiss Me Kate*
Prebble, Lucy – *Enron; A Very Expensive Poison*
Puccini, Giacomo; Illica, Luigi, Giacosa, Giuseppe – *La Bohème*
Rogers & Hammerstein – *Carousel*
Rose, Peter – *Snatch*
Rwothomack, John – *Far Gone*
Seneca – *Thyestes*
Shaffer, Peter – *Amadeus*
Schnitzler, Arthur – *La Ronde*
Shakespeare, William – *Hamlet; Romeo and Juliet; Julius Caesar; A Midsummer
    Night's Dream; Macbeth; King Lear; Love's Labour's Lost; A Winter's Tale; Titus
    Andronicus*
Sirett, Paul – *Reasons to be Cheerful; The Big Life; Bad Blood Blues; Rat Pack
    Confidential; The Iron Man; Skaville; A Night in Tunisia; Worlds Apart*
Sondheim, Stephen – *Into the Woods*
Sondheim, Stephen; Bernstein, Leonard; Laurents, Arthur – *West Side Story*
Sophocles – *Oedipus Rex; Trackers*
Stephens, Simon – *Heisenberg*
Strindberg, August – *A Dream Play*
Thomas, Dylan – *Under Milk Wood*
Thomas, Preston – *Cambises*

tucker green, debbie – *Random*

Vogel, Paula – *The Long Christmas Ride Home; Indecent; Baltimore Waltz; How I Learned to Drive*

Wade, Laura – *The Watsons*

Waller-Bridge, Phoebe – *Fleabag*

Walsh, Enda; Hansard, Glen; Irglová, Markéta – *Once*

Webster, John – *The Duchess of Malfi*

Wilder, Thornton – *Our Town; The Long Christmas Dinner*

Williams, Roy; Dyer, Clint – *Death of England*

Zeller, Florian – *The Father*

INDEX